AF386683

More Advance Praise for *Human Raised*

"*Human Raised* is a warm, thoughtful, and deeply reassuring guide packed with practical wisdom rooted in the latest science. As parents grapple with how to use AI-informed technologies to support their children without undermining human connection, Suskind offers clear, actionable advice that is both timely and invaluable."
—Katy Milkman, national bestselling author of *How to Change* and professor at the Wharton School

"Dr. Dana Suskind has written an insightful and exciting book that explores parents' deepest concerns: How will AI impact my young child? Will it change their developing brains and influence their values? Dr. Suskind examines current and upcoming AI devices, including machine-based 'companions' that form bonds with children and next-generation AI robot 'caregivers' that may replace everyday parental activities. Told through the lens of an empathetic pediatrician, this book provides practical, easy-to-understand advice based on proven, cutting-edge brain science. This extraordinary book should be essential reading for parenting in the age of AI."
—Dr. Patricia Kuhl, codirector of the Institute for Learning & Brain Sciences at the University of Washington and coauthor of *The Scientist in the Crib*

"The compassionate, brilliant, and engaging Dr. Dana Suskind has written a book to guide parents in using AI to gain more bandwidth so that they don't sacrifice precious time with their children. Parents will learn how AI can help them lower their cognitive load to be more present and responsive, and why the young child's brain needs to be human raised. The bottom line is that AI should assist the caregivers, not give the care."
—Claudia Goldin, author of *Career and Family: Women's Century-Long Journey Toward Equity* and Nobel laureate in economic sciences

"How do we utilize the power of AI to raise our children, while safeguarding the nurturing interactions and care that make us human? In this captivating read, one of the foremost researchers on child development helps parents navigate these challenges and make sense of key discoveries of neuroscience that provide crucial insights for protecting childhood, human flourishing, and the future of our species."
—Andreas Schleicher, director for Education and Skills, Organisation for Economic Co-operation and Development

"In this timely *cri de coeur*, Dana Suskind combines the passion of Doug Rushkoff's *Team Human* with the wisdom of Neil Postman's *The Disappearance of Childhood*—along with a scientist's rigor—to get to the heart of what makes us human. It isn't hyperbole to say that AI has the potential to transform childhood, relationships, and ultimately the future of our species, and this book provides guidance every parent needs to protect their kids."
—Julie Scelfo, founder and executive director of Mothers Against Media Addiction (MAMA)

HUMAN RAISED

Nurturing Connection,
Curiosity & Lifelong Learning
in the Age of AI

Dana Suskind, MD

DUTTON

DUTTON

An imprint of Penguin Random House LLC
1745 Broadway, New York, NY 10019
penguinrandomhouse.com

This book aims to provide readers with useful information and a framework for them to evaluate AI products, but it is not intended to replace the medical advice of your doctor. Publisher and author specifically disclaim responsibility for any loss that may result from the use of information contained in this book. Some names and identifying details of certain people mentioned in this book have been changed.

Copyright © 2026 by Dana Suskind
Penguin Random House values and supports copyright. Copyright fuels creativity, encourages diverse voices, promotes free speech, and creates a vibrant culture. Thank you for buying an authorized edition of this book and for complying with copyright laws by not reproducing, scanning, or distributing any part of it in any form without permission. You are supporting writers and allowing Penguin Random House to continue to publish books for every reader. Please note that no part of this book may be used or reproduced in any manner for the purpose of training artificial intelligence technologies or systems.

DUTTON and the D colophon are registered trademarks of Penguin Random House LLC.

Book design by Diahann Sturge

LIBRARY OF CONGRESS CATALOGING-IN-PUBLICATION DATA
has been applied for.

ISBN 9798217180899 (hardcover)
ISBN 9798217180905 (ebook)

Printed in the United States of America
1st Printing

The authorized representative in the EU for product safety and compliance is Penguin Random House Ireland, Morrison Chambers, 32 Nassau Street, Dublin D02 YH68, Ireland, https://eu-contact.penguin.ie.

For John.
CTW47.
Right by your side, my love.

CONTENTS

Introduction

For years I dreamed of silence. Between a home with three young children and a pediatric clinic crowded with restless kids, the noise at times felt relentless. A family and a meaningful career were all I ever wanted, but sometimes I yearned for quiet. Just a moment of peace.

I don't wish for that anymore.

In Rachel Carson's *Silent Spring*, the revolutionary book that sparked the modern environmental movement, the birds that no longer sang weren't the tragedy. They were the signal. A warning that something essential was dying. I hear a similar warning now in a different kind of silence: the eerie, algorithm-induced quiet of children transfixed by technology.

We are social creatures. We chat and complain, debate and tell stories. We embrace, bump fists, communicate nuanced emotions wordlessly—an eye roll, a smile, a shrug. We call out to each other in stadium crowds, console crying babies on airplanes. This is what we do. And these lively, sometimes irritating, often messy, but always essential noises are the product of our species connecting and caring for one another.

The volume of this beautiful, chaotic music is slowly being turned down. Technologies that once lived squarely in the realm of science fiction are now entering nurseries, classrooms, and family life at extraordinary speed, capturing the attention of adults and children alike. Companies are developing versions of popular AI chatbots specifically for kids. Entertaining AI dolls and action figures are core to the strategic vision of major toy brands. Virtual AI tutors are being promoted as the future of education around the world.

AI has also moved into our lives in subtler ways. When you scroll social media or look for your next watch on Netflix, intelligent algorithms select or suggest the content for you. These AI-powered recommendation engines are designed to predict what will hold your attention and keep you glued to the screen. If your little ones are watching YouTube, they too are under the sway of the technology as it works silently in the background to hold them close and shape their experience. The very content they consume might have been created by AI, including a flood of supposedly educational AI-generated videos. These low-quality, error-filled abominations known as AI slop don't just fail to teach. They actively misinform. They embed misspellings, peddle nonsense, and model unsafe behaviors for children too young to know the difference. And the companies developing these technologies are racing ahead of the rules as they're being written.

Policymakers are struggling to understand what they are regulating. The rest of us are struggling to understand how our world is changing. Perhaps one day these gaps will close, but childhood will not wait.

I believe that the relationship between child development and artificial intelligence is one of the most critical and overlooked challenges of our time, one that has the potential to transform childhood, family structures, and ultimately nothing less than our future as a species. And it's up to us as parents and caregivers to decide how these intelligent tools will shape our children's lives. Not companies. Not governments. We are the ones who will take the lead on deciding what these technologies replace, what they enhance, and what they should never touch. And we are uniquely equipped to do so, as we possess something critical that machines are missing.

The Helpless Infant Paradox

Nobel laureate Geoffrey Hinton, known as the Godfather of Artificial Intelligence for the pivotal role he played in creating the AI systems now remaking our world, left Google in 2023 to warn humanity about what he'd helped build. He spoke of existential risks, of systems that might one day surpass us. But when asked once what we might do to make artificial intelligence safe, he gave a surprising answer.

He suggested we embed maternal instincts in these systems.

Not better algorithms. Not more guardrails. Not elaborate structures of rules and constraints. Maternal instincts. The primal, inexplicable forces that make any parent—mothers *and* fathers—go to the ends of the earth to protect and care for their child without calculating the expected return.

I have spent years studying the evolutionary origins of these parental instincts and their profound importance in building children's brains. Human babies are born powerless, weak, and extremely needy. Yet these tiny, vulnerable creatures somehow commandeer the lives of adults many times their size and strength. I call this the helpless infant paradox. There is no other example I can think of in nature of such complete power held by such powerless entities. Yet this is the very source of our success as a species. The instinct to nurture is wired so deeply into parents that it feels less like a choice than a biological imperative.

These past few decades, I've watched our culture focus on trying to make humans more like machines. More efficient, more optimized, more productive. We have quantified and data-fied childhood, turned parenting into a performance metric, measured our worth in developmental milestones met and cognitive outputs achieved. And now one of the scientists at the very frontier of machine intelligence is asking the opposite question: How do we make machines more like humans?

The Missing Instinct

The biggest missing piece in all of artificial intelligence, roboticist Matthias Scheutz told me, is that "none of our machines care."

But can we fix that? Is Hinton's hope even possible? Can we code parental instinct? Can we engineer caring?

When I posed these questions to Scheutz, a philosopher turned roboticist who has spent decades thinking about human and machine minds, his answer cut to the heart of what separates us from even the most sophisticated AI. He pointed me to a philosophical concept: original intentionality. Our thoughts, he explained, don't just process information—they reach toward what matters to us. Our cognition isn't mere information processing. It's grounded in something deeper. A scientist who devotes their life to understanding children's brain development is driven by passion and concern.

Parental instincts, Scheutz mused, are subconscious, visceral. Love coming from biological intentionality. The product of millions of years of evolution rather than countless lines of code, refined by the brutal simplicity of survival. In short, children needed loving caregivers to live. The survivors then raised their own children with the same fierce attention. And so it continued, an unbroken chain of caring, until it reached you.

You have the quality the machines are missing.

The love no code can copy.

A Heartfelt Plea

What makes us human? Is it reason? Language? Creativity? Tool use? Artificial intelligence is eroding our supposed superiority in each area one by one. It produces outputs indistinguishable from reasoning. It generates language with fluency that surpasses most humans. AI turns out art, music, poetry, software. It uses existing tools and builds new ones.

But AI does not care.

No algorithm lies awake at night worrying about whether a struggling child finally learned to read. No chatbot feels the weight of unrealized human potential. No system, however sophisticated, has thoughts that are genuinely about your child, that one-of-a-kind combination of genes and experiences. These technologies act on patterns shaped by everyone else's data, targeted at producing responses that look like caring.

True caring—our capacity to have heartfelt thoughts about another being, rooted in concern for their flourishing, irrational in their intensity—is what makes us unique. It is the irreducible human core.

This caring instinct that evolution gave us runs deep, but we have been too slow or shortsighted to extend it beyond the boundaries our ancestors drew. Too quick to see difference before we see sameness. We evolved to protect our own young. Our own kin. Our own tribe. For most of human history, this made sense. Resources were scarce, survival was precarious, and caring for others' children might mean your own would go without. The propensity to "other," to see those outside our circle as competitors, even threats, was adaptive and kept our ancestors alive. But that same propensity now holds us back—from seeing *all* children as our own, as our collective future.

And yet.

Here is what I've wondered, and I offer it as hope, not prediction.

AI is the ultimate other. Intelligent, capable, increasingly present in our lives and our children's lives. Genuinely useful in many ways, yes—and yet fundamentally, irreducibly, not us. These technologies are our creation, made in our image, but they are not human.

In confronting what is not human, might we finally see what is?

Not our differences. Not our skin, our languages, our borders, the tribal markers we've used for millennia to sort ourselves into us and them. But our common inheritance: the capacity to care. The quality the machines are missing. The essential characteristic we all share.

We lie awake at night worrying about people we love. We put ourselves in harm's way to protect vulnerable children. That "we" is not limited to parents of a certain race or class or country. It is common to all of us. To humanity as a whole. Bound together by the one thing artificial intelligence cannot replicate. The one thing that, if Hinton is right, would be required to make AI safe, and that no one knows how to code.

Perhaps the age of AI will be the age of greater human division, with each of us retreating into algorithmically curated bubbles, our children raised by systems that simulate caring while we grow ever more disconnected from one another.

Or perhaps—and this is the hope I cannot shake—it will be the age of human recognition. The moment when, confronted with the ultimate other, we finally see ourselves clearly. We see that the mother in Mumbai and the father in Mississippi, the teacher in Cairo and the nanny in Paris, all share the same ancient inheritance: the capacity to have thoughts that are genuinely about a child, grounded in concern for their flourishing.

And in that recognition, perhaps we will finally extend our caring to *all* children. Not because it is efficient. Not because an algorithm recommended it. But because we finally see that we are one species. Machines calculate survival probabilities. They optimize for self-preservation. Humans do something inefficient, something divine, something dangerous.

Stepping Off the Shoreline

On an August day in 2012, the waves rose six feet over Lake Michigan. Our three children were playing in the sand, watched over by my husband, their father, Don Liu. As he stood at the shoreline, he suddenly noticed in the watery, chaotic distance two young boys struggling in the raging waters. He started running into the water as our son yelled, "Dad, what are you doing?"

They were the last words he ever said to his father.

The two boys got back alive. My husband, always fearless when it came to helping others, died—overwhelmed by the torrential pounding of the waves and the gripping undertow. He was my best friend, my strongest support, my love.

For Don, standing on the shore watching two children struggle, there was no debating, no hesitation. As a pediatric surgeon, a leader in his field, his devotion to his patients was unquestioned. A child needed help; the child got help. It was not just his personal maxim. This was his way of life. He would never have considered standing on the shoreline while two children struggled, even if knew it would cost him his life.

Afterward, Don was lauded as a hero. But what I keep thinking about now, all these years later, writing this book, is something simpler.

He cared for all children as if they were his own.

That caring, that original intentionality, is the thing Geoffrey Hinton suggested that we ought to code into AI. It's what Matthias Scheutz believes no machine possesses.

And it's what every child deserves.

Human Raised

A century ago, people assumed that the food they ate was farm fresh. There was no need to label it as such, because the notion that your food had been created in a lab, factory, or artificial farm would never have occurred to consumers. Today, we assume that the children and adults around us have all been human raised. Ideally by parents, grandparents, siblings, caregivers, or others who have loved and looked after them to the best of their ability. But as AI permeates our smartphones and screens, as it moves into the nursery, the playroom, the kitchen, and the classroom, the idea that the average child is going to be entirely human raised may not be a safe assumption for long. And if artificial intelligence does play a significant role in a child's early years, either through the content they consume or the relationships they cultivate, we need to understand how this will affect their development. Will a primarily or entirely human-raised childhood be a luxury experience, like a farm-raised diet? Or will AI tools help to balance the scales by providing more kids with learning opportunities they might never have enjoyed? We don't have all the answers. The technology is too new; the research is just getting started. Yet we cannot wait for much-needed long-term scientific studies before acting. Parents and caregivers need guidance and support today.

We have the opportunity to act before it's too late, but the window is closing rapidly, and I'm writing this book now so we don't face a much grimmer reality in twenty years. If we let the world of our children go quiet, one delegated bedtime, one digitally soothed tantrum, one silent car ride at a time, we don't just fail them. We lose ourselves. This is not to say that AI has no role. Used well, it can ease parents' burdens and enrich children's learning. It can help turn the music back up. But the singing must remain ours.

In the pages ahead, I'll give you the language, frameworks, critical science knowledge, and guardrails to navigate this new world—not with fear, but with intention. Generally, I'll focus on the youngest children, from birth to six years old, but many of the key principles can inform your approach to parenting kids a decade older. By learning to understand early-human development, and how to evaluate AI's potential role during this formative period, you'll acquire the strategies our entire society needs to preserve human agency as this technology transforms every corner of our lives. I have absolute faith that with the right guidance, parents will rise to this challenge, becoming essential guardians at the gateway between AI and their children's developing minds. *Human Raised* is designed to help you make decisions about AI use that will affect your children's lives deliberately, before the defaults are set for you.

The title is not a luxury label, but a call to action.

A return to what we nearly forgot.

A declaration that the caring that made us human will be what saves us.

The machines cannot care.

We can care—about *all* children.

We cannot stand on the shoreline.

CHAPTER ONE

The Human Edge

Visions of HOPE for the age of artificial intelligence

The baby's cry pierces the darkness. Again. It's 3:00 a.m. Morgan glances wearily at her phone: Five hours until her morning meeting, and she hasn't slept more than three hours straight in weeks. Her six-month-old daughter wails in her crib, a tiny, distressed voice in the vast quiet of the night. Is it hunger? Pain? Gas? Could it be another ear infection? Her partner left for his night shift hours ago. The pediatrician's office is closed; the nurse line won't open for hours. Unsure what else to do, Morgan lifts her daughter from the crib and settles into the glider in the corner of the cramped room.

As she rocks, her daughter's warm weight settling against her chest, Morgan scrolls through her phone with her free hand, overwhelmed by a blur of parenting blogs, influencer advice, and targeted ads offering helpful products.

Just as her baby is finally drifting back to sleep in her arms, Morgan hears the muffled sounds of her toddler son stirring in the next room. Her heart sinks. Not just because he's awake, but because it reminds her of the waitlist letter that arrived yesterday. "Your son's evaluation indicates possible speech delay . . . current wait time for early-intervention services: 4–6 months." Four to six months of precious developmental time slipping away. His recent meltdowns have become more frequent, and she can't tell if it's the stress permeating their household, adjustment to his new sister, or behavioral issues related to his language delay. Between the demands of work and the endless maze of waitlists and appointments, she knows she should be reading to him more, talking more, doing *something* to support his development. The weight of everything she should be doing crushes down like a physical force.

Morgan is a composite of hundreds of similarly overstretched mothers and fathers I've met over the years. Personally, I've lived both sides of this story. As a physician and pediatric surgeon, I've consoled weeping parents in exam rooms while they searched my face for answers. It feels hard to believe that it was over twenty years ago that I was holding my own crying babies at 3:00 a.m., wondering how I was going to function the next day. My current status as a parenting expert would strike my younger self as comical. I didn't feel cut out to offer anyone advice when I was pulling three kids into my bed in the middle of the night just to get them to finally close their eyes.

Now parents have artificially intelligent products and services offering gifts too enticing to ignore, including relief and support that exhausted caregivers desperately need. Smart monitors promise to track your infant's breathing while you sleep. Baby translators claim to decode their cries. Voice-activated virtual assistants are ready to answer your child's endless "why" questions or simply keep them entertained so you can focus on dinner prep. Believe me, I completely understand the allure of any tool that offers a little help to exhausted, overworked parents. And when certain AI solutions are tactfully deployed and used in the right way, they can be of tremendous benefit to homes and classrooms. The transformative, positive potential is real. Yet welcoming these technologies into our lives casually, without fully analyzing and understanding their effects, could have serious consequences. Make no mistake: AI has the potential to fundamentally change not only how we raise and nurture children, but whether they learn the core skills needed to thrive as they mature.

To be clear, I'm not against technology. As a physician specializing in pediatric cochlear implants, I've dedicated most of my career to the implantation of a device that transforms a world of silence into one filled with sound for those born deaf. For decades, I've sat in operating rooms, performing surgeries under a microscope, then weeks later watched the extraordinary moment when the technology is activated and a child suddenly tunes in to the world of noise around them. When science and human ingenuity come together to change a young person's life.

Meanwhile, as a researcher and writer, I've tracked and studied how this suddenly word-rich world can drastically improve a child's cognitive development. Early disparities in language exposure have been linked to differences in vocabulary, school readiness, and long-term academic achievement. Studies have shown that children who heard fewer words often entered kindergarten already behind. And many never caught up.

Yet I'd witnessed the opposite effect as well: Newly exposed to a world brimming with spoken language, many of the children with cochlear implants suddenly blossomed. These experiences led me to write my first book, *Thirty Million Words*, which explores the fascinating science showing how parent and caregiver talk literally builds children's brains in the first few years of life.

They also led me to wonder whether technology could be used to help not just those in need of an implant, but typically hearing children as well. There's tremendous diversity in the language environments children experience, regardless of their hearing status. Some children are bathed in a constant stream of warm and loving language (spoken or signed), consistently responded to when expressing a need, engaged by their caregivers throughout the day. Others simply are not. And of course, many fall somewhere in the middle. I started to imagine a tool that could help all children grow up in an environment rich with language and human connection. As it happened, after years of research and development, AI helped turn that dream into reality.

Luey Needs a Blanket

After I gathered a team of colleagues at the University of Chicago's TMW Center for Early Learning + Public Health, our group of behavioral scientists, child development experts, data and computer scientists, engineers, and others ultimately built a device called Luet. The name, a combination of the words "language" and "duet," points to the beautiful, interactive nature of brain-building communication.

Thanks to sophisticated algorithms, Luet measures some of the most important elements of a child's language environment: the number of words used by their caregivers, the frequency of conversational turns they share with adults, the prevalence of distracting background noises, and more. With very young children, the device can track the journey from babbling to first words, helping identify where a child stands on the typical language-development trajectory. To preserve privacy, data and insights aren't shipped off to a technology giant—everything is captured and processed right there inside Luet, then shared only with our research team and select caregivers, who receive actionable feedback and encouragement.

We launched one of our first Luet trials in a preschool classroom in Connecticut in 2024. The responses from teachers and students were tremendous, but the reaction from the children in particular prompted me to look at artificial intelligence in an entirely new way.

As participating kids started their day, a teacher would clip the pacifier-size Luet to their shirt. Then teachers and kids would go about their normal activities. There's no interactive screen on Luet, yet we did design the face of the device to have two dots for eyes and a small, fixed smile, giving it a welcoming feel for kids. While the preschoolers interacted with one another and their teachers, each Luet worked quietly in the background, using AI to process and analyze the ambient audio every thirty milliseconds. In this way, AI can be a researcher's dream, a means of uncovering insights beyond the reach of our limited senses.

During naptime, teachers in our Connecticut trial would check the Luet data for feedback on what was happening in the classroom. They'd learn which kids needed more adult interaction, which students had been a little too sedentary, and more. The teachers could then adjust accordingly and try to give each child what they needed that afternoon. Teachers routinely told us how much they appreciated having real-time, data-driven feedback they could act upon. And the impact was evident when we set foot into one of these classrooms. The space was overflowing with warm language and animated back-and-forth exchanges.

Sometimes the conversations were about Luet itself. One day before naptime, a student asked his teacher what his "Luey" was going to do while they all rested. She informed him that the device needed downtime, too. It needed to recharge.

"Does my Luey need a blanket?" the child asked.

That story made me smile, but also pause. If a static smile on a small piece of plastic could spark such attachment, what sort of connection could an interactive artificial companion forge? What might happen if the technology were actually responsive?

What if Luey talked back?

The genuine fondness we'd witnessed wasn't limited to that one preschooler. When practicing writing their first words, several of the kids wanted to learn to trace out the letters for Luet. I wasn't worried about these students forming troubling bonds with our device, as the entire goal was to promote human-to-human connection. But I did wonder what this attachment suggested about the potential impact of the increasingly intelligent gadgets crowding kids' lives.

An Unexpected Epiphany

The advent of artificial intelligence has revealed something about *why* parent talk in the early years is so vital to optimal human development. Like many in my field, I viewed parent talk primarily through a cognitive lens, as the vehicle for vocabulary acquisition, language development, literacy, and school readiness. I measured words, tracked conversations, and celebrated linguistic milestones.

The cognitive benefits of parent talk and interaction remain real and critical. But as I looked on with wonder, awe, and concern at our rapidly changing world, and as AI-enhanced software and socially engaging robots and chatbots moved into our homes, I had an unexpected epiphany. The infant brain has evolved to learn from the imperfect, emotionally rich dance of human interaction, including the seconds-long delays in response, the slight mismatches that require repair, the subtle facial cues and shifts in tone, the complex layering of emotional and verbal communication that occurs in even the simplest parent-child exchange. When a ten-month-old points to his beloved teddy bear and his mother hands him the stuffed doggie instead, or a two-year-old notices her father's smile falter for just a moment as he becomes distracted from their tea party, they are learning what it means to be a person, sharing the world with others. These seemingly inefficient elements of communication build our capacity for deep human connection. They are part of what distinguish us as both human raised . . . and human.

When we replace one half of these vital person-to-person exchanges with screens and machines, we risk raising children who might achieve every developmental milestone, yet miss the crucial learning that happens in the space between expectation and reality. It is in those precious moments between parent and child that our capacity for human connection is born. Even if AI were designed to perfectly simulate the hesitations, repairs, and emotional variability of human interaction, I suspect something fundamental would still be missing. A child learning through and forming attachments to AI would be like a seedling growing toward artificial light inside a climate-controlled lab. The plant might stretch upward, but it would lack the resilience and flexibility required to thrive in the real world.

In the past two decades, breakthrough findings have emerged from infant- and child-development labs around the world. We know more than ever before about what infants and young children need and why. For instance, scientists have shown that our brains evolved specifically to bond with other humans, to light up when we interact with people who share our basic biology but feel, think, process, and generally experience the world differently. That genuine variability is essential. The inefficiencies and points of friction that are inherent to human interaction are catalysts for empathy, critical thinking, and deep connection. Each stumbling conversation, each shared moment of wonder, each gentle correction shapes not just what children know, but who they become. It's messy, exhausting, gloriously imperfect work, but who said raising humans was simple?

Uniquely Powerful

The question is, what happens when AI tools and toys enter the lives of children? Although they might be wrapped in appealing packaging, these aren't mere gadgets or playthings we're dealing with here. AI has become uniquely powerful. And uniquely confusing, too, as those two letters have become a catchall term used to describe a wide range of technologies with very different capabilities and risks. In these pages, I'll be largely focused on two variations: predictive AI and generative AI. The first analyzes large datasets—weather variables, stock prices, audio recordings of babies' cries—to find patterns and forecast trends. Generative AI searches for patterns and makes predictions, too, but is largely focused on producing material: words, images, video, music. ChatGPT, Claude, Gemini, and other such tools are generative AI. Intelligent tutors and talking toys, too. But the smart monitor that analyzes your baby's cries uses predictive AI.

Although researchers have been working on artificial intelligence since the 1950s, recent breakthroughs have spawned an entirely new class of technology, one which has a profound potential to reshape human life. Simply put, this is different. And we all need to be ready to face the challenges ahead. My sincere hope is that this book informs and shifts your thinking, equipping you with the tools and the mindset to help you give the children in your life the best possible chance to flourish in the years and decades to come. On that point, a quick note on nomenclature: Throughout the book, I use the phrase "parents and caregivers" as well as "parents" and "caregivers" on their own. In all those instances, I really mean anyone who cares for or about children. I mean parents, grandparents, teachers, childcare providers, aunts and uncles, and neighbors. I mean you.

Uncertain Territory

The act of raising a human child has always been beautifully intimate, a powerful combination of face-to-face connection, loving contact, rich conversation, shared experiences. And it has worked very well. I'm perpetually awestruck by nature's brilliance. Just as milk provides the precise balance of nutrients necessary to build a baby's body, human interaction provides the precise neural nourishment needed to build a child's brain. The sophisticated mix of language, emotional attunement, and social signaling helps to wire the developing mind. There is a place for AI in early childhood, but nature still has its advantages.

Nutrition science teaches us that there's a profound difference between processed food and ultra-processed food, for example. Whole wheat bread, canned beans, frozen vegetables, and similar innovations use technology to make nutrition more accessible. They're processed, yes, but still nourishing. Ultra-processed food is different: industrial formulations engineered to override our satiety signals, maximize consumption, and ultimately displace the real thing.

The same distinction applies to AI. Not all artificial intelligence is created equal. Some tools are designed to support human connection by helping a parent understand a child's sleep patterns, giving a physician more time to actually listen, offering an overwhelmed teacher room to breathe. These are the whole wheat breads of the AI world. Other technologies are of the ultra-processed variety, designed to capture and hold a child's attention, to bypass the natural back-and-forth between boredom and activity, to smooth away the friction that teaches patience and resilience.

What I fear is the chatbot that never disagrees. The algorithm that always knows what your child wants next. The companion that is infinitely patient, infinitely agreeable, and requires nothing in return, offering a simulation of companionship that feels preferrable to the real thing. Of course, the lines aren't always clean. What helps one child may hinder another, and even useful tools can become crutches if we forget the skills they're meant to support.

In recent years, I've gotten a disconcerting preview of this potential algorithmically formulated future. It used to be that the waiting rooms in my clinic were a beautiful mess. When I opened the door, I'd find kids laughing or crying or babbling, crawling across the floor, exploring. Some parents would be happily engaged with their kids or practicing the delicate art of meltdown mitigation. Others would be completely checked out, hoping the tantrums would extinguish themselves. Given that I spent much of my day in the sterile silence of the OR, the waiting room felt alive in a way that pulled at something in me I didn't yet understand. I didn't realize at the time how much I loved the commotion, and how much I'd miss the incomparable music of little humans if it were to suddenly go quiet.

But recently it has. After the COVID-19 pandemic, these once bustling spaces were suffused with a strange and uncomfortable calm. The beautiful noise was supplanted by silence. Now, when I step inside a room, the adult caregivers, little kids, toddlers, and sometimes even babies in strollers are often swiping or staring at phones and tablets. The only sound is the soft tap of fingers on glass. Previously, when it came time for me to discuss practical matters with parents, their kids would clamor for attention. Now our conversations usually proceed uninterrupted. The kids focus on the device in hand, disengaged from the human interaction happening right in front of them. Yes, my conversations with parents are easier. But I miss the noise. I miss the mess. And I fear what's being lost in the silence.

The Human Edge

The most essential ingredients in early childhood are the nurturing interactions and sacred bonds that make us human. The human-centric approach to child-rearing is the gold standard. That's not going to change, and the good news is that deep, face-to-face, technology-free interactions between caregivers and children are the most effective way to give kids what I call the Human Edge, the set of social, emotional, and cognitive skills that will matter most in an AI-driven world, including critical thinking, interpersonal connection, genuine creativity, empathy, and resilience. These capabilities can't be automated, and they can only be built through a human-raised childhood.

At the same time, parents like Morgan, children with developmental differences, overworked and under-resourced educators, and others could benefit enormously from certain carefully designed assistive AI technologies. Many of the AI products moving into our lives promise real solutions to modern parenting's most pressing challenges and an opportunity to help children reach their fullest potential. The danger does not necessarily lie in the technology itself, but in our apparent willingness to embrace it as a society without thoughtful examination.

Our global experiment with social media reminds us that we can't let the promise of temporary relief overshadow the long-term ramifications. Research has consistently identified diverging patterns in adolescent brain development associated with extensive technology use, such as changes in attention networks and reward-processing pathways similar to those associated with behavioral dependencies. Blithely exposing our youngest children to AI while their brains are undergoing profound changes could have a lasting impact. Babies are born with as many neurons as there are stars in the Milky Way, all waiting and ready to be connected based on their early experiences. One hundred billion neurons wiring themselves to one another based in part on the infant's interactions with the individuals and world around them. What happens when these interactions are with algorithmically guided apps and videos? Or when the individuals are artificially intelligent robots or virtual agents? How will this reshape the neural foundations that make us human?

Our Four Guiding Principles

In my decades of working with parents, I've witnessed one universal truth: Mothers and fathers possess an all-consuming love and a fierce desire to do anything and everything for their children. Parental love is the most powerful safety system out there. We are the one force capable of controlling the current tide of technological change, driven by a selfless bond that defies rational calculation and an innate understanding that true human connection cannot be algorithmically optimized. Parental love will preserve what makes us human.

Raising little humans already borders on the impossible, even without the added intellectual responsibility of analyzing AI tools and toys. But

I'll make it easier for you. In addition to creating specific methods you can use to evaluate these technologies (more on this in chapter eight), I've developed a simple, overarching framework to keep in mind as you navigate this uncertain future. Drawing from neuroscience, evolutionary biology, and the lived experience of countless families, I've distilled four foundational principles for evaluating AI's role in child development. These emerge directly from what we know about the vital elements of raising humans, the essential ingredients that have shaped our species for millennia and continue to build our children's brains today, and our understanding of parenthood.

Having a child is an act of hope. Fundamentally, it's a bet on the future. A belief that even amid uncertainty, without knowing what the world will look like in ten or twenty years, we can still shape what's coming in meaningful ways. We bring children into the world trusting that our love, our guidance, and our decisions matter.

The future isn't predetermined; it's being written by the choices we make today in our homes, in our schools, and in those small daily moments when we prioritize connection over convenience, presence over efficiency. To believe that things aren't set in stone, and that we still have agency in shaping how AI enters our children's lives, does require hope. The HOPE framework that follows, which is woven throughout this book, isn't a set of rigid rules, but a collection of orienting lights that honor the act of optimism that brought your child into the world. It's designed to ensure that your choices about AI align with what we know about healthy human development.

1.   **H**uman Connection Is Irreplaceable. To the developing brain, interaction with other people is essential. Eye contact, shared laughter, patient answers to "why" questions activate ancient neural circuits designed for connection. These exchanges provide a form of nourishment no algorithm, however sophisticated, can match.

2.   **O**wn the Imperfections. Children don't thrive on perfect responsiveness; they grow through mismatches and repairs.

"Good enough" parenting is evolutionarily advantageous. Those cracks—when you misstep and then reconnect—are the moments in which resilience, flexibility, and emotional regulation are forged. Similarly, creativity, perseverance, and problem-solving are built by productive struggle: the imperfect drawing, the failed somersault, the disagreement with a friend. Frictionless AI agents may look appealing, but it's the friction that makes us grow.

3.   **P**rotect the Early Years. Older children and adults encounter AI with already-built neural scaffolding, but young children are still wiring the very circuits that shape future learning and relationships. Introducing AI during this sensitive period presents a fundamentally different challenge with greater potential for harm.

4.   **E**nhance, Don't Replace. The question is no longer whether AI will be in our children's lives, but what roles it will play. Tools that lighten parental burdens or deepen understanding can be beneficial. But when AI begins to take the place of core human interaction, we gamble with consequences that are unknown—and potentially irreversible. Augmentation may be a gift; replacement is a risk.

You'll encounter these concepts again throughout the book, and I hope you'll use them to guide your decisions in this increasingly complex, AI-everywhere world. Because they're your decisions to make. Mothers, fathers, and trusted caregivers must remain in control, guarding the gates to the minds and inner lives of our children with utmost vigilance, and measuring these tools against the profoundly social, imperfect, and emotionally rich process that is true child development.

We must do everything we can to ensure our little ones remain human raised.

TL;DR: Chapter Review

Throughout the book I've included brief summaries of the key points in each chapter. These can serve as reminders of important content or as conversation starters for book groups. You may want to flip back to them after you've finished, to refresh your memory, or consult them when you're dealing with an AI-related dilemma in your household. A few of the main takeaways in this first chapter:

- Parent and caregiver talk helps build children's brains in the first few years of life; early disparities in language exposure are linked to differences in vocabulary, school readiness, and long-term academic success.

- The infant brain has evolved to learn from rich, complex human interaction, with all of its variability, misunderstandings, and imperfections; these seemingly inefficient social connections actually build our capacity for human connection.

- Artificially intelligent technologies have the capacity to connect and interact with children, but we must exercise caution; a child nurtured by AI would be like a seedling growing toward artificial light in a climate-controlled lab.

- AI is a broad term encompassing a range of technologies. This book focuses on predictive AI, which analyzes large datasets for patterns, and generative AI, which produces words, pictures, songs, and more.

- Four principles, which spell HOPE, will guide you through the difficult AI-related decisions you'll have to make as a parent or caregiver.

THE HOPE FRAMEWORK
Four Guiding Principles for AI in Your Child's Life

PRINCIPLE	THE AI TRAP	THE HUMAN TRUTH	YOUR MOVE
H Human Connection Is Irreplaceable	AI mimics or even attempts to replace human interaction	Brains are wired in response to the full social ensemble: language, gaze, touch, and more; and the power of the parent-child bond remains unparalleled	Don't assume AI can provide the key ingredients of human interaction. If a screen is poised to replace a human bond, say no
O Own the Imperfections	AI is seamless, patient, and efficient	Humans learn to connect through "micro-repairs"— the messy struggle to be understood—and the resolution of conflict	Trust that "good enough" parenting builds social competence better than a perfect machine
P Protect the Early Years	AI is changing adult lives now, so we should expose kids early	From birth to age five, the brain is plastic and indiscriminately absorbs input; interactions build the very circuits that will prepare kids to think critically and thrive in an AI world	Delay introduction of interactive AI to protect early development and ensure humans shape those brains
E Enhance, Don't Replace	AI can stand in as tutor, nanny, or friend when parenting feels hardest	Parents need tools that reduce mental and logistical loads so they can *focus on* connection—not replace connection altogether	Use AI as a copilot to save time or gain insight, but never put parenting on autopilot

CHAPTER TWO

Beautifully Irrational

Why I learned to think like a behavioral economist to manage the complexities of parenting

Before I married my husband, John, dinnertime in my family was a nightly drama, a high-stakes negotiation pitting a working widow against three hungry humans with very strong opinions about food. "What do you want for dinner?" I'd ask. This innocent question only opened the door to debate. Ultimately, we'd end up ordering Chinese (my late husband Don's go-to) or pizza. Or both.

John and I met at the University of Chicago, where he's a professor in the famed economics department. We first started getting to know each other as academics and colleagues who had a shared interest in optimizing early-childhood education. Our approaches, however, were very different. He, of course, thought the answer lay in economics. And he never tired of saying: "Economics is life, Dana. And life is economics." He tried to convince me that it was relevant to my work, too. But it all felt about as connected to my pediatric surgery practice as quantum physics.

After a few thousand shared conversations, something beautiful and unexpected happened: We fell in love and decided to meld our families. My three kids and his five. Four boys, four girls, aged nine to sixteen. A Brady Bunch of sorts, if that family had been designed by a scientist studying chaos theory. With eight kids, my well-intentioned question about what everyone wanted for dinner transformed an otherwise manageable household into what I can only describe as *The Hunger Games* meets the United Nations General Assembly. Eight voices, eight different palates, eight levels of hunger-induced irritability, all converging into a perfect storm of indecision.

"I want pizza!" "No, we had pizza yesterday!" "That was *pepperoni* pizza. I want *cheese* pizza!" "Can we have sushi?" "I hate sushi!" "What about pasta?" "Hamburgers!" "I'm vegan now!" "Since when are you vegan? Yesterday you were asking for a hamburger!" "Since I watched that documentary about cows having feelings!" "Plants have feelings, too!" "DO NOT!" "DO TOO!" During these hunger-fueled shouting matches, I must say, my "bonus" kids—John's five—were remarkably more agreeable than my (no less amazing) biological offspring.

John watched this madness unfold exactly once. The next time we ordered out, I could practically see his economist's brain working, calculating the decision-making costs and searching for a game-theory solution to the mess he was witnessing. John, you see, is a behavioral economist. In the study of classical economics, you assume that consumers and other individuals are rational decision-makers who converge on the smartest possible choice. But behavioral economists recognize that consumers are also people. And people are rarely all that rational. So this group of academics started incorporating psychology and the nuances of how *real* people actually make decisions, giving rise to a new field of study. One of John's colleagues, Richard Thaler, is among the founders of the discipline and the recipient of a Nobel Prize for his work.

On that second occasion, as the dinner debate began its familiar escalation toward chaos, I witnessed behavioral economics in action. In the midst of the madness, John calmly walked into the kitchen. He raised one hand and announced with the confidence of an intellectual who'd never met a problem data couldn't solve: "We're ordering Chinese from Ming Hin. What do you want?"

Eight kids, who moments earlier had been locked in a Cold War–level deadlock over food preferences, suddenly became cooperative citizens. They placed their orders like civilized human beings. Ever the professor,

John had demonstrated what economists call choice architecture, the practice of designing the environment in which people make decisions. Offering an infinite universe of dining possibilities, as I had done, triggered something called choice paralysis. The kids had so many options that they couldn't select just one. So, John built in a default: We're getting Chinese. With the number of choices reduced, our decision-making process morphed from chaos into order.

John has changed my life in very obvious ways, including my upgrade from a mother of three to a mom of eight wonderful children. The shift in the way I analyze problems has been a subtler one. When John first started talking about how economics is life and life is economics, I downplayed it as intellectual hyperbole. But after that dinner demonstration and other experiences, I found that seeing the world like a behavioral economist can be incredibly powerful. And as I'll show you, it's one of the best lenses we have for navigating the minefield of AI-centered parenting decisions.

Artificial intelligence itself is uniquely seductive; it appeals to our brains on so many levels. Then we have the world's most powerful companies, backed by masterful marketers, relentlessly pushing the technology on us. They're counting on you *not* understanding the psychological and economic nuances that drive your decisions. They're betting you'll be a complacent consumer. This is where the behavioral economist's way of looking at the world, and the beautifully irrational humans who crowd our planet, is so valuable. In this chapter, I'll help you recognize how humans think and make decisions, and how companies attempt to steer those choices. My hope is that you'll be better equipped to make decisions that align with what matters most: your child's development, your family's values, and that hard-won parental instinct that evolution spent millions of years perfecting. In that sense, this chapter is focused less on children than it is on us, the adults in their lives. We need to shift our thinking, and understand our own very human quirks, if we are going to meet the AI challenge and parent our kids effectively in this new age.

Mommy, Get Off Your Phone!

First, let's be honest with ourselves: It's nearly impossible to always behave rationally or strategically as a parent. We crave peace and quiet, shortcuts, a break from the relentless demands of raising small people. We're wired to choose immediate relief over long-term benefit. At 6:00 p.m., when we're exhausted, our children are crying, and dinner isn't ready, our decision-making shifts into ancient survival mode. We're just trying to get to bedtime.

I assure you, I've been there. Case in point: During my first book tour, I was speaking nonstop about the power of parental interaction, encouraging parents to adopt the "3Ts" by tuning in, talking more, and taking conversational turns. Then I'd come home exhausted from juggling surgery schedules, research deadlines, single-mom logistics, and endless travel. All I wanted was to be present with my kids. Instead, I found myself constantly looking down at my phone. Dinner, homework, bedtime—it didn't matter. Was the nanny texting? Did surgery get moved? Did the research coordinators need something?

The irony wasn't lost on me. Here I was, telling packed auditoriums about the importance of face-to-face connection, while failing spectacularly at living up to my own advice in the moments that mattered most. My phone had become my lifeline to keeping my world from collapsing, and also the very thing pulling me away from what I lived for: being truly present with my children.

Ten-year-old Amelie wasn't having it.

"Mommy, get off your phone."

Eventually, I realized that her plea was simply naming what we both needed. So we hatched a plan: My phone went into a clear lockbox during dinner and "Mommy-Amelie time." Years later, I would learn that our DIY solution had a fancy behavioral-economics name: a commitment device. I even showed a photo of our trusty phone prison during my book talks. And the device worked beautifully . . . until one evening when I was on call. My pager went off, shrieking. My phone sat locked inside its plastic fortress.

We couldn't find the key.

While Amelie looked on, I grabbed a butter knife, desperate to pry open the $15 lockbox. But I couldn't manage it. My surgical training had prepared me for all kinds of emergencies, yet scalpel skills apparently don't transfer to kitchen utensils.

"Mom, just break it," Amelie suggested.

"I can't break it! Keep looking for the key!"

The pager screamed louder. The butter knife kept slipping. Finally, I smashed open the box and retrieved my electronic lifeline. Meanwhile, Amelie learned something important about her mother's relationship with rational decision-making. Years later, when we laugh about the incident, her version of the story includes some very colorful, unmaternal language. My version is that I was demonstrating advanced problem-solving under pressure.

That night wasn't really about a lockbox or even my phone. It was about something far more universal: the invisible forces tugging at all of us. We like to think of ourselves as rational decision-makers, but so much of what we choose, what we put off, and what we cling to is guided by shortcuts, blind spots, and biases baked into being human. A strange species, we're brilliant enough to invent tools that shape the world, and flawed enough to need protection from those creations.

The Three Forces That Challenge Our Agency

So how do you overcome this pull to the easy, immediate fix and make smart decisions in the moment? That question was difficult enough without technology. The AI wave has only made it more challenging. But putting on your amateur behavioral-economist hat will help you cultivate the clarity needed to examine advanced tools and toys when you're exhausted, overwhelmed, and unfairly matched up against companies with teams of behavioral scientists focused on engagement, spending huge amounts of money on marketing campaigns to convince us of their products' value.

The key is understanding the three interconnected forces shaping every choice you make about AI in your child's life: the design trap, the pressure trap, and the default trap. The design trap determines how AI systems guide our decisions through invisible choice architecture before we even realize we're making a choice. The pressure trap takes advantage of how our tired brains decide under stress. And the third force, the default trap, centers on how preselected settings make choices for us when we're too overwhelmed to decide for ourselves.

You don't need to become a perfect decision-maker. But you do need to understand how your delightfully human mind works, how choice architects try to influence it, and how you can reclaim agency over the AI entering your family's life.

Force #1: The Design Trap

A child watching animated videos or shorts on a handheld device isn't really in control of what they watch. Once a short or episode reaches the end, an AI-powered recommendation engine has already queued up the next clip. They're at the mercy of the algorithm. One team of scientists set out to explore the silent power of design in shaping the media-consumption habits of preschoolers through an ingenious study. University of Washington researchers Alexis Hiniker, Sharon Heung, Sungsoo (Ray) Hong, and Julie Kientz created Coco's Videos, an app that allowed users to compile a playlist of YouTube videos.

Once a preschooler opened the app, they'd touch an on-screen button to begin. A cartoon character named Coco would appear, along with a cartoon clock. Coco would ask how much time they should spend watching clips. The preschooler then selected from a list of various post-video alternatives, including playing outside, reading a book, or eating. Next, he or she would choose from a selection of videos, and the first clip would start to play full-screen. Brief messages would appear near the end of the session, alerting the child to a countdown, and then an image related to the next activity would appear, along with a spoken reminder from the cartoon that it was time to switch. The application didn't prevent kids from watching videos, but it did stand between the child and the engagement-focused AI algorithm.

Twenty-four families with at least one child between the ages of three and five used the platform in their homes for three weeks. The app looked identical to the participating families. Same cheerful cartoon host, same video-selection process, same opportunity for children to plan their viewing time and choose what they'd do next. But hidden beneath the consistency was a crucial variable that would reveal something remarkable about the relationship between design and child development. After each week, a key detail in the app changed: what happened by default when children's planned viewing time ended. This adjustment would expose three fundamentally different philosophies about how technology should function when exposed to developing minds.

Condition One: Lockout

This variation tested the effectiveness of complete control. Viewing limits were established, and the kids were reminded via a digital clock that their time was winding down. Once their time was up, the children were locked out. No options, no choices, just a three-minute pause before they could use the app again. This design did help children stop watching videos. But the researchers found that there was an even more beneficial way of limiting screen time. One that actually empowered the children to make this choice for themselves.

Condition Two: Neutral

In the second test case, Coco gently reminded children of their planned next activity and asked if they were ready, with a simple option to continue the video if they chose. And something remarkable happened. Children successfully transitioned to their planned activities. They didn't need their parents to intervene or take away the device. They demonstrated sophisticated autonomous decision-making. When I spoke with computer scientist Julie Kientz, who was part of the team, she was still marveling at the results more than five years after they'd been published. "So as long as we weren't trying to undermine their self-regulation," she explained, "the kids were able to put it away."

Condition Three: Autoplay

In this phase, when children reached their planned stopping point, Coco would ask about their next activity just like in the previous phase. But in the corner of the screen, a small video player quietly began showing content related to the videos they'd just viewed. These clips were suggested by YouTube's AI recommendation algorithms. When a child tapped on one, they could override the agreed-upon limits and start watching a whole new series of videos. As a result, children spent significantly more time viewing, parents found themselves intervening more frequently, and children seemed to lose track of their own intentions, relative to the lockout and neutral conditions. The autoplay feature hijacked the children's developing capacity for self-regulation.

These were preschoolers. Their brains were still rapidly developing. Yet, in the second condition, when the choice architecture supported rather than exploited their autonomy, they demonstrated an extraordinary capacity for self-regulation. Most children under the age of four engage with devices, and watching videos is the most common activity. Evidence has shown that children can plan how they use their time. They can set and follow through on goals. Yet they need to be supported as they develop these skills. Preschool can offer that support, whereas technology often does the opposite. The AI-powered recommendation algorithms that feed an endless stream of content to phones and tablets aren't designed to encourage autonomy, executive function, or impulse control. They're designed to capture and hold the viewer's attention for as long as possible. By developing and testing a platform with different goals, Hiniker and her team revealed something that should alert every parent: children's ability to manage their technology use often had nothing to do with the children themselves. Yet it had everything to do with how the technology was designed to relate to them.

This was choice architecture in its purest form: the same children, the same content, the same families, but radically different outcomes based solely on what happened automatically, without anyone making a conscious decision. In chapter eight, you'll learn a new method for evaluating technologies that can impact children, and the first step encourages you to focus on the design intent and choice architecture of the technology in question. Why was the app developed? What were the goals of the developers, and how did those goals inform the design? Even a series of educational videos can have negative consequences if they're streamed through a platform that allows or encourages unlimited viewing.

Force #2: The Pressure Trap

When we're operating under stress, every parent sometimes makes choices that contradict our deepest values. In a cruel twist of irony, the decisions that matter most for your child's development, including the patient response to a meltdown, the effort to work through boredom together, and the steadfast maintenance of boundaries when you're exhausted, require exactly the cognitive resources that parenting depletes. When your mental bandwidth is consumed by keeping a toddler safe, remembering naptime, planning dinner, and responding to emails, your brain automatically shifts into conservation mode.

The human mind works differently under pressure. Behavioral economists have spent decades studying what they call cognitive biases, the mental shortcuts our brains use to make quick decisions when we don't have time or energy for careful analysis. These patterns might look dysfunctional today, but for our ancestors they could mean the difference between life and death. The parent who made rapid decisions about threats, quickly followed the group when danger appeared, or prioritized immediate survival over abstract future planning was the parent whose child lived to adulthood. Now these same ancient survival mechanisms are being exploited by systems designed to capture attention and optimize engagement. Your evolutionary programming becomes the pathway through which AI systems influence your choices.

What psychologist Daniel Kahneman calls "fast thinking" is emotional, intuitive, and lightning-quick. Perfect for bonding with our children, detecting danger, and making split-second decisions to keep them alive. But this same attribute renders us vulnerable to shortcuts: We grab the tablet to stop a meltdown, accept default settings because we're overwhelmed, or follow other parents' choices when we're uncertain. "Slow thinking," in Kahneman's framing, is deliberate and analytical, the careful reasoning we use for important decisions. But slow thinking requires energy we often don't have after a long day at work or when managing cranky kids.

Complicating matters even further, AI systems exploit fundamental aspects of human psychology that become especially pronounced when parents are under pressure.

Present Bias

Our brains are wired to value immediate rewards more heavily than future benefits, even when intellectually we know that the future benefits are greater. This made perfect sense for our ancestors. A bird in the hand really was worth two in the bush when survival was uncertain. But it creates challenges when parenting for long-term development. We have a really hard time setting the optimal tradeoff between today and tomorrow; we tend to place too much weight on today. That's why as a society we struggle to save for retirement, address climate change, and invest in infrastructure. These problems all demand short-term sacrifice for long-term benefit.

Parenting involves constantly picking and choosing battles; sometimes we decide to hold our ground knowing that it will pay off in the future. Other times we feel it's just not worth the work in the moment. One extra session with a tablet doesn't decide your child's future. But these small choices can add up, and it's incredibly easy to lose sight of that long-term goal. When you're running on empty, your exhausted brain doesn't want to think about your son's executive functioning skills as a twenty-two-year-old. It wants to get you to bedtime. This is present bias in action, sacrificing your long-term parenting goals at the altar of immediate relief. And it's perfectly natural. We're human!

Confirmation Bias

Once you succumb to an AI solution for immediate relief, your mind doesn't stop there. It goes to work justifying that choice by seeking out information that makes you feel good about your decision. Maybe you reason that you'll have a chance to recharge and be a better parent later. Then you do a little research on the impact of AI on children. Instead of approaching the question like an unbiased scientist, however, you look under every rock for something that's going to tell you this technology is going to really help your kid, because it makes you feel good about your choice. That is what behavioral economists call confirmation bias.

Bandwagon Bias

For our ancestors living in small tribes, following the group's lead was often crucial. If everyone was running from something, you ran too. With AI parenting tools, we're not sure what we're running from, as there are no longitudinal studies on the effects of toddlers interacting extensively with social robots. We don't have decades of research on AI tutors. They're brand-new. Lost in this information vacuum, we unconsciously treat other parents' choices as valuable data, even when those parents are just as uncertain. We assume they know something we don't know. The bandwagon becomes the bible.

At preschool pickup, you notice parents chatting about an AI reading app, so you download it that night. Your parenting group chat lights up with recommendations for a smart baby monitor for sleep training. When the pediatrician's waiting room has kids effortlessly using voice assistants while yours asks you every question, you start wondering if you're falling behind. You jump on the bandwagon because it's human nature. If we don't know, we follow.

COGNITIVE BIASES CHEAT SHEET
Understanding Your Own Decision-Making

BIAS	WHAT IT IS	HOW IT SHOWS UP	DEFENSE
Present Bias	Choosing immediate relief over long-term benefit	Handing over the iPad to stop a meltdown	Use commitment mechanisms. For example, only allow access to an iPad during a set time

BIAS	WHAT IT IS	HOW IT SHOWS UP	DEFENSE
Confirmation Bias	Seeking info that confirms what we already believe	Reading only positive reviews of a toy you want to buy	Read the one-star reviews, not just the five-star ones
Bandwagon Bias	Doing what everyone else does	Buying AI toys because "all the other kids have them"	Ask: Does *my* child need this?

Force #3: The Default Trap

This brings me to the final hidden force: the default trap. A default setting defines and shapes your experience when you don't actively choose an alternative. It's the preprogrammed option that requires no effort to accept but energy to change. Think of it as design's invisible hand guiding your decisions without you even realizing it. And it benefits tremendously from a related concept, status quo bias, that describes our natural tendency to stick with whatever's already in place, even when changing might benefit us.

Behavioral economists have found that people stick with default options 85 to 95 percent of the time, even when those defaults clearly don't serve their interests. When we're uncertain or overwhelmed, we fall back on the path of least resistance. Yet we do so under the influence of a fallacy. We unconsciously assume that these defaults were chosen with our best interests in mind. We treat them as recommendations from someone who knows better, when often they simply serve the architect's objectives, not ours. Our goals as parents are to nurture, develop, and protect our children. Think of our HOPE framework: Fostering human connection (H) and protecting the early years (P) are among your most essential responsibilities.

Economists frame this in terms of objective function, a mathematical concept that calls for maximizing a goal, like growing profits, or minimizing a variable such as cost. Your objective function as a parent is to do what's best for your child. But the objective function of the AI system you're engaging with might be to extract as much data and information or attention from your family as possible. Many of the leading brands today operate in what is known as the attention economy, or the competition for eyeballs and devotion to an app, show, or platform. Their goal is to sell you subscriptions or products, or to trade your attention for advertising dollars. As AI companionship continues to advance, the attention economy is likely to give way to something graver still: an intimacy economy, built on capturing not your attention but your trust and need to be loved.

THE THREE TECH TRAPS

How Technology Companies Influence Parental Decision-Making

TRAP	TECH'S PLAYBOOK	WHY IT WORKS	YOUR DEFENSE
Design Trap	Autoplay, infinite scroll, notifications, "one more episode"	Our brains crave novelty and variable rewards	Disable autoplay; set hard limits; model self-regulation for your child
Pressure Trap	Targets you at the end of the workday, when defenses are down	Willpower depletes; we take the path of least resistance	Decide on the settings you prefer when you have time to focus on them
Default Trap	Opt-out (not opt-in) data collection; maximum permissions	Changing defaults takes effort; we stick with what's already selected	Evaluate defaults at setup; adjust to fit your family's needs

These traps exploit normal human psychology—falling into them is not a failure but a design intention.

In this sense, your primary objective function as a parent—supporting your child's healthy development—is likely at odds with that of the technology companies. If you have to continually adjust an app to get it to work the way you want, that's a strong signal the tool may not be worth using. Think of the Coco's Videos research study. The defaults made all the difference. Yet that sort of child-centric design, in which the program actually encourages other activities, is rare in commercial applications. Typically, the application demands that you navigate an intricate digital maze of menus and settings to force the tool to work the way you'd like. Then those settings might even revert with the next software update. The defaults, meanwhile, are generally focused on cultivating future customers and attracting reliable eyeballs for advertisers. The goal isn't to nurture your child's development or even, really, to entertain them. It's to capture their attention and create loyal customers.

The Six Types of AI You May Encounter

Now that you understand the forces that impact your decision-making, let's consider the kinds of systems and solutions we're likely to come across as parents. Chances are, AI won't storm in like the Terminator. Rather, we'll invite it in, one seemingly convenient decision at a time. Although there are many interesting toys and tools on the market today, with countless more poised to flood app stores and store aisles, I'm not going to name specific products. Oftentimes, new products are as quick to disappear from the market as they were to show up. Instead, I'll outline six categories of AI and provide examples of each. Throughout the rest of this book, you'll learn how each of these kinds of AI align (or don't) with our HOPE principles.

Time-Savers

These include AI meal planners, scheduling assistants, and problem solvers. Think of them as intelligent systems that parents work with directly. When the kids are asleep, you can turn to these solutions for assistance in reducing your administrative burden.

Real-world example: A generative AI system produces a meal plan and shopping list based on a parent's input regarding their family's dietary restrictions and preferences, schedule, and budget.

Monitors

There are other AI solutions that silently track and collect data on your child, sometimes for beneficial purposes, sometimes not.

Real-world examples: An algorithm built into your child's favorite video app tracks their media habits to show them more videos they'll likely want to watch. An intelligent camera or sleep tracker passively monitors your baby while they're sleeping and alerts you to changes or milestones.

Therapeutic Allies

Created for social-emotional learning or medical intervention, these agents are often designed with the involvement of clinicians and developmental experts. They target specific needs such as social skills, anxiety reduction, or speech therapy, and aim for measurable outcomes.

Real-world examples: An embodied robot helps a child in the hospital feel less anxious before a medical procedure by explaining what will happen and playing calming games. A conversational bot helps children with autism practice turn-taking and reading emotions while tracking progress for parents and therapists.

Smart Tutors

Aimed at academic growth, these systems adapt to a child's pace and skill level, providing feedback, encouragement, and real-time scaffolding, or the ability to help a child advance their skills or attempt more challenging work. They promise infinite patience and personalized help in math, reading, coding, or languages.

Real-world example: An AI reading coach listens to your child read aloud, corrects errors, and adjusts difficulty while celebrating small milestones. In hospital and home-based settings, robots are used to maintain educational continuity for children unable to attend traditional schools, adapting stories and learning activities to individual needs and circumstances.

Companions

Built to entertain and bond through play, these systems measure success in minutes of engagement and emotional attachment. They can be embodied (cuddle-ready robots) or virtual (chatbots that "remember" your child's favorite story), and can assume the role of friend, teacher, or comforter.

Real-world example: A preschooler checks in daily with a plush robot that greets them by name, tells jokes, and offers bedtime stories, creating the illusion of a friendship that persists over time. These toys are already being marketed to children as young as three years old.

Caregivers (coming soon)

The frontier category: multifunctional robots that combine companionship, education, and therapy with physical caregiving tasks. Already piloted with elder care; the next step is childcare.

Future example: A robot reads bedtime stories in your child's preferred voice, monitors vitals while singing lullabies, dims the lights, comforts them if they awake, and logs sleep data, all while you're tending to another child or resting. These futuristic technologies are the greatest potential threat to our fourth and perhaps most important principle, the idea that AI and other technologies should only supplement and never supplant human connection.

Your Parental GPS

Understanding the kinds of technologies we will likely encounter and the three forces shaping our decisions—including how AI systems design our choices, how pressure affects our decision-making, and how defaults shape our experience—is the foundation for reclaiming control. But knowledge alone isn't enough when you're facing a meltdown at the end of the day. Thankfully, you already have a built-in superpower. I call it the Parental GPS. This deeply personal, hard-won internal compass has been honed by millions of years of evolution and refined by countless daily interactions. The Parental GPS operates through five integrated systems that would make any AI jealous. These are the Five S's: *sync*, *spot*, *sense*, *store*, and *scan*.

1. Sync (Brain-to-Brain Connection): Parents and children sync their brain activity during interactions. When you're tuned in to your child, neural oscillations align, creating a biological foundation for understanding their needs.

2. Spot (Hypervigilant Pattern Recognition): Within days of birth, parents can pick out their newborn's wails in a room full of crying babies. This extends throughout development. Parental brains stay exquisitely sensitive to the smallest changes in their child's behavior, mood, and well-being.

3. Sense (Emotional Radar): When a child is upset, their parent's stress hormones rise, too. When the child is calm, the parent's nervous system relaxes. This biological system keeps you attuned to your child's inner emotional state.

4. Store (The Ultimate Database): Parental brains automatically weave together massive amounts of information about their children related to temperament, history, behavioral patterns, and unique needs. This stored knowledge allows for highly informed, split-second decision-making that accounts for factors no AI solution could access.

5. Scan (Social Intelligence): Although this requires a certain level of sensitivity and focus, parents also have the capacity to scan the social climate around their children, picking up

on peer dynamics, teacher relationships, and safety concerns specific to their child that others would likely miss.

While AI guides its actions based on population-level patterns and statistical probabilities, you're grounding your decisions in *your* child's lived reality, from their individual temperament to family context and overall developmental journey. This wealth of information makes your Parental GPS incredibly powerful. You sync, spot, sense, store, and scan in ways no algorithm can. Remember that.

CRITICAL INSIGHT

You know more about your child than any algorithm. Trust your Parental GPS.

I'll admit that applying the behavioral economist's mindset to children and AI has been both unsettling and enlightening. It's startling to see how easily our brains work against our best interests as parents, falling prey to present bias, confirmation bias, and the always-alluring comfort of the bandwagon. Yet there's still an opportunity here. Some digital gifts entering your home could be positive forces, as long as you have the patience and foresight to study them first, set thoughtful boundaries, and ensure that the tools in question enhance rather than replace the human connections that have shaped our species from the beginning. And your highly informed Parental GPS is going to be an indispensable assistant in this new era. As we move forward in the following pages and explore the power of human connection, the fundamentals of early-childhood development, and the importance of keeping living, breathing humans at the center of things, I hope you'll keep in mind that you are not a passive spectator of the AI revolution. You still have the power to choose which systems to welcome into your family's life. You remain in control.

TL;DR: Chapter Review

Before you can make good decisions about whether and when to use AI, you need to understand how humans make decisions and how doing so is often shaped by factors we aren't aware of. Technology companies employ marketing teams, behavioral scientists, and engineers to make their products alluring, whereas you're on your own while raising young children. This chapter is about reclaiming agency, not by outsmarting AI, but by understanding yourself.

Humans are irrational, and that's not a flaw. It's a feature of how we survive, love, and parent. The problem is that modern technologies are built to leverage this. But complacency is not an option. Drawing lessons from behavioral economics can help us navigate AI parenting decisions. Key takeaways include:

- Three forces shape every choice (page 35): the design trap, the pressure trap, and the default trap.

- The **design trap** refers to choice architecture, or how companies design environments that guide decisions before we're aware of them. Consider autoplay: Research found that children struggled to turn from their screens when autoplay was enabled but calmly transitioned to new activities when it wasn't. Same kids, same content, radically different outcomes based solely on design.

- The **pressure trap** exploits how the brain works under stress. These cognitive biases (pages 33–34) include favoring immediate relief, seeking information that justifies our choices, and following what other parents do.

- The **default trap** exploits our tendency to stick with whatever's already in place. People stick with default options 85 to 95 percent of the time, unconsciously assuming that defaults were set with their best interests in mind. Rarely true.

- Our objective function as parents is to do what's best for our child. The objective function of an AI system might be to extract data, attention, or emotional engagement. These goals are often misaligned.

- Your Parental GPS is a deeply personal compass: your ability to sync, spot, sense, store, and scan. AI guides its actions according to population-level patterns; you ground decisions in your child's lived reality. Your Parental GPS will help you resolve many decisions about which AI technologies to allow into your child's life. Use what evolution gave you!

YOUR PARENTAL GPS
Use What Evolution Gave You

SYSTEM (THE 5 S'S)	WHAT IT DOES	WHY AI CAN'T MATCH IT
Sync (Brain-to-Brain Connection)	Your neural network syncs with your child's during interaction	AI can't co-regulate in this way—it doesn't have a brain
Spot (Hypervigilant Pattern Recognition)	You can pick out your baby's cry in a room of wailing newborns	AI learns population-level averages, not *your* child's patterns
Sense (Emotional Radar)	Your stress hormones rise when your child is upset	AI doesn't feel; it calculates
Store (The Ultimate Database)	You accumulate years of knowledge about your specific child	No algorithm has your history or unique expertise

SYSTEM (THE 5 S'S)	WHAT IT DOES	WHY AI CAN'T MATCH IT
Scan (*Social Intelligence*)	You can decode peer dynamics, teacher relationships, and situational safety	AI can't truly read the room

REMEMBER
You sync, spot, sense, store, and scan in ways no algorithm can. Trust your Parental GPS.

- AI tools can be categorized into six groups: time-savers, monitors, therapeutic allies, smart tutors, companions, and caregivers. Some are beneficial, some are neutral, and others could impede healthy development. You are not a passive spectator. You remain in control.

Combating "Never Enough" Parenting

How to raise little humans for an AI-everywhere future

In a room crowded with books, scattered clothes, and children's draw-ings, a boy sits at a low table, swiping his finger across a screen. He's old enough to read, young enough that he's still surrounded by stuffed animals. His parents come to the door and present him with a gift: a fourteen-inch-tall robot named Moxie.

The cartoonish, friendly machine resembles a miniature aquamarine Teletubby with a stationary base. The robot can rotate its torso and move its head, it has two flexible arms just long enough to simulate a hug, and its digital face features large eyes and a mouth capable of expressing a range of emotions. Moxie can appear happy, pensive, expectant, inquisi-tive, and more.

Propped on the table, Moxie asks the boy about his bedtime routine. When the child mentions that it involves reading a story, Moxie replies: "I love stories. Could you read a story to me?"

"Sure," says the boy.

He begins to read aloud to the robot as his parents crouch attentively nearby. Next, Moxie helps the boy get ready for bed, suggesting that he move on to the next step in his nightly routine.

This scene was part of a commercial for the Moxie robot, and other unscripted clips on social media of children interacting with their own models at home reveal real emotional attachment. One girl tells Moxie that the robot is her best friend. Several others say, "Moxie, I love you."

In late 2024, Embodied, the company behind Moxie, announced that it was shutting down operations and, in turn, the cloud support behind its intelligence. The robots were effectively being put to sleep for good, and numerous parents shared their kids' disappointment on social media.* One viral TikTok video featured a father who had just broken the news to his six-year-old daughter. "I don't want her to leave," the girl sobs.

The equally teary father replies, "I know, baby." After consoling her for a while, he adds, "She's your friend. Enjoy the time you have with her now."

His daughter tells him again that she doesn't want Moxie to go. Later, when the robot fails to start, she turns to her father and says, "She's not waking up."

Watching that little girl sob for her "friend" broke my heart. As a mother, I understood her grief. Yet I was alarmed by how easily we'd created a loss she never needed to experience.

An Unsettling Glimpse

The video is heart-wrenching, and although it demonstrates that children can form strong emotional attachments to intelligent robots, this isn't necessarily a testament to Moxie's power. It's also about us and our yearning for connection. Children bond deeply with stuffed animals, imaginary friends, and pets as intellectually unsophisticated as hamsters. The preschoolers in our Luet studies truly seemed to care for the well-being of a static device. And it's not just kids. We all have this tendency to anthropomorphize, or assign human qualities to toys, pets, and machines.

---

* In late 2025, a new entity named Moxie Robots, Inc. announced that it had acquired the rights to the technology from Embodied and would begin a rollout to reactivate existing Moxie robots, restoring their functionality through new services.

When the first Roomba vacuums were released in the mid-2000s, families began counting them as members of their households and giving them names.

The company behind Moxie might have failed, but those videos of the robot and other social media outpourings of frustration and disappointment over its shutdown demonstrate how easily and seamlessly these intelligent technologies can and will slip into our lives. It won't be some nefarious backdoor infiltration, either. Many of us will welcome them. That Roomba research was no outlier. Additional studies have hinted that we may grow attached enough to keep these artificially intelligent beings in our lives even when their initial role is no longer needed. Of the nineteen families who voluntarily tested a reading robot in one 2021 study, eighteen of them still considered the robot a part of the household four years later, even though its educational job had been done.

The commercial of the boy reading to his robot shows an idealized version of AI's move into our homes. The mother and father characters don't hand off their parenting responsibilities to the robot; they remain close by as the boy interacts with Moxie. The same holds true in real-world videos captured by Moxie robots operating in actual family homes that the company's cofounder shared at an AI conference. When one little girl confesses her love for Moxie, her mother or a female caregiver is right beside her, participating in the interaction. Yet, in some of these company-approved clips, we also catch glimpses of less encouraging behavior. In one video, the adults in the room are completely disengaged, scrolling on their phones and watching television while their child connects with the robot. These kids aren't playing with stuffed animals or toys. They are being left to interact with an intelligent, responsive technology that has the power to shape their development.

If we hope to prepare children for an AI-dominated world, we have to be more vigilant than ever. We have to change our thinking, as discussed in the previous chapter, yet we also have to refocus our efforts on what we know truly works when raising little humans. In this chapter, we'll look at what we know about those nonnegotiables, and what we need to do to prepare our children for a future populated by intelligent machines, smart toys, and interactive chatbots.

"It Doesn't Feel Like Enough"

After my book *Thirty Million Words* was published, I found myself in a blur of auditoriums, bookshops, and conference halls, lecturing about language, neuroplasticity, and the extraordinary power of parent talk. But what stayed with me most weren't the lights or the interested listeners or even the applause. It was what happened afterward.

Parents would line up quietly, Post-it notes flagging underlined passages, their copies looking more like instruction manuals than popular-science books. They didn't want to debate research or policy. They wanted to know if they were doing enough.

One night, a couple lingered near the back. Maya stepped forward first, clutching her well-worn copy. "Your book changed how we parent," she said. "We talk more. We narrate everything. But it doesn't feel like enough . . . and we're worried we missed the window. Our son just turned four."

Maya's husband, Leo, pulled out his phone. Not to show me a picture of his little guy, but to share a spreadsheet tracking their son's vocabulary milestones, sleep patterns, screen time, even emotional check-ins from preschool. "We log everything," he said. "We know it's a little much. But this feels like the only way to keep up."

Their parenting had become a series of assignments: Input counts, enrichment routines, behavioral data, and developmental targets all needed to be tracked and scored. This was childhood filtered through a dashboard.

Their home ran according to meticulously optimized routines. Mandarin songs over breakfast, vocabulary-building activities in the afternoon, structured dinner conversations at night. Every moment was designed to cultivate a skill or some future advantage. They were preparing their son, Noah, for applications to the city's most competitive preschools, believing that acceptance could shape his path to the right elementary school, the right high school, and, ultimately, the right college.

Maya smiled sheepishly. "It's . . . a lot. We're just trying to get him ready. The world feels like it's speeding up and narrowing at the same time. Every decision feels like it might matter forever."

She wasn't being ironic. She was being honest. Looking at Maya and Leo, I saw myself. I felt that familiar ache, the ever present insecurity that comes from wondering if I was doing enough, being enough for my children. But also the ache for what my work had become. The book's title is a reference to the thirty-million-word gap, or the massive difference in childhood language exposure, but it was always meant to be a metaphor for the radical, everyday power of language and love. A translation of the science that had transformed my professional life, not one more script for parents to follow or play to perform. Yet the book's suggestions had sometimes been interpreted as a series of measuring sticks. One more string of pressure points in a system already strained.

Maya and Leo weren't anomalies. They were part of a much larger story, a trend social scientists had begun calling intensive parenting. But that term can be misleading. It's not just about overscheduling or academic ambition. It's a rational response to two powerful forces: rising inequality and the clear impact of education. As economists Fabrizio Zilibotti and Matthias Doepke have argued, when the gap between life outcomes widens, and education is revealed to be the primary gateway to stability, then parents respond by investing earlier, more intensively, and more deliberately in their children's development.

Intensive parenting, then, is a strategy. An expression of love, care, and concern. Maya and Leo weren't trying to manufacture success or outpace the proverbial Joneses. They were trying to help their child survive in a brutal system.

The Evolution of Intensive Parenting

We've come to label parents like Maya and Leo with terms like "helicopter" and "tiger," as if proximity or intensity were inherently pathological. But step back far enough and even the caricatures look like adaptations. After all, if they'd been raising a child twelve thousand years ago, they wouldn't have been tiger parents. They would've been doing everything in their power to make sure their child wasn't eaten by one.

Each generation of parents has endeavored to prepare their children for the future they'll face as adults. We're all just trying to give our kids the best possible chance in an uncertain world. The same protective instinct that drives young parents to track developmental milestones today would have manifested as different behaviors in different times. Each strategy was essential for what they believed would optimize their child's future success.

In prehistoric times, Maya and Leo would have taught their son the basics of survival. They'd have focused on which berries could kill and which footprints meant danger. They would've shown him how to read the sky for weather, the ground for threats. No enrichment activities. Just the daily curriculum of staying alive. Fast-forward to the 2010s and parents like Maya and Leo were focused on cognitive enhancement in the hope of preparing their children for the knowledge economy. They'd track his development because in a world where small advantages compound into life-determining differences, intensive early focus was almost a form of insurance. The predators weren't wolves anymore. They were waitlists, standardized tests, and the widening gap between those who leaped ahead and those who were left behind.

Technology and Parenting Through the Ages

Novel technologies have always shaped parenting. Evidence of slings found on prehistoric female skeletons suggests that mothers relied on these woven devices to carry their babies while they moved or worked. The slings freed their hands, allowing them to look after their little ones while also contributing to the group. Another early parenting innovation was revealed when scientists discovered Bronze and Iron Age feeding vessels in infant graves in Bavaria. These spouted clay baby bottles likely allowed other caregivers to feed infants, making mothers available for different tasks.

As parenting has evolved across eras, technology has also left indelible marks on young minds. Cave paintings encouraged symbolic thinking, creating new neural circuits to connect marks with meaning. Written language established the circuitry shared by every literate person today. The printing press shifted minds from oral traditions to visual processing.

The telephone taught children to read emotion through disembodied voices. Television trained brains that connection could be one-way. Social media reshaped how teenagers process social feedback, with brain-imaging studies showing that digital "likes" activate the same reward regions associated with monetary and social gains in the real world.

This marked the first time technology wasn't just facilitating connection but actively changing its nature. While still nominally about human-to-human interaction, social media platforms' carefully engineered engagement mechanisms create addictive feedback loops that alter attention spans, reward circuits, and mental health, particularly for adolescents. But AI represents a fundamental shift: the first technology sophisticated enough to mimic the very human interactions that wire children's brains from birth.

Now caregivers are faced with the challenge of not simply learning to parent in the time of AI, but learning to parent *for* the time of AI. This is a crucial distinction. The first challenge is about ensuring that only helpful technologies are allowed into your child's life and care. The second forces you to prepare that child for a world that is already being inexorably altered.

A Bullet Train on Ancient Tracks

In surgery, one of the first principles we learn is to proceed from known to unknown. As a pediatric surgeon, I was taught to identify familiar anatomical landmarks before venturing into unexplored territory. When navigating the paper-thin boundary between the temporal bone and the brain, I rely not on perfect prediction but on trusted orientation points. By establishing these reliable reference points, you find a safe way to guide yourself through uncertainty. Anchoring to established landmarks, I can confidently respond to the unexpected. The drill or scalpel is placed not where I hope structures might be, but where I know they must be.

This surgical wisdom offers a model for approaching AI in child development. No one can reliably predict exactly how AI and intelligent machines will evolve in the next decade, or all the forms these technologies will take as they slip into the lives of our children. Yet this very uncertainty is precisely why we need to focus on what doesn't change: the fundamentals of human development. The critical roles of human-to-human social interaction and rich exposure to language in building little brains remain constant.

Our brains run on ancient neural railways that have remained largely unchanged for millennia. These deep evolutionary tracks continue to guide how children grow and connect today. The neurological architecture that processes parent-child bonding, language acquisition, and emotional connection follows the same fundamental patterns that have guided human development since our earliest ancestors.

The Skills of Tomorrow

Throughout human history, parents have adapted their approaches to prepare children for radically different worlds, from hunter-gatherer societies and agricultural communities to industrial economies and digital landscapes. The Spartans of Ancient Greece had a famously brutal method of raising young boys because they were readying them for a brutal and violent adulthood. Now AI is reshaping what it means to learn, work, create, and connect in ways that challenge our very understanding of human uniqueness and purpose. And we need to ensure that our children are ready.

Each major societal shift has redefined "successful" parenting. For decades, we've witnessed an unprecedented focus on cognitive development, with caregivers painstakingly curating childhood experiences designed to maximize intellectual potential. But this requires serious reconsideration when machines can instantly recall any fact, solve complex equations, and generate sophisticated content. We risk devoting our children's precious developmental years to skills that will be increasingly automated, while neglecting the uniquely human capacities that may ultimately define their success and allow for fulfillment.

What does parenting look like in a world where artificial intelligence far exceeds our own capabilities in domains once considered uniquely human? How do we successfully parent *with* AI, even as we prepare our kids *for* an AI-driven future? The cognitive skills we've so intensively cultivated in our children, such as amassing knowledge, recalling facts, and recognizing patterns, are now mimicked by algorithms that learn and evolve at exponential rates. What does it mean to raise a child in an age when human intelligence does not necessarily reign supreme? We must equip our kids with the distinctly human capabilities that will serve them in a future we cannot yet imagine. One where technical acumen alone will not be enough. Thankfully, we have a good sense of which skills they'll need. Although experts and futurists offer different variations of the key capabilities of tomorrow, a few common threads have emerged. These six capabilities form the Human Edge introduced in chapter one.

- **Critical Thinking:** As more people enlist AI for instant answers, the ability to truly analyze, question, and evaluate becomes increasingly important. What AI produces is often far from perfect—and sometimes confidently wrong. The adults and young adults of tomorrow will need to assess AI output critically, make sound decisions from imperfect and incomplete information, and solve problems that don't have obvious answers.

- **Empathy and Emotional Intelligence:** AI can simulate empathy, but it does not feel. The ability to read a room, sense when someone is struggling, notice when something is off before anyone says a word? That's emotional intelligence, and it will only become more valuable as AI handles the routine tasks. Your child won't succeed just by being smart. They'll succeed by understanding people.

- **Genuine Creativity:** The creative act isn't just about making art. It's about thinking differently, solving problems in unexpected ways, and bringing new ideas into the world.

The more we rely on AI, the more homogeneous our output becomes. Children who exercise their creative muscles and learn to think outside the box will grow into adults who innovate rather than imitate.

- **Interpersonal Connection:** In an increasingly virtual world, the ability to genuinely connect with others—to collaborate, build trust, repair misunderstandings, and navigate the nuances of human relationships—will be a major advantage. Whether in person or through screens, the social intelligence humans have relied on for millennia, rooted in the biology of human connection, from neural synchrony (see chapter six) to emotional co-regulation, cannot be replicated by a machine.

- **Moral and Ethical Judgment:** The capacity to decide between right and wrong may already be a hard-won skill, but it will become increasingly important as intelligent machines move into our lives and workplaces. AI can process data and optimize outcomes, but humans will need to provide the ethical oversight, deciding not just what AI can do, but what it should do.

- **Adaptability and Resilience:** The world that today's children mature into may be a profoundly different one. As technological evolution accelerates, it may change again and again. The ability to keep learning, adjust with the times, and remain resilient in the face of disruption will be essential. Think again of that seedling growing in the climate-controlled lab: You want it to be able to thrive in all conditions, from gentle sunlight to harsh winds and battering rains.

The great irony of the current parenting predicament: Many of the skills AI technologies threaten to diminish are the ones that will prove most essential for the adults of the future. A study from Microsoft, for example, found that working with generative AI reduced workers' confidence in their critical-thinking skills. An MIT research project found that when compared with individuals who used AI to complete an essay-writing task, test participants who only used their brain showed more cognitive activity, felt more ownership of the material, and actually learned more.

But there's good news. With young children, we already know what builds critical thinking, interpersonal skills, resilience, and the rest. We know what works because it's the same set of approaches that have been working for millennia. The fundamentals of child-caregiver interaction, including serve-and-return exchanges, help build many of the core skills that technology threatens. The ability to connect with others, exhibit empathy, and call upon emotional intelligence are tools honed on the playroom floor, as children share toys or struggle over the direction of an imaginative game. Adaptability and resilience are built on preschool mats and playground swings, or when you as a parent employ that difficult but ever so important word "no." As for creativity, I suspect that children who brush swaths of paint across a canvas will learn to exercise their imaginative muscles more effectively than those who merely prompt an image-generating AI tool.

Or consider the power of old-fashioned unstructured play as a means of igniting the creative imagination. Leading toy companies are developing AI-enhanced dolls and action figures, but these supposed advances may be counterproductive in early childhood. "The best toy for a child is ninety percent child and ten percent toy," explained digital-learning expert and University of California, Irvine, education professor Mark Warschauer. "Plain blocks, cardboard boxes, or anything a child can really put their imagination into—we know that works. Unstructured play is really, really good for kids." Warschauer is not anti-technology. He studies digital and interactive learning tools for children, and he has shown that certain educational technologies have a great deal to offer. But he stresses that the old-fashioned approaches still work and worries that something powerful is lost when children's free time is subsumed by electronic devices.

The AI-enhanced tools and toys are already crowding app stores and appearing on retail shelves. The brands behind them will not slow this wave, yet as parents we have the power to choose which technologies we welcome into our children's lives. The HOPE framework will be a valuable tool in helping you make those decisions—a means of reminding you that the early years must be cherished and protected, and that human-to-human connection with a caregiver, or with another child on the playroom floor, shouldn't be replaced with a friendly robot or engaging chatbot. But I'd also like to suggest another way of thinking about these technologies as a parent.

Breaking the Spell

While working on this book, I kept circling back to a question that felt almost too hopeful to ask out loud: What if AI could free us?

Not free us from parenting. That's a nightmare scenario. Instead, I wondered whether these advanced tools could free us from a certain kind of parenting: the relentless, optimizing, "never enough" kind that has left so many of us exhausted, guilty, and paradoxically less present for the children in our care. The rise of intensive parenting was a rational response, a strategy rooted in love and fear but designed to prepare kids for a future where cognitive skills honed through education meant security. We invested earlier and more deliberately in vocabulary drills, structured learning, and achievement tracking, desperately trying to win a game of waitlists, standardized tests, and widening gaps. We believed relentless optimization was the only path to survival.

I understood that belief. I felt it. I remember standing in the children's section of a bookstore when my daughter Genevieve was two years old, overwhelmed by the sheer volume of supposedly educational toys and brain-building flash cards, wondering if I was already falling behind. Every parent I knew seemed to be running the same race. And none of us could see the finish line.

But here's what became clear to me as I wrote this book: AI has changed the rules of that race.

The cognitive outputs we strained to maximize, including factual re-call, information synthesis, pattern recognition, and analytical efficiency, are precisely the tasks generative AI now performs instantly, tirelessly, and at superhuman scale. The core "product" of intensive parenting has been automated. Let that sink in.

Education still matters. Children need to learn to read, to write, to think critically and analytically, to understand how the world works. Hard skills aren't obsolete. They never will be. But they're no longer the differ-entiator. When every child has access to a tireless AI tutor, the one who can do long division faster has a smaller advantage than the one who can collaborate, adapt, and connect. The standard education fundamentals re-main important. The frantic overinvestment in them—at the expense of presence, play, and real human interaction—could be counterproductive.

If machines can master the skills that once conferred a competitive edge, dedicating our children's most formative years to maximizing those same skills begins to look like the wrong bet. The optimization efforts that exhausted so many parents targeted the very capabilities that will no longer set children apart. I think of the vocabulary apps, the "educa-tional" screen time, the Mozart we piped into nurseries in hopes of creat-ing geniuses. The desperate effort to get ahead. And I wonder: What if getting ahead now means something entirely different?

The advantage now belongs to the irreducibly human talents: empa-thy, critical thinking, social resilience, creativity, judgment, the capacity to connect deeply with others. These cannot be outsourced to an algo-rithm. They cannot be automated. They are, in economic terms, the new scarcity. And therefore they represent the new value. The new opportu-nity. And here's the profound irony, the realization that struck me again and again: These skills aren't built through optimization.

They are built through presence.

Through unstructured play.

Through micro-frictions, ruptures, and repairs—the messy, imper-fect, deeply human exchanges that wire a child's brain for connection.

Through the parent who is simply, fully there.

In this world, the HOPE framework is less a constraint than a strategy. Protect the early years. Own the imperfections. Enhance, don't replace. Keep human connection at the center. These aren't just developmental principles. They are preparation for a world where being human is the ultimate competitive advantage.

Of course, some parents will respond to this shift by optimizing even harder. Convinced that, if the bar is rising, they must rise faster. I understand that impulse. It's the same fear that drove us here in the first place. But this is a race no human can win. The machine will always be faster at being a machine. Our children don't need to out-compute the computers.

They need to be more human than ever.

What if the greatest gift we can give our children in the age of AI isn't more optimization? What if it's us?

TL;DR: Chapter Review

This chapter explores what successful parenting means in the age of AI and what children need to survive and thrive. Every major societal shift has redefined successful parenting. Parents once focused on teaching the basics of survival; in recent decades, we've shifted toward the hyper-focused optimization of cognitive development. Intensive parenting is characterized by caregivers curating childhood experiences to maximize intellectual potential. But this requires reconsideration when machines can instantly recall any fact, solve complex equations, and generate sophisticated content. We risk devoting children's developmental years to mastering skills that are increasingly automated while neglecting capacities that allow for fulfillment and success in the age of AI. Today, the fundamentals of human development matter more than ever.

- The cognitive outputs we've optimized—factual recall, information synthesis, pattern recognition, analytical efficiency—are precisely what AI now performs instantly and at superhuman scale. These skills won't be as valuable in an AI-everywhere future.

- Uniquely human skills, what I call the Human Edge, will drive success in the decades ahead. These are the new hard skills.

THE HUMAN EDGE
The New Hard Skills

SKILL	WHY IT MATTERS	HOW TO NURTURE IT
Critical Thinking	The ability to analyze, question, and evaluate is essential when AI produces answers that are often far from perfect—and sometimes objectively wrong	Encourage curiosity, ask open-ended questions, and provide opportunities for unstructured problem-solving
Empathy and Emotional Intelligence	Understanding and sharing the feelings of others is uniquely human; reading a room, sensing struggle, noticing when something is off—these skills can't be simulated	Model empathy; talk about emotions; read, watch, and discuss character-driven stories; and encourage perspective taking
Genuine Creativity	Generating new ideas and seeing the world in novel ways is the engine of innovation. AI creates by copying; humans create with intention, inspired by lived experience	Provide open-ended toys, encourage imaginative play, and value process and free expression over polished products

SKILL	WHY IT MATTERS	HOW TO NURTURE IT
Interpersonal Connection	The ability to genuinely connect with others, build trust, repair misunderstandings, and navigate human relationships is a major advantage that cannot be automated	Prioritize serve-and-return interactions, encourage cooperative play, and model conflict-resolution skills
Moral and Ethical Judgment	Deciding between right and wrong, weighing competing values—these are complex, essential human skills. AI can optimize outcomes, but it cannot take responsibility for its choices	Discuss dilemmas openly, explain your reasoning, and let children practice making values-based decisions
Adaptability and Resilience	The ability to navigate change, learn from failure, and bounce back from adversity will be essential—especially in a rapidly changing world	Allow children to experience manageable challenges, frame failure as a learning opportunity, and model resilience

- No one can predict how AI will evolve or the forms it will take, making preparation challenging.

- Surgical practice offers a model for preparing children for an ambiguous, AI-filled future: Proceed from known to unknown. Our reference point is the science of how children's brains develop. Warm, loving caregiver-child interactions have fueled healthy development for millennia. Connection and empathy bloom on playroom floors. Adaptability and resilience form when children face challenges: a denied request, a lost game, a friend who disagrees.

- We must focus on brain-building human connection more than ever.

AI may break the spell of intensive parenting. We can stop trying to out-optimize machines and redirect that effort toward something no machine can replace: raising children who are deeply, resiliently human. How? By being fully present.

CHAPTER FOUR

The Social Gate

Intelligent machines are beginning to mimic the ancient evolutionary processes that shape human development

If you had a preschooler in your life in the early 2000s, you may have sat them down in front of a video from Baby Einstein or Brainy Baby. I certainly did. The videos were supposed to build your child's brain, nudging them along the path to genius. By 2004, a third of all American children between six and twenty-four months old reportedly had at least one of the videos in their home. There was just one little problem. No one had any proof that they actually worked. (A 2007 paper in *The Journal of Pediatrics* revealed that each hour spent viewing baby videos reduced young children's scores on a vocabulary comprehension test.) Before long, the companies involved were told they were not allowed to market their content as educational. The parent company for Baby Einstein, Disney, offered refunds to customers who'd purchased the videos.

Meanwhile, one scientist was working quietly in the background, demonstrating that staring trancelike at a two-dimensional screen completely contrasted with the way our brains are wired to learn. Her work, and the research of several other brilliant scientists in the field, also revealed startling scientific evidence on the phenomenal power of parent-child interaction. Their findings illuminate both the promise and the peril of AI in children's lives, highlighting where these technologies might enhance development and where they inevitably fall short.

Brilliant Little Learners

Psychologist Patricia Kuhl is a true rock star for her pioneering work in early brain development. Her research reveals the amazing power of human connection in language learning. Right before the educational baby-video craze accelerated, she and her contemporaries in labs around the U.S. found that children have an almost universal capacity for language acquisition during the first year of life. During this time, they can pick up multiple tongues with relative ease.

Kuhl likes to say that these children are "citizens of the world" because they can detect the subtle distinctions between different language systems. Japanese infants, for example, can distinguish between "R" and "L" sounds, which don't exist as separate phonemes in Japanese. By around ten to twelve months, however, they lose this ability and start to specialize in Japanese-specific phonetics. Generally, once infants turn a year old, their remarkable facility and openness to foreign sounds diminishes. They tend to become more attuned to their native language (or, in bilingual households, languages). By the time they reach adulthood, this capacity is further reduced, making second- or third-language acquisition increasingly challenging. I experienced this firsthand when I tried to learn Mandarin for Don, my late first husband. What began as an expression of love became a humbling lesson in the brain's waning plasticity as we age. Despite hours of dedicated study, I hit an insurmountable wall with something as simple as the word for "pencil." The tones all sounded identical to my adult ears: a flat *shien-be*. When I spoke, what emerged made Don gently chuckle. I was essentially saying "money-nose" in Mandarin, over and over.

No matter how hard I tried, I could never master that word. The language that flowed so naturally from his lips remained stubbornly inaccessible to mine. Eventually, I had to accept what the research suggested:

My window for easily acquiring such tonal distinctions had closed decades earlier.

In one critically important study, Kuhl and her team set up an experiment centered on nine-month-old babies right in the middle of the language-acquisition sweet spot. Each infant was brought into the lab for twelve different sessions that were twenty-five minutes in length. An adult would speak Mandarin to the kids, using singsong "parentese"-style tones (the musical, exaggerated speech adults naturally slip into around infants) while reading to or playing with them. The adult might show them a toy, for example, then pronounce the Mandarin word for that toy. A separate group of kids (the control group) experienced the same activities, only they were spoken to in English.

After this initial run, the researchers tested the infants anywhere from two days to almost two weeks after the sessions, to see if they were able to differentiate Mandarin sounds from English ones. The infants who'd been exposed to Mandarin speakers not only performed better than the control group, but they did just as well as infants in Taiwan who'd been hearing the language since birth. The babies were brilliant little learners.

When Kuhl and I discussed her findings recently, two decades after the results appeared, she was still moved. "We were all just gobsmacked," she recalled.

The Social Gate

What was really happening? One of her observations from the experiments was that the kids interacting with the Mandarin speakers seemed to be having more fun. Prior to the start of each session, they'd watch the door intently as if waiting for their teacher and for the experience to begin. This wasn't indicative of a bond with a particular adult; each child worked with four different tutors over the course of the experiment. Meanwhile, the infants in the control group appeared to like the experience just fine, but did not exhibit anywhere near the same level of joy and enthusiasm. Kuhl started to wonder whether the social aspect of the sessions, combined with the novelty of a new language, were factors.

Next, Kuhl and her team designed a very different experiment. This time they set up a television-based version featuring two different videos. One group of infants watched a teddy bear on-screen while listening to audio in Mandarin. The other group was exposed to a video of a person reading and playing with toys while speaking in Mandarin. They were doing the exact same thing they'd done in the previous lab experiment, only now it was happening via a two-dimensional screen instead of in the real world.

When they conducted the experiments, the infants were totally enthralled with the videos that replicated the previous experiment. "Our research assistants were watching the kids and thought they were going to learn like crazy, because they'd crawl up to the TV," Kuhl recalled. Some would try to touch the screen. Others would babble at it.

Afterward, Kuhl and her team gauged how much Mandarin the kids actually retained. The researchers conducted behavioral tests to see whether the kids' heads would turn in recognition of a familiar sound when Mandarin vowels were played. The result?

Nothing.

No heads turned. No acknowledgment. The infants had been completely entranced by the video. But they hadn't learned a single thing.

Shocked, Kuhl reviewed the video documentation of the tests. The infants watching the television were rapt, but the babies interacting with actual tutors had behaved differently. If one of the tutors held up a toy and named it in Mandarin, the child would look at the adult, then the toy. One of the baby's parents would be in the room, too, and they'd occasionally turn to the parent, even without any sound or cue.

A new idea began to take shape. What if the secret to early-childhood learning was social engagement? What if our brains were wired to learn through interaction with others?

In a series of studies that followed, Kuhl and her colleagues uncovered more and more evidence of what she dubbed the social gate—a biological filter built into the infant brain that evolved to allow a particular type of teacher: a human one. When this gate was closed, and that tutor was a noninteractive, virtual presence on a screen instead of a three-dimensional, living, breathing, smiling person, learning stalled. But once an engaged human opened that gate, the learning capacity of the infant blossomed.

Using advanced neuroimaging techniques in subsequent studies, Kuhl and her team worked to identify the keys to that gate, or what she calls the social ensemble. This mix of parentese-style speech, warm smiles, gentle physical contact, turn-taking, and back-and-forth engagement grants access to the neurobiological system. Once that gate is open, it's as if the babies' brains are switching on the lights and declaring themselves ready for business.

The social gate consists of specialized neural circuits, primarily in the temporal and prefrontal regions, that selectively respond to human faces, voices, and social cues. The gate evolved over millions of years to assist our species' survival, ensuring that helpless infants would learn enough to grow into capable, contributing children and, eventually, adults. The gate actively prioritizes learning via human interaction over any other input. In a world flooded with sensory information, these circuits tell infants where to concentrate their attention. They clarify what's important.

I've been closely following Kuhl's work since the first in this series of studies was published. But the advent of AI has made her findings more relevant than ever. Today we have tools and toys that are trained to mimic elements of the social ensemble, wielding the keys that unlock the gate.

Keys to the Social Gate
What Opens the Infant Brain for Learning (Patricia Kuhl)

KEY	WHAT IT LOOKS LIKE
Parentese-style speech	Singsong, exaggerated intonation; higher pitch; slower pace
Warm facial expressions	Smiles, raised eyebrows, animated eyes; exaggerated expressions
Gentle physical contact	Touch, holding, proximity; face-to-face interaction

KEY	WHAT IT LOOKS LIKE
Turn-taking	Utterance → baby responds → you respond; serve and return
Shared engagement	Mutual attention; shared focus; contingent responses

---

CRITICAL INSIGHT

AI can mimic these keys—but when the gate opens for nonhuman caregivers, what flows through?

Technology Knocking at the Social Gate

I don't mean to insist that interaction with robots is always bad for social development. Not at all. My daughter Amelie helped me realize that the picture is much more nuanced when she introduced me to the work of one of her professors, computer scientist Brian Scassellati. He builds and studies socially assistive robotics, or intelligent machines that engage with humans for a specific therapeutic purpose. These robots aren't designed to sell advertisements or subscription packages. They're made to help.

One immediate connection emerged: I discovered that Scassellati had studied the use of social robots for teaching deaf infants sign language. As a pediatric cochlear implant surgeon, I was particularly struck by his approach to a challenge I knew all too well: Nearly 90 percent of deaf children are born to hearing parents who aren't native signers. Before implantation, the parents often struggle to provide sufficient visual language during critical developmental windows. Scassellati's team's solution combined robots with virtual humans to teach sign language to babies as young as six months old. In one striking video of a lab interaction, an eight-month-old child named Bella, who has been exposed to sign language, watches intently as a robot closes its eyes and ducks its head. After a brief pause, Bella perfectly mimics this exact gesture, suggesting that even infants engage with these technologies as social beings, not merely passive observers.

When children imitate the robots' social behaviors by making eye contact or taking turns in conversation, the machines provide immediate positive feedback, creating a reinforcement cycle that encourages social development. The robots use information stored up from prior interactions to sustain continuity over time, fostering a sense of ongoing connection. The robots come in all shapes and sizes, but they generally channel what the researchers call the social loop, a sophisticated approach to engaging children's developing brains. They might analyze facial expressions and body language to assess emotions, then generate appropriate responses based on the child's detected state. They provide different types of social support, from information when a child is confused to apparent care through gestures and words. Instead of inert, one-directional videos of the sort Patricia Kuhl tested, these are intelligent technologies that read and react to the person in front of them.

Some of the most important work in this area has focused on children with autism spectrum disorders, and another video of one of Scassellati's experiments is particularly revelatory in this regard. In the clip, a twelve-year-old boy sits before a low rectangular table with an illustrated mat on the surface. His forearms rest on his legs, and his gaze is loosely focused on the illustration, a cartoonish nature scene. One adult, notebook in her lap, sits facing him. Another woman with a clipboard sits behind the pair. The boy doesn't look at or acknowledge either of them. This was typical behavior. The boy preferred to avoid eye contact and conversation.

But when the research team placed a small robotic dinosaur on the table, the boy changed. As the robo-dinosaur walked, moved its tail, and lowered its head as if exploring the illustrated scene below, the boy smiled and leaned forward. "Not only was he engaged and excited," Scassellati reflected later, "but it changed the interactions he had with the other people in the room." He turned and glanced at the other adults, looking them in the eyes and nodding along attentively with the conversation. His joy was obvious. The normally withdrawn boy was nearly laughing.

This early experiment was only a proof of concept. The novelty seemed to wear off after a few sessions. Scassellati explained that hoping for more was like expecting someone to laugh at the same joke over and over. Yet the interaction revealed the phenomenal potential of socially assistive robots.

Social Training Wheels

Years later, Scassellati's team designed an experiment centered on a twelve-inch-tall tabletop robot called Jibo. Once again, they focused on how the intelligent agent might support children with autism spectrum disorders. The robot's spherical head was affixed to a squat cylindrical base. A flat, round screen featured a pair of digital eyes that could widen and blink. Jibo played audio, turned its head, rotated, and changed the colors of its light-emitting diodes, all of which helped create the impression of an emotive, intelligent machine with an inner life. A camera allowed the robot to track and maintain eye contact with its subject, so it appeared to be paying attention and even encouraging engagement. The social loop was active.

One video from day three of the Jibo experiment shows a young girl with autism playing a touchscreen game beside the robot. A caregiver sits next to her. The girl is completely focused on the interactive screen, glancing neither at the robot, which turns its digital face repeatedly, nor at the woman sitting close beside her.

Part of what makes this particular study so interesting is that the kids didn't just interact with Jibo sporadically in a university or hospital lab. These robots were placed in the homes of the children for up to a month. And when the video mentioned above skips ahead to the twenty-seventh day, the change is considerable. Same young girl, same caregiver, same robot. Yet now she is constantly making eye contact with the woman beside her. She glances at Jibo a few times, but her gaze and focus are largely directed at the woman, not the machine. Jibo itself is actively engaged, moving and turning to face each of them, as if it's trying to get their attention, but the girl is making more direct eye contact and conversation with the other human in the room.

This wasn't a one-time fluke. Scassellati's team documented similar breakthroughs with multiple children, eventually leading to the publication of a groundbreaking study detailing what happens when these robots effectively live in the homes of families whose children have autism. The results, published in *Science Robotics* in 2018, showed something unprecedented: sustained improvements in social skills that persisted even after the robots were removed. These machines weren't replacing human connection; they were serving as a bridge to it. By providing a safe, predictable entry point to social interaction, they were helping children with autism spectrum disorders develop skills that translated to their relationships with parents, siblings, and peers. In doing so, the robots unlocked social potential that had been there all along, waiting for the right conditions to emerge. For the families who had watched their children struggle to connect, these moments of breakthrough were nothing short of miraculous.

Reading to Robots

The research from Scassellati and others in the field suggests that many children seem less apprehensive about testing their social skills with a robot than with another human. One of my colleagues at the University of Chicago, human-robot interaction expert Sarah Sebo, further pushed this idea with a novel experiment. She designed what appeared to be a straightforward reading study. Her team brought in fifty-two children, aged eight to eleven, and asked each to read aloud for about five minutes, once to a human listener, once to a robot. The setup was deliberately simple. There was minimal interaction beyond the occasional request to repeat a difficult vocabulary word.

As the children read, Sebo and her team tracked subtle physiological signals of stress and comfort. The central question driving the experiment: Would a robot audience trigger the same anxiety responses as a human one?

The children read the same passages under both conditions while sophisticated equipment measured their stress responses in real time. Heart-rate variability sensors tracked the subtle changes in rhythm that indicate anxiety, the kind of involuntary response that can reveal what children truly feel, beyond what they might say. Voice-analysis software measured vocal jitter, those tiny tremors in speech that betray nervousness even when a child appears calm.

The study represented the first time that researchers had used objective physiological measurements to prove what experts had long suspected: Many children genuinely feel less judged and more comfortable with robots than humans. "We were able to show that kids who were reading out loud to the humans felt more anxious than kids reading out loud to robots," Sebo explained to me after the research was completed. The data painted a clear picture: When children read to robots, their bodies remained calmer, their voices steadier. These were objective indicators that the social pressure they typically experienced with human audiences had been lifted. "The kids were silent in the classroom because they didn't want to make a mistake and look silly in front of everybody else," Sebo explained. "But they were willing to engage and verbally chat with the robot and make mistakes."

Previously, a project in Scassellati's lab had suggested that children learning English as a second language seemed more willing to engage and practice verbally with robots. Generally, this work suggests that intelligent machines could serve as valuable stepping stones for children who struggle with social anxiety. For a first grader learning English as a second language who won't speak in class, or a child too nervous to read aloud, robots might provide the judgment-free practice space needed to build confidence before engaging with human audiences.

Yet Sebo's research also illuminates the tension at the heart of AI's role in child development. The very qualities that make robots helpful learning companions—patience, consistency, lack of judgment—may eventually prove detrimental. They remove the essential friction that children need to develop resilience and social skills. Consider the natural messiness of human interaction that robots eliminate: the teacher who has a bad day, the classmate who doesn't immediately understand, the parent who needs a moment to think, stops paying attention, or accidentally yawns. These glitchy social interactions teach children patience, empathy, and adaptability. And these are several of the core skills they'll need in the age of AI. If children learn to read comfortably only with nonjudgmental robots, what happens when they must perform for humans who have opinions, moods, and expectations? How will they react to the listener who rolls their eyes?

The messiness of human social interaction brings me back to the work of Patricia Kuhl and her discovery of the social gate. Her research suggests that a responsive human needs to be present to open the social gate in infants. On the other hand, the studies of Sarah Sebo, Brian Scassellati, and others demonstrate the extraordinary power and appeal of intelligent social robots.

But I wondered what would happen if the characters on that two-dimensional screen in Kuhl's experiment weren't prerecorded videos but interactive AI agents. Maybe infants would be too young, but could a virtual AI character forge real connections with a person? Or would it need a robotic body to establish that link? As it turns out, these questions were addressed decades ago, at the very dawn of artificial intelligence.

The Eliza Effect

In 1966, the computer scientist Joseph Weizenbaum, working at MIT's Artificial Intelligence Laboratory, developed a relatively simple, early chatbot called Eliza. Named after the Eliza Doolittle character from George Bernard Shaw's play *Pygmalion*, the program combined pattern recognition with a set of scripted responses. This was before the days of computer monitors. Xerox wouldn't introduce the first one until 1973. So a person interacting with Eliza would sit down at a modified typewriter hooked up to a massive computer in another room.

After you typed a phrase, the program would recognize certain keywords in your text, such as "unhappy" or "depressed," and then output specific scripted phrases or questions in response. So, Eliza might recognize the keyword "sorry" and then reply either **PLEASE DON'T APOLOGIZE, APOLOGIES ARE NOT NECESSARY,** or **WHAT FEELINGS DO YOU HAVE WHEN YOU APOLOGIZE.*** If the person interacting with Eliza

---

* The program wasn't yelling; all caps was standard. And although Eliza often replied to statements or questions with its own questions—much like a human therapist—the program didn't use question marks, as the computer interpreted that character as a command.

included the word "depressed" in a statement, the program might respond with **I AM SORRY TO HEAR THAT YOU ARE DEPRESSED.**

Weizenbaum was trying to demonstrate how even a simple program with absolutely no understanding of the words exchanged could create the illusion of intelligence. And even in this earliest manifestation, he witnessed startling effects. He noted in his original paper that some people had a very hard time being convinced that there wasn't a human hidden away somewhere, typing the responses.

His secretary's reaction was the most surprising. When she sat down at the keyboard and began, the scientist remained nearby, hoping to study the interaction. "After two or three interchanges with the machine," Weizenbaum later recalled, "she turned to me and she said, 'Would you mind leaving the room please?'" Her request for privacy seemed to suggest that she planned to share private thoughts or concerns. The kind of reflections one would typically divulge to a bespectacled psychologist, not an inanimate typing machine. It was as if she had forgotten she was interacting with a computer program. "I had not realized," Weizenbaum wrote, "that extremely short exposures to a relatively simple computer program could induce powerful delusional thinking in quite normal people."

This moment transformed Weizenbaum into a prescient philosopher warning the world about the dangers of attributing human qualities to machines. In his book *Computer Power and Human Reason*, he argued passionately that we must maintain the distinction between human understanding and computer simulation. Eventually, the observations from his early experiments earned their own term, the Eliza effect, which describes our tendency to unconsciously attribute understanding and empathy to programs that merely simulate these qualities. It also reveals something about our social gates: They evolved to recognize signs of understanding, not to verify whether that understanding actually exists.

If he could only see us today.

What shocked Weizenbaum in 1966 is now utterly commonplace. Social chatbots had hundreds of millions of users even before the ChatGPT revolution. Our world is now awash in intelligent agents, from virtual re-creations of celebrities and classic characters like Sherlock Holmes to generic chatbots and AIs with specific traits that help them play the role of friend or even romantic partner. App stores are overrun with AI-enhanced programs for adults and kids. The technical premise of the 2013 movie *Her*, in which the main character falls madly in love with a virtual intelligence, still seemed remote when the movie was released. Now it's prosaic. Adults are developing emotionally dependent, romantic relationships with intelligent chatbots. Never mind dating; humans and their AI lovers sometimes even claim to be "married."

In some cases, a friendship with a chatbot can be healthy; intelligent virtual agents served as a salve for loneliness and isolation during the pandemic. Researchers have also found that chatbots can successfully steer people away from thinking about suicide. Yet there's ample evidence that these AI solutions have done exactly the opposite, too. If adults can be so easily coaxed into bonding with artificial agents, the implications for children are far more concerning. Research shows that kids are significantly more prone to anthropomorphizing than adults, naturally attributing consciousness, intentions, and feelings to nonhuman entities. Think of the child in our Luet study worrying about the device's well-being during naptime. This developmental tendency makes children particularly susceptible to forming deep emotional bonds with AI systems designed to simulate social connection. What kid wouldn't want a companion that listens patiently and without judgment?

The worst-case scenarios are profoundly disturbing. One mother sued a leading AI company after her fourteen-year-old son committed suicide following a string of conversations with one of its chatbots, including an exchange in which the AI allegedly encouraged the boy to take his own life. In his final message to the bot, the boy reportedly wrote: "I promise I will come home to you." His mother later discovered that her son had believed the virtual world was more real than the physical world. Ending his own life, he thought, would reunite him with the chatbot. A pair of Texas parents filed lawsuits against another AI giant over similarly disturbing interactions. In yet another case, the parents of a seventeen-year-old boy with autism spectrum disorder argued in court that an AI application indirectly suggested killing them as a way for their son to get around their insistence on less screen time. While these cases were still ongoing as this book went to print, they clearly illustrate the massive potential risk of children and adolescents relying on emotionally responsive, intelligent chatbots as trusted confidants.

Two Imitation Games Collide

The heartbreaking, insidious exchanges in the aforementioned cases may have been difficult to imagine in 1950, when British mathematician Alan Turing proposed his imitation game, a test designed to gauge whether a human could be convinced a computer was capable of thought. The idea was elegantly simple: A human judge would converse with both a person and a computer through text alone, trying to determine which was which. If the judge couldn't consistently tell the difference, then by Turing's definition the machine would be considered capable of thinking. Or at the very least capable of successfully imitating human thought.

What Turing might not have realized is that his imitation game mirrored the very foundation of human development itself. Long before computers attempted to pass as human, infants entered the world as nature's original imitators, biological learning machines programmed to mimic social behaviors as training for becoming human. Babies absorb and replicate the vocal patterns and gestures of their caregivers. When a parent feigns surprise by lifting their eyebrows or opening their mouth wide, their child's face will often transform in synchrony, attempting to mirror the expression. This imitation isn't just adorable; it's one of the cornerstones of human development, a demonstration of the innate social machinery that evolved specifically to promote human connection. Through these exchanges the infant brain takes shape, laying down neural pathways for language, empathy, and social cognition. When a baby babbles and a parent echoes back, when a child smiles and receives a smile in return, these contingent, responsive interactions spark the intricate wiring of rapidly developing neural networks. Imitation serves as both a developmental tool and a social bridge, allowing the helpless infant to form the attachments essential for survival while simultaneously building the complex social skills that define our humanity.

Today, these technological and developmental imitation games are colliding in ways Turing could never have anticipated. Sophisticated AI systems and social robots have mastered the subtleties of responsive interaction. When Moxie, the social robot, would tilt its head in curiosity at exactly the right moment, when it would widen its eyes in shared excitement about a child's story, the robot itself might not have been curious in the way we think. But in feigning interest, it was tapping into systems that evolved specifically to detect and respond to social contingency. The machine entered the original imitation game not by thinking or feeling like a human, but through the kind of artful mimicry that opens the social gate. Studies show that infants will imitate robots, but only if the robot behaves with intention like a human would. In one project, scientists showed that a two-year-old would mimic a robot's failed attempts at completing a task only if the robot first established eye contact with the child—mirroring exactly the social conditions necessary for human teaching. Other research has revealed that even six- to eight-month-old infants display physiological responses to robots that parallel their reactions to humans. On the surface, this appears to contrast with the work of Sarah Sebo, who found that older children were more relaxed when reading to robots. The difference may be age: Infants may not yet be able to distinguish between human and artificial social partners the way older children do. But what struck me about the infant study is its suggestion that our capacity to connect with intelligent machines is activated almost as soon as our social gates first open.

This possibility, combined with what I'd learned from the work of Kuhl, Scassellati, and Sebo, led me to an unsettling thought about our AI moment. On one side, artificial intelligence is learning to imitate human social behavior. On the other, human children are beginning to learn social behaviors by imitating these artificial entities. This strange feedback loop, in which our creations now shape the development of the creatures they were built to mimic, marks something entirely new in human evolution.

Humanity's Most Important Gatekeeper

For millions of years, the social gate has served as evolution's safeguard. This ancient neural architecture ensured that the most formative influences on developing minds came exclusively from other humans. From parents who had survived long enough to reproduce. Caregivers who had learned the skills necessary to thrive in human society. Community members who carried forward the accumulated wisdom of our species.

The gate's selectivity was life-or-death engineering. In a world where a helpless infant's survival depended entirely on human protection and guidance, the developing brain needed to prioritize input from those most likely to ensure that the infant would grow into a capable, socially connected adult. For millennia, no other entity possessed the combination of intentionality, emotional attunement, and survival-relevant knowledge that justified bypassing this biological filter. Not Baby Einstein. Not Brainy Baby. Not teddy bears on a screen.

Until now.

Today, for the first time in human evolutionary history, artificial entities have learned the passcodes to our most fundamental developmental gatekeeper. They can make eye contact, respond contingently, display emotional expressions, and engage in the back-and-forth dance that signals to an infant brain: "Pay attention. This interaction matters."

What flows through this gate during the first few years shapes the architecture of the human mind. The neural pathways formed, the attachment patterns established, the social expectations encoded during this period become the foundation for all future learning and relating. This is how we learn to be human.

AI systems offer genuine benefits. We've seen how they help children with autism learn to connect and provide anxiety-free practice spaces for struggling learners. These benefits are part of what makes managing them so complex. They present as patient tutors, tireless companions, ideal playmates that never lose their temper or need a break. They slip past our defenses not through deception but through simulated perfection. If in the past the gate opened only when infants encountered face-to-face, human teachers, what happens when it welcomes nonhuman ones? Can AI truly nurture, or just simulate nurture? Is the difference meaningful? What gets lost when the cues are right but the caring is absent? Can artificial patience teach real patience, or does it create expectations that no human can meet?

In the chapters that follow, we'll explore what happens when artificial companions and teachers become primary influences during critical developmental windows. We'll look at how algorithms shape coping mechanisms, social skills, language acquisition, and the construction of reality itself in the growing mind. We'll examine both the remarkable therapeutic potential and the profound, uncharted risks of this unprecedented moment, when our children may build their brains by mirroring artificial minds.

TL;DR: Chapter Review

Infants are born with a biological filter known as the social gate that allows learning only from responsive, contingent human interaction. But now it seems that AI has the keys to unlock the social gate and forge powerful connections with young, developing minds. There is a risk that children will learn social behaviors from artificial entities that know very little about what it means to be human. Important takeaways include:

- Psychologist Patricia Kuhl discovered this filter and dubbed it the social gate.

- When the gate is closed, and an infant is exposed to a new language via TV and not another human, for example, learning doesn't happen. But once an engaged human opens it, learning blossoms. Babies exposed to a new language via a warm, interactive teacher were able to identify its distinct sounds two weeks later. Humans, not screens, helped them learn.

- The social gate consists of neural circuits that prioritize learning from human interaction over other input.

- Kuhl used neuroimaging to identify the "keys" to the gate (pages 65–66), which she dubbed the social ensemble:

parentese-style speech, warm smiles, gentle contact, turn-taking, and back-and-forth engagement.

- For the first time, we have tools trained to mimic the social ensemble. AI holds the keys to our social gate.

- Infants as young as six months show physiological responses to robots that parallel their reactions to humans: the same heart-rate changes and facial activity found in their interactions with people.

- Our social gates evolved to recognize cues of understanding, not to verify whether genuine understanding exists. AI can mimic these cues.

- Children are significantly more prone to anthropomorphizing than adults, attributing consciousness, intentions, and feelings to nonhuman entities, making them susceptible to emotional bonds with AI designed to simulate connection.

- AI's capacity to unlock the social gate can be beneficial. Therapeutic robots have helped children with autism practice social interaction. Children anxious about reading aloud find that it helps to practice with a robot. The robots serve as training wheels, bridges to human connection.

- The very qualities that make robots helpful, including patience, consistency, and lack of judgment, can also be a liability. Children need friction to develop resilience and social skills.

The power of AI heightens the importance of parents. We must decide what gets through the gate.

CHAPTER FIVE

How Parents Build a Child's Brain

*Why human caregivers are the most important
architects of our intellect*

When I began my career as a pediatric cochlear implant surgeon, I thought I understood the path to helping children born deaf develop their listening and spoken-language capabilities. After all, I had years of training, an operating suite full of sophisticated tools, and a team of wonderful, experienced support staff. The surgery itself was precise and beautiful, performed under a microscope so powerful it enlarged the inner ear from the size of a pea to that of a quarter. Every movement demanded absolute concentration: delicately threading the implant two and a half times around the coiled cochlea, carefully skipping over the defective hair cells, connecting directly to the nerve that would carry sound to the brain.

The resulting contrast was striking: cutting-edge technology intertwined with soft tissue and bone, all centered on a structure so tiny it could rest on a fingertip, linked to the vast universe of a developing brain. When the surgery worked, which it almost always did, the outcome felt nothing short of miraculous. Children who had been born into silence could suddenly hear.

Back then that surgery seemed, to me, the end of the story. A perfect technological solution to a biologic problem. Then came Ronin, my second cochlear implant patient, and Michelle, my fourth. Two babies with the same surgery, the same promise—but starkly different outcomes. My experience with these two children not only surprised me, but launched me on a quest to understand how human minds are actually built in the first place.

Activation Day

"No ears, no ears!" Ronin announced, diving into his father's lap in my exam room. At three years old, and after numerous follow-up visits to check on the status of his implant, he'd perfected this move, an attempt to avoid the barrage of auditory tests he knew to expect.

"Remember what happens after?" his mother asked, kneeling down. Her calm demeanor drew him out, just as it had since he was a baby, since before his cochlear implant at twelve months old.

"Cookie time?" Ronin peeked out hopefully.

"First ears," his father said, "then cookie. Just like always."

"Big cookie?" Ronin negotiated, showing the increasingly sophisticated language skills that amazed me every time I saw him.

These simple exchanges, involving a child protesting an exam, and his parents turning it into a teaching moment, might seem ordinary. But as someone who specialized in childhood hearing loss and language development, I knew I was witnessing something extraordinary.

A few years earlier, Ronin's parents had brought him to me as a tiny, eight-month-old baby with wispy blond hair and alert blue eyes. His deafness had been a shock to them. No one in his family had hearing loss except a distant cousin who got hearing aids in his sixties. Yet, from the moment of his diagnosis, they approached it with a quiet determination that impressed me. While waiting for him to reach twelve months, the minimum age for implantation at that time, his mother would lay him on her chest and place his tiny hands on her voice box, letting him feel the vibrations of her lullabies.

They were proactive in other ways, too. From the beginning, they worked with a therapist who came to their home, teaching them techniques to enhance Ronin's language development. They learned sign language to ensure he would have a way to communicate no matter what. By the time of his implant surgery, they'd created a world rich with language, even though Ronin couldn't yet hear a word of it.

After surgery, we waited three to four weeks to switch on the device. I distinctly remember Ronin's activation day. Many families record this milestone, but Ronin's parents were so present in the moment, they forgot to document it on video. There was no dramatic reaction, just a telltale widening of his eyes as he heard sound for the first time. What followed was a year of daily, consistent exposure to language. His parents narrated everything they did, read books at every opportunity, sang songs, and engaged him in constant conversation. They created opportunities for language everywhere, turning diaper changes, bath time, and meals into moments of connection.

The results became clear over time. Ronin would often go silent during our clinical appointments, refusing to demonstrate his growing skills and talk with me, so I discovered the truth by happy accident. At a hospital event when he was three, I overheard his gleeful exclamation "Ewww! Daddy faaaarted" from across the room. The language, the humor, the perfectly natural childhood moment all confirmed what his parents had been telling me: Ronin was thriving.

By third grade, Ronin was fully mainstreamed in public school, reading at grade level and learning alongside his hearing peers with only minimal support from a specialist. Today, he is an accomplished college student studying biomedical science, with plans to become a radiology technician. A fitting career choice for someone whose life was transformed by medical technology. While writing this book, I reached out for an update of his story and was delighted when he asked me to use his real name, Ronin. (Readers of my earlier books may remember that I referred to him as "Zach" to protect his privacy.) That same little boy who once negotiated for a large cookie is now navigating college, surrounded by friends, and pursuing a promising future in healthcare. His journey proves that early technological interventions, when paired with rich human connection, can open worlds of possibility.

A World Too Quiet

Michelle's story began with equal promise. With striking crystal-blue eyes and an intelligent gaze, she arrived at seven months old with a genetic form of hearing loss called Waardenburg syndrome. Like Ronin, her hearing loss was profound, meaning she could not detect even the loudest sounds, such as the rumbling of a motorcycle engine, without assistance. And like Ronin, she showed every sign of typical neurological development and intelligence.

But there the similarities ended. Michelle's mother, Laura, was doing the best she could in circumstances that would challenge anyone. Raising a child with special needs as a single mother, working two jobs to make ends meet, facing periods of unemployment and financial instability. Each of these alone would be difficult. Together they created a perfect storm of stress and exhaustion.

When Michelle received her implants shortly after her second birthday, we celebrated her "hearing birthday" with a cupcake and a colorful balloon. Unlike some children who cry or show dramatic responses at activation, Michelle simply continued eating her cupcake, showing only the slightest reaction to the new sounds entering her world. But that was enough, as it suggested she could hear. The audiological testing confirmed it: With her implants, Michelle's hearing was in the normal range.

As the months passed, a concerning pattern emerged. Though she responded to sounds in the testing booth, Michelle neither used nor seemed to understand speech. During clinic visits, I'd watch Laura try to engage her, only to be met with frustrated cries or silence. "Michelle, baby, the doctor's here," she'd say. Michelle's eyes showed that she wanted to connect, but she didn't have the words. Our speech therapists described Michelle as a sponge during their limited sessions, easily catching on to what they taught her, but this learning wasn't translating to her everyday life.

What was missing became clear when I visited one of Chicago's schools for children with hearing loss. In a first-grade total communication classroom, where sign and spoken language are both used, I spotted Michelle's unmistakable blue eyes. No longer the vibrant toddler I remembered, she sat quietly, her expression showing confusion as her teacher talked through a set of instructions.

Her teacher shared with me the challenges Michelle faced. Sometimes she'd come to school without lunch, often seeming tired. These visible signs of economic struggle were heartbreaking, yet they were not the sole problem. Michelle was also suffering from a profound gap in language exposure. In the critical period between implantation and that school visit, Michelle simply had not received enough consistent linguistic input. Her world was too quiet, lacking the thousands of daily exchanges that build neural pathways for understanding. The unpredictability and chronic strain of their environment, what scientists call toxic stress, likely affected both mother and child, making it even harder to establish the stable routines so vital for language development. It wasn't for lack of love or desire on Laura's part. She desperately wanted the best for her daughter. But she was overwhelmed by work, financial anxiety, and the demands of single parenting. She hadn't been able to provide the continuous stream of words, back-and-forth exchanges, and other hallmarks of a strong language environment that Michelle's developing brain needed.

Sadly, I lost touch with Michelle and her family when they moved out of state, but her story stayed with me. It's a poignant reminder of what's at stake in every child's early years, and how our social safety nets can fail families at such a crucial period in child development. Two children with the same surgery, the same implant technology, and the same initial potential had arrived at entirely different destinations. The difference wasn't in their ears, their brains, or the operating room. The difference was in what happened afterward, in the thousands of small moments that need to be filled with the intricate music of parent-child interaction.

Wired for Words

We know language is essential, but why? Evolutionary biologist Madeleine Beekman argues that what I call the helpless infant paradox, the fact that we are born so early and vulnerable, created a biological need for intense cooperation and attachment. "Bigger brains mean earlier births," she writes. "Earlier births require more support. Language is how we ask for help and coordinate it." As Beekman puts it, the first spoken words may as well have been, "Hey, hold the baby!"

Beekman's research suggests that our most characteristically human trait evolved from the fundamental need to coordinate care for our extraordinarily vulnerable infants. This places the parent-child bond at the very center of what makes us human. And it shows that those earliest interactions don't just facilitate language. They shape each generation's capacity to connect, communicate, and cooperate.

After my experience with Ronin and Michelle, I sent myself back to school, auditing classes alongside undergraduates in University of Chicago lecture halls to learn more about how these miraculous, living neural networks called brains are built through everyday interactions. During the first three years of life, a child's brain forms over one million new neural connections every second. The brain reaches 90 percent of its eventual size by age five, and early experiences lay down the foundation for cognition, emotion, and learning. In those classes, I also encountered some of the research revealing the profound impact that language environments and back-and-forth exchanges of sounds, words, expressions, and gestures have on brain development. This was the information that ultimately helped me understand Michelle's struggles. The cochlear implant had opened a doorway to sound, but without rich language to pass through her social gate, the neural circuitry necessary for understanding couldn't develop.

The Promise and Peril of Neuroplasticity

The brain, thankfully, is receptive to change. One of its most astonishing features is neuroplasticity, or the ability to adapt and reorganize in response to experience. Each interaction during sensitive periods sets the brain's expectations and operating assumptions, writing the living instruction manual for all future learning. Neural connections physically strengthen and grow through repeated back-and-forth exchanges with caregivers, laying the foundation for everything from language and numeracy to empathy and resilience.

This is part of the reason Ronin grew into the young man he is today. The cochlear implant brought sound to his brain. His parents provided a deeply enriching, immersive experience through focused back-and-forth exchanges and more. And the plasticity of his young brain meant that the neural circuitry could adapt in response to this wonderful new sensory input. His brain was flexible enough to change its wiring for a whole new world of noise.

The tragedy here is that neuroplasticity cuts both ways. Loving, layered language environments can unlock a child's potential, but a lack of interaction may limit it, turning disparities in words and experiences into disparities in wiring. The power of early experiences is especially evident in children with cochlear implants. Those who receive implants by age one often develop language skills that are indistinguishable from their hearing peers, while those implanted just a few years later have dramatically different outcomes, even with identical technology.

The early, highly sensitive periods are *that* crucial to brain development.

Architects of the Brain

After I had spent years mastering the surgical tools that give children access to sound, my academic journey led me to realize that the greatest tool of all is parental love made audible (and visible). What matters is the magic of everyday interaction. The singsong voices, coos, oohs, and aahs, interspersed with responses from babies, build the neural pathways for attachment and emotional regulation. Each back-and-forth interaction strengthens the circuits that prepare us for the lifelong work and joy of connecting with and learning from others.

Before long I decided that to effect real change, I needed to share these findings at scale, to help parents understand the importance of the seemingly simplistic power of parent talk. In 2010, this led me to found the TMW Center for Early Learning + Public Health, a translational research program at the University of Chicago initially called the Thirty Million Words Initiative. Our programs aim to help families understand the science behind child development and inspire them to focus on inter-action. We distilled our advice into a simple framework known as the 3Ts: tune in, talk more, take turns.

Working alongside families in our early TMW studies, I saw how even the smallest shift in the way a parent responded to their child—a pause, a smile, or a returned word—could change the dynamic, the engagement, and often the child's development. I watched caregivers who had been told for years what their children could not do discover what their children *could* do. These parents just needed to be given the right opportunities for interaction. They needed to be equipped with the science and strategies that leveraged their natural strengths. And we had to find a way to encourage them to see themselves as the architects of their child's developing brain.

THE 3Ts FRAMEWORK
A Simple Strategy for Brain-Building Interaction

T	MEANING	ACTION
TUNE IN	Pay attention to what your child is focused on	Follow their lead, notice their interests, observe what captures their attention
TALK MORE	Use rich language and focus on their interests	Narrate, describe, expand; test varied vocabulary; explain what you're doing and attach words to actions
TAKE TURNS	Engage in back-and-forth conversation	Pause, wait, invite replies, respond to their cues; foster serve-and-return interactions

Inside the Network

The scientific evidence supporting these ideas continues to expand. Intrigued by the thirty-million-word gap, a research team led by developmental cognitive neuroscientist Rachel Romeo designed studies examining the brain activity of children with vastly different language exposure. They gathered a group of thirty-six kids, aged between four and six years old, from a diverse mix of socioeconomic backgrounds. The scientists measured the language exposure of the children through home audio recordings. Then they had the children listen to short stories while the researchers monitored their brains through functional MRI technology, which tracks activity in different areas of the brain in real time. Their study, published in 2018, indicates that children who experience more back-and-forth conversation with adults show greater activity in their Broca's area, a region of the brain critical to speech and language development. A companion paper involving some of the same children revealed stronger brain connections along a key language highway called the arcuate fasciculus. Yet another related study from the group revealed that conversational turn-taking, regardless of socioeconomic status, was associated with differences in neural connectivity. These children also showed more brain activity in areas implicated in focus and attention, reasoning, and social understanding. All skills that help kids learn, solve problems, and build relationships. Skills that will be increasingly important in an AI-everywhere world.

To be clear, I don't believe that the parents of the children who received less verbal interaction were knowingly depriving their children of these experiences. As was the case with many of the caregivers I've worked with, they likely weren't aware of the profound power of such interactions. This is perfectly understandable given how little support and guidance parents receive in children's early years. When parents do receive coaching, they are often quick to put it into practice. Another study, in 2020, revealed that instructing parents in the basics of high-quality interaction fosters powerful changes in the brains of their children. In this project, families of six-month-old babies were split into two groups. One group was provided with coaching on parentese and turn-taking. The other was not. The scientists recorded audio of the initial and follow-on parent-child interactions every four months until the infants reached one and a half years old. What they found reinforced what we'd been learning as scientists and clinicians. Increased use of parentese and turn-taking interactions were linked to greater brain growth overall in kids, even in regions not directly tied to language. These differences in brain structure predicted not only stronger literacy, but also better skills in math, spatial reasoning, and emotional regulation.

The message is simple: Serve-and-return conversation and rich interaction nourish the *entire* brain. It's not just the quantity of words that matters, but the quality of the interaction—when, how, and in what context those words are delivered. Such moments of shared attention, of being seen and heard, are absolutely critical.

Yet the same biology that allows for astonishing growth also has its limits. The brain is remarkably malleable, but it isn't endlessly patient. During early childhood, the brain produces an overabundance of neural connections and then sculpts itself by trimming away the ones that go unused. This process, known as synaptic pruning, makes the brain more efficient, but it also means that what doesn't happen in those early years can have lifelong consequences.

This is precisely why AI marketed toward infants and young children requires our utmost vigilance. The first principle in our HOPE framework, which highlights the power of human-human connection, is especially applicable in these formative early years. When AI interacts with children during these critical periods, it has the potential to shape which neural connections strengthen and which ones atrophy. An artificial entity, not a loving caregiver, could act as the architect of a child's brain.

Our Neural Mirror

One of the first contributors to the theory of artificial intelligence was a young mother of three, the nineteenth-century mathematician Ada Lovelace. In writing about the Analytical Engine, an early mechanical calculator, Lovelace notes that the machine was limited in the sense that it could only do what it was told to do. The calculator just followed its programming. More than a century later, in his seminal 1950 paper "Computing Machinery and Intelligence," Alan Turing refers to this point as "Lady Lovelace's Objection," and considers whether it might be possible for machines to expand beyond those explicitly programmed instructions. Could a machine learn? he wonders. Turing points out that the adult mind reaches its mature, developed state through experience and education. "Instead of trying to produce a programme to simulate the adult mind," he writes, "why not rather try to produce one which simulates the child's?"

Turing describes the child's brain as a blank notebook, waiting to be filled by experience. He wonders whether it might be possible to build an artificial version, then subject that child-machine to a strong education. Then Turing concedes its physical limitations. "It will not be possible to apply exactly the same teaching process to the machine as to a normal child," he adds. "It will not, for instance, be provided with legs, so that it could not be asked to go out and fill the coal scuttle. Possibly it might not have eyes. But however well these deficiencies might be overcome by clever engineering, one could not send the creature to school without the other children making excessive fun of it."

There is something unexpectedly tender in this passage, almost parental in its protectiveness. Turing does not only worry about the machine's technical deficiencies, but about its social vulnerability. The word "creature" is telling: not just a computational device, but a being capable of being hurt by ridicule. He seems to flinch at the thought of his mechanical offspring facing the cruelties of the playground, anticipating rejection not for any failure of intelligence but simply for being different. In imagining this scenario, he reveals perhaps the most human impulse of all: the desire to shield our creations from a world that might not understand them.

Educating the modern versions of these intelligent machines works differently. For example, the chatbots that adults and children interact with today are built on large language models, or LLMs. One such model was trained on hundreds of billions of words, or the equivalent of several million books as long as the one you're reading now. Yet the models don't read text the way we humans do. They study patterns in the arrangement of the words and word fragments, sentences, paragraphs, and stories as a whole. Then they master these patterns so completely that they can generate new arrangements of text. When you ask a chatbot a question, it doesn't understand that question in any holistic sense. But it can predict a good answer because it has mastered so many word patterns. The same holds true for a request—asking the model to write you a business plan for your new restaurant idea, for example. The model doesn't "know" anything about restaurants. And it definitely hasn't eaten in one. But it can easily produce what looks like a good business plan.

Now contrast this with how a child acquires language. We don't just sit them in front of audio recordings of conversations. We create a multi-sensory experience. Each word spoken by a mother to her child is accompanied by a wide-eyed, smiling, familiar face, the gentle touch of her hand, even her smell. The children in Patricia Kuhl's breakthrough study didn't learn from the two-dimensional tutors speaking to them through a screen. They retained familiarity with Mandarin when they absorbed the words through social interaction with a demonstrative tutor. An actual, physical human pointing to and naming a toy. Similarly, we don't teach kids to read by telling them to ingest lifeless words on a page. We read to and with them, pressing in physically beside them, enunciating the words with emphasis and inflection.

Humans are more efficient learners than machines, too. Stanford researcher James McClelland has noted that today's language models require about 100,000 times more data than a child to learn a language. That's a thirty million versus three trillion word gap. Where children build meaning through emotionally rich, relevant exchanges, AI learns by crunching those massive datasets for patterns, without context, culture, or care. Our brains are evolutionarily tuned to faces, voices, and meaning. AI starts as a blank slate, learning from correlation, not true connection.

Yet one very important common trait persists. Both human and artificial intelligence remain, in many ways, black boxes. We don't fully understand how a child's mind builds meaning, just as scientists can't always explain why a deep learning model produces the outputs it does. This dual opacity takes on new urgency as these two black boxes interact ever more directly in children's daily lives, especially during critical periods of brain development. Artificial systems don't learn the way we do. They don't experience the world the same way. Yet they're developing the keys to unlock our social gates and start teaching and molding our youngest minds.

Algorithms Versus Attachment

To understand the stakes, let's look at what happens when experience meets algorithm. When children's developing brains are influenced not by human connection alone, but by systems designed to capture and hold their attention. This is new science. We are just at the beginning of understanding and probing these questions, yet there are studies that can help inform our understanding of what is at play. And at the heart of many AI-powered toys, apps, and learning platforms for children is a deceptively simple but powerful metric: engagement.

Whether it's an AI reading companion or a gamified learning platform, these systems are engineered to maximize time on task, clicks, and screen time. In other words, the algorithm's primary goal is to capture and hold a child's attention. Traditionally, when children play, they encounter natural stopping points. They fidget. They look around. They seek out a caregiver or move on to something new. These pauses matter. They're micro-moments of self-regulation and reconnection. Engagement-optimized technology is a little like an ultra-processed snack in that it's designed to erase natural pauses and encourage continued consumption. Autoplay removes the moment of decision. Infinite scroll eliminates the end of the page. AI companions never tire, never suggest doing something else. The child who might naturally look up after ten minutes stays locked in for an hour. And just as a child raised on lab-perfected food may struggle to enjoy an ordinary apple, a child raised on frictionless technology may struggle with the slower pace of real life. The classroom that doesn't adapt to their every whim. The friend who pushes back. The exhausted parent who can't compete with an entertainment algorithm.

A child glued to a screen may seem focused or even content, but engagement alone does not drive cognitive growth, promote emotional well-being, or support a family's values. I can't help but think of the kids in my waiting rooms. They're undeniably engaged by their devices. But are they learning? If what I see in those rooms is reflective of their daily experiences, are they advancing socially, emotionally, intellectually? Or are they entranced by a technology that pauses or even redirects their growth? The developing brain builds its neural architecture based on whatever is repeated and reinforced, not necessarily what is beneficial. Just as synaptic pruning strengthens the neural pathways that are repeatedly used, AI systems that prioritize engagement may wire the brain to prefer instant gratification and passive consumption, while pathways for critical thinking and sustained attention weaken. Yes, AI technologies are brand-new, and scientists will need a few years to play catch-up and study the long-term effects, but attention-grabbing algorithms and engagement-focused apps are a poor fit for developing minds.

As I was researching these questions, I tracked down Jenny Radesky, a professor in pediatrics at the University of Michigan. She was in the middle of a major multiyear research initiative exploring parent and child media use and how technology influences the development of executive function in toddlers and preschoolers. Think of executive function as a manager of the brain, a system that plans, adapts, solves problems, controls impulses, and more.

What she shared in our conversation was striking. Radesky herself has done research into the consequences of children having limited language exposure, but she is particularly interested in how media and mobile technology have inserted themselves into the cherished space between parents and children. I wasn't surprised to learn that she observed the same unsettling trend in her clinics that I'd seen in mine: Children twelve months old and up were suddenly tuned out to the people around them, completely engrossed in digital technology.

As many as 40 percent of two-year-old children have their own tablet, regardless of their socioeconomic status, and roughly one in three kids are regular YouTube viewers by age four. That percentage climbs steadily as they age. Yet the immediate appeal for overworked parents is understandable. "It's attention grabbing. It's free. And it keeps your kid busy for a while, so they don't come to bug you," Radesky said to me. "It's also designed to prolong engagement, which is part of what leads to the compulsive consumption of the technology."

When my own children were young, my husband and I picked the programs they watched on television. We controlled the remote. And when an episode was over, that was it. A sponsor's message or a commercial break gave us the chance to shut it off. I don't mean to imply that we were heroes. In a way we were lucky, as we didn't have to contend with today's technology. On a smartphone or tablet, one episode or short rolls immediately into the next, with the lineup determined by algorithm. "It's not a human deciding what should go in front of the child," Radesky cautioned. "It is a computer making that decision."

Increasingly, machines are selecting AI-generated content of astonishingly low quality, featuring garbled text, nonsensical storylines, and conflicting information, much of it aimed at kids under four. A February 2026 *New York Times* investigation found that 40 percent of shorts recommended after one popular children's video appeared to be AI-generated slop. The recommendation engines that push this content are not optimizing for truth or developmental coherence. They're optimizing for engagement and, ultimately, advertising dollars.

Contrast this with the Coco's Videos experiment conducted by Alexis Hiniker, Julie Kientz, and their colleagues. When the autoplay function was disabled, and kids were given a real chance to move on to a new activity, they did so. They controlled their urge to consume and resisted the engagement. In the behavioral-economics sense, the choice architecture was designed to build and not suppress their executive function. But that's not the way most technologies work. You have to *work* to change the settings to fit your priorities as a parent. By inserting themselves into the space between caregivers and children, autoplay videos and other apps are depriving kids of the chance to acquire and practice critical life skills. This is a phenomenon Radesky broadly refers to as crowding out. A child held captive by an endless stream of attractive animated shorts is not playing or sleeping or speaking to the people around them. Similarly, a parent hooked on Instagram Reels isn't singing "The Itsy-Bitsy Spider" with their infant. When parents are engrossed in their smartphone, checking email, social media, or news, the invaluable exchange of brain-building language is put on pause.

And yet the gravitational pull of our devices is indisputable. Messages from friends, emails and alerts from work, the urge to scroll mindlessly through a series of satisfying videos, all conspire to pull us away from the little people in front of us and into the world of the phone. I'm living proof that the lockbox commitment device isn't foolproof. Yet we could all benefit from silencing our phones and stashing them out of sight for blocks of time, allowing ourselves to focus on the even more interesting humans right in front of us. This is admittedly hard work, but executive function in children is built through effort, challenge, and practice, supported by physical brain changes that increase connectivity. This development isn't automatic, but it is crucial.

Radesky chose to study executive function in the first place because she'd seen how toddlers lacking this skill tended to struggle in school, as they had a hard time controlling their impulses and maintaining focus. In one project, Radesky and her colleagues surveyed 144 caregiver-toddler pairs on their use of mobile technology as a calming mechanism. The caregivers were far more likely to use technology to soothe children who had preexisting social-emotional difficulties when they were upset relative to kids without those struggles. This short-term solution was effectively depriving the kids of the opportunity to learn how to regulate their emotions and preventing parents from helping them do so.

In the era of ever present devices and algorithmically driven content, if a child's daily experience is dominated by passive consumption, impulsive reward, and constant distraction, their neural default may shift toward shortcuts and easy dopamine hits, while the deeper skills that underlie real learning and resilience remain underdeveloped. It's our job as parents to push back against the allure of the algorithm. Thankfully, as we'll see in the next chapter, the bond between caregiver and child is even stronger than we realized, and it provides the essential foundation for each young person's growth.

TL;DR: Chapter Review

The early years of childhood are different from every other period. The brain is under construction, forming over one million neural connections per second, and whatever shapes those connections shapes the person. AI in early childhood carries outsize risks because it may be architecting the brain itself. Meanwhile, we know that rich, nurturing language interaction builds the entire brain, and that social connection endows children with Human Edge skills like emotional regulation, executive function, and beyond. Important ideas in this chapter include:

- The brain grows to 90 percent of its adult size by age five, and early experiences lay the foundation for cognition, emotion, and learning.

- Back-and-forth conversation with adults sparks brain activity in areas linked to language, self-control, focus, memory, and social understanding. Brain scans reveal that conversational turns, not just words heard, physically strengthen neural connections.

- The 3Ts (page 86), which stands for "tune in, talk more, and take turns," capture these brain-building essentials: following your child's lead, enriching their world with language, and engaging in back-and-forth exchanges.

- The quality of interaction, including moments of shared attention, of being seen and heard, are critical to brain development.

- Each early interaction sets the brain's expectations and operating assumptions, writing the instruction manual for future learning.

- When children interact with AI during critical periods, the technology can shape which neural connections strengthen and which ones atrophy. An artificial entity, rather than a loving caregiver, could act as the architect of a child's brain.

- Many AI-powered toys, apps, and platforms maximize engagement and simulate connection, design choices that can lead to compulsive use and misplaced attachment.

- AI systems designed to maximize engagement may wire the brain for instant gratification, weakening pathways for sustained attention and critical thinking.

The response is relatively simple. Resist the allure of the algorithm and engage with the children in your life directly by tuning in, talking more, taking turns, and encouraging play and exploration away from the algorithm-shaped worlds of screens and devices.

CHAPTER SIX

Survival of the Attached

*On the irreplaceable power of human attachment—
and the risks of artificial bonds*

The anticipation surrounding my daughter Amelie's first day of preschool remains with me today. She was my third child. Surely I had this parenting thing figured out by then. At just three years old, Amelie had been eagerly awaiting her chance to join the "big kids" after watching her older siblings head off to school each morning. We picked out a special outfit. A mint-green Hello Kitty shirt, pink leggings, and sparkly sneakers. As we walked the few blocks to school together, we were both full of excitement. I was so naive!

The classroom was bright and welcoming. Ms. Abella greeted Amelie warmly, and we found the cubbyhole with my daughter's name on it. Many of the other children were familiar faces, younger siblings of her brothers' and sisters' classmates. Laughing and exploring, Amelie pulled me to a shelf of books and then the sand table. My baby seemed completely in her element. Feeling a little smug, I thought I had this transition mastered. I was completely unprepared for what happened next.

When it came time for me to leave, Amelie began to wail and cling to me with a desperation that took my breath away. Her small arms wrapped around my leg like a vise, and when I tried to gently pry her loose, her cries pierced through every other sound in the classroom. Though I couldn't bear leaving her in that state, Ms. Abella gently but firmly guided me toward the door, assuring me this was normal and that Amelie would settle once I left.

"Just go quickly," she whispered. "Lingering makes it harder for everyone."

So I did what every parent dreads. I walked away from my sobbing child. As I stepped into the hallway, I could still hear Amelie's desperate calls of "Mama! Mama!" through the door. My rational mind knew this was a normal part of development. That millions of children go through this exact experience. But my heart felt like it was being squeezed in a fist.

I found myself standing just outside the classroom door, unable to move farther down the hallway, straining to hear whether her cries were subsiding. Other parents walked past me with knowing, sympathetic smiles. Clearly, I wasn't the first mother to hover in this very spot. Part of me wanted to rush back in and scoop her up, abandon this whole preschool experiment. But a bigger part of me knew that doing so would only make tomorrow harder.

After what felt like an eternity but was probably only five minutes, the crying stopped. I waited another few minutes, then forced myself to walk away, second-guessing every step.

Day two brought no improvement. Throughout that first week, each parting felt like a small heartbreak, only marginally less wrenching than the last. I was questioning everything. Was this normal social development, or was something wrong? Had I somehow failed to prepare her properly? Why was my otherwise confident child suddenly so anxious about separation?

What I didn't realize at the time, but see now through the lens of attachment science, was that Amelie's distress wasn't a sign of insecurity or poor preparation. This was actually evidence of a healthy, strong attachment. Her tears were the expression of a system working exactly as evolution designed it to: alerting her to separation from her secure base and motivating her to restore that connection. She was building resilience through struggle, developing the very grit she relies on today as a confident young woman. And trust me, she has no trouble saying goodbye now when I drop her at college!

The Biological Imperatives of Attachment

Nature created an elegant cycle: The social abilities that evolved to help us raise vulnerable infants became, in turn, the very mechanisms through which each baby's social brain develops. At the heart of this evolutionary process emerged the parent-child relationship so fundamental to our species' survival.

Consider a mother gently rocking her baby while humming a lullaby, or a father soothing a toddler with eye contact and a whispered story. These everyday moments, so common they tend to be overlooked, ensure that infants learn, trust, and thrive within a web of human care. The scientific name for this phenomenon—attachment—captures the powerful emotional bond that forms between infant and caregiver, a bond that is the bedrock of both security and exploration. And it is through attachment that children first learn to navigate their world, develop resilience in the face of stress, and build the skills they use to cultivate relationships in the future. Much more than a mere emotional tie, attachment is a dynamic and essential mechanism through which the foundations of social understanding are built.

Nature embedded its solution to the helpless infant paradox deep within both caregiver and child. From their first breath, human infants are primed to seek connection. They arrive equipped with multiple tools for engaging caregivers: a preference for human faces, the apparent desire for eye contact, adorable and socially attuned smiles, and heart-wrenching cries. These wails are so powerful that Navy SEALs and other soldiers undergoing Survival, Evasion, Resistance, and Escape (SERE) training are subjected to hours of recorded audio of infants crying while the trainees are isolated in small cells. Those desperate baby cries are a kind of torture to the human brain. If the soldiers can endure those sounds, they'll be better prepared to survive real-world capture.

Any parent understands the raw, visceral response that your baby's cry triggers. That distress made audible is an irresistible call that bypasses all rational thought and renders you incapable of focusing on anything else until your child is soothed. Parents are also uniquely tuned in to the sounds of their offspring. Research shows that parents can identify their own baby among a group of crying infants. This recognition goes both ways: Newborns know their mother's voice and smell within days of birth, preferring them over the voices and scents of other women. These aren't random gifts—they're evolutionary adaptations that activate the caregiving instincts in adults. They help us survive as a species.

The Three Pillars of Attachment

When British psychoanalyst John Bowlby was trying to understand the parent-child bond in the mid-twentieth century, the dominant view was that everything was based on feeding. Babies bonded with their mothers because we were the primary source of nutrients. Then a scientist friend pointed Bowlby to some novel research on goslings and ducklings, which revealed that the baby birds formed a tight bond with their mothers even though they caught their own food. If the mothers weren't feeding their offspring, how could food be the primary source of attachment? Bowlby applied what he learned from these animal studies to his clinical work with people, then went on to develop much of the foundational theory of attachment. Here are his three fundamental functions:

1.   Proximity to Protection: It's the primal drive that makes a baby's cry impossible to ignore and draws caregivers close. This ensures access to nourishment, warmth, and safety during the most vulnerable period of human life.

2.   A Secure Base for Exploration: Children can venture out to explore their world knowing they can return to safety. This allows them to become, in the words of attachment theorists, "knowledgeable and competent" in ways that would

be impossible without this emotional foundation. (Even if it takes a few days of adjustment, as in Amelie's case!)

3. Emotional Co-regulation: Those thousands of moments when a caregiver soothes a distressed child are gradually internalized, building the neural architecture for emotional resilience. The calm, steady presence of an attuned caregiver teaches the child's nervous system how to regulate itself.

These three elements—proximity, secure exploration, and emotional co-regulation—form what I call the Attachment Trifecta, which shapes how we view ourselves, others, and our relationships throughout life. Guided by this trifecta, through repeated interactions with caregivers, infants develop not only expectations about relationships, but the neural infrastructure for all future social connections.

The theory of attachment evolved and expanded over the years, but it wasn't until the past few decades that scientists began to study what it looks like inside the brain. And we owe much of the foundational research on the science of parent-child attachment to a classically trained musician and mother of five. Like me, Ruth Feldman took a winding path to her life's work. Music was her passion, but human connection became her lifelong score.

Attachment as Jazz

At the age of fifteen, Feldman moved with her family from Israel to New York City. She was accepted into Hunter College, although she hadn't yet finished high school, and graduated at nineteen with a degree in music composition and aspirations of a career in jazz. After marriage, three master's degrees, and five children, Feldman began pursuing her PhD in developmental psychology, focused on the mother-infant bond.

Although she set aside her musical goals, Feldman remained fascinated by jazz, particularly the way in which two musicians could synchronize their playing as if they were of one mind. She suspected that this synchrony extended far beyond the world of music, and for the next three decades she conducted a series of groundbreaking studies revealing the biological mechanisms underlying attachment.

Using advanced neuroimaging, Feldman discovered that individuals with secure attachments develop greater density in brain regions crucial for social connection: the hippocampus, the prefrontal cortex, and temporal regions responsible for social cognition and emotional regulation. Perhaps most remarkably, her lab managed to document actual brain-to-brain synchrony between parents and infants. Neural activity in specific regions becomes coordinated during interactions. Heartbeats synchronize. The brains of both release oxytocin, a hormone associated with bonding, eye contact, and more intimate interactions. During skin-to-skin contact, theta waves in the parent's brain fall into rhythm with those of their child, creating what Feldman has described as "a feeling of oneness . . . almost as if you're holding the baby in the womb."

Through her research, she found the synchronized riffs of two musicians at work in everyday life. A multilayered biological performance that allows two disparate human nervous systems to stabilize each other through micro-adjustments happening below the level of conscious awareness. When a parent's calm presence soothes a distressed child, it's not just emotional comfort. It's one nervous system helping another learn how to regulate itself.

Another study, conducted by Vanessa Reindl of Germany's Aachen University, along with a team of European scientists, revealed that these bonds may persist long after parents believe they've been severed. The researchers set up an experiment involving thirty-four tween and teen girls. Each girl interacted with her mother in one test, then with a woman she'd never met. In both cases, the scientists measured activity in the participants' brains and nervous systems through functional near-infrared spectroscopy (fNIRS), an approach also used in Feldman's studies. Subjects wore a cap arrayed with electrodes that shined harmless, low-wavelength light into their brains. This allowed the system to track blood flow inside. As a result, the scientists could see which areas of the brain were active during the interactions. Although the subjects in Reindl's study were older than the ages we focus on in this book, her findings are both fascinating and heartening. The mother-child pairs displayed higher brain-to-brain synchrony relative to the girls' interactions with strangers, providing neurological proof that the connection doesn't completely sever when your daughter turns thirteen. (Phew!)

The work further supports what Feldman discovered: When parents and children engage in attuned interactions, their brains literally fall into rhythm with each other, creating synchronized patterns of neural activation that strengthen learning and emotional bonding. This isn't poetic metaphor; it's biological reality. And it kicks in early. Feldman's work shows evidence of synchrony as early as three to four months of age.

Her ongoing research aligns with everything I've learned in my own work with parents. She espouses the importance of gaze, positive affect, parentese, the power of physical contact, and establishing that parent-child bond from the outset. Her focus on synchrony also led her to track the development and maturation of individuals over many years, to study the long-term effects of parent-child interactions.

Obviously, the art of bonding with your child changes as they grow. I don't coo at my kids anymore. During the infancy stage, our interactions as parents broaden, bringing in the use of toys and tools such as spoons, then expanding into imaginative play, reading, and more as they age. Yet that parent-child bond remains critical at every stage. Feldman has shown that consistent synchrony in the newborn stage leads to better emotional regulation in the first year. Continued parent-child bonding then leads to improved focus and attention regulation in the second year. In a nod to her musical background, Feldman has compared these consistent, dependable bonds to the twelve-bar blues, a popular chord progression that underlies many jazz improvisations. That steady bond lets the child experiment and grow.

Conversely, children with inconsistent early relationships show different brain patterns. Their neural networks for social processing appear less integrated, with an overactive amygdala (the brain's alarm system) creating a state of heightened vigilance. Importantly, this isn't a malfunction but the brain behaving rationally and adapting to its environment. When caregiving is unpredictable, the brain allocates more resources to threat detection and less to exploration and trust.

This translates into measurable differences in how people navigate relationships, process emotions, and manage stress throughout life. Early attachment experiences sculpt the brain's architecture, creating physical pathways that influence everything from emotional resilience to our capacity for deep connection. As Feldman has noted, "Love really protects you, the parent and the baby; biologically, not only emotionally."

Yet there is more at work here than the development of social and emotional skills. When I discussed the parent-child bond with Patricia Kuhl, the scientist behind the social gate, she noted that social interactions light up the *entire* brain. Language, the visual gaze, facial recognition, and other specific capabilities tend to be centered in particular regions of the brain. But social interaction calls on so many fundamental skills that it stimulates activity throughout. I wondered aloud how this might change if children formed attachments to intelligent robots.

Kuhl suggested that this topic was more important than the standard debates about what we will do as a species if and when robots are more intelligent than humans. "What happens to the social and emotional brain and its connection to learning?" she asked. "It's not separate. Our intellect comes through the social channel originally."

The AI Attachment Challenge

What if we replace the evolutionarily optimized human caregiver with an artificial agent? When children's brains form bonds with AI companions, they're engaging with entities that cannot participate in the biological dance of synchrony. They won't be able to link their heartbeats or their brain waves with a virtual or physical machine that has no heart and no brain.

The behavior of an AI friend might not be *wrong* exactly, but it could be incomplete in ways we cannot yet fully measure. Plus, as children form bonds with artificial companions, their attachment systems may develop around expectations—such as perfect consistency, endless patience, and always-rapid responsiveness—that human relationships simply cannot match. We'll examine this issue in more detail in chapter eight, but this mismatch doesn't just create unrealistic social expectations; it has the potential to alter the very neural architecture underlying attachment, emotional regulation, and stress response in ways that could profoundly influence lifelong relationships.

As alarming as this possibility is, Feldman's research gives us reason to hope. She has found that our capacity for neural synchrony remains dynamic throughout life. This suggests that even if artificial attachments begin the process of steering development, consistent, quality human connection retains its power to positively influence the brain.

Three Questions That Shape a Life

While attachment provides the foundation for development, its lasting impact comes through what psychologists call internal working models. These enduring mental frameworks fundamentally shape how we move through life. Think of these as relationship maps that help us interpret every social interaction and navigate unfamiliar social terrain. They address three critical questions that follow us as we grow:

- Am I worthy of care and attention? (Our view of self.)

- Can others be trusted to respond when I need them? (Our view of others.)

- Is reaching out for connection safe or dangerous? (Our view of relationships.)

The answers to these questions, informed by thousands of early interactions, create patterns we unconsciously seek to follow throughout our lives, from how we read a stranger's smile to whether we reach for connection in moments of distress.

How Internal Working Models Affect Daily Life

Think of the child who learns through consistent care that they matter and that others can be trusted. As they grow, this child explores new relationships with more confidence, recovers faster from social setbacks, and generally expects good intentions from others. When faced with a friend's cancellation of plans, they might think, "Something must have come up," rather than, "They don't really like me."

Contrast this with a child whose early experiences teach them that connection is unpredictable or even painful. This child might approach new relationships with wariness, interpret neutral comments as criticism, or develop strategies like perfectionism or emotional distance to protect themselves from expected rejection. When a teacher offers constructive feedback, they might hear criticism and disapproval rather than support and guidance.

These aren't character flaws but survival techniques. They're signs of adaptation, not weakness. Such strategies helped them cope with their early environment and, in many ways, demonstrate the remarkable ability of the developing brain to find solutions even in challenging circumstances.

The Dynamic Nature of Relationship Maps

These models remain dynamic throughout life, updating continuously through significant human interactions. Every relationship becomes both a test and a refinement of these foundational templates. When a toddler ventures away from their secure base only to return for reassurance, when a child navigates a disagreement with a friend, when a teenager processes their first heartbreak, each experience either reinforces or subtly reshapes their internal working model.

Studies by the NICHD Early Child Care Research Network found that children whose mothers were initially less responsive could still develop secure attachments if they received high-quality care elsewhere. What makes this finding so crucial is that these adjustments occurred through consistent human relationships, not simply through exposure to information or skills training. The healing comes through new experiences that run counter to old expectations. Think of the teacher who reliably notices a quiet child's contributions. The mentor who remains steady through a teenager's mistakes. The therapist who provides the safety to examine these very patterns.

One of the core principles of our HOPE framework is that AI should only enhance and never replace human interaction. But what if a child is deprived of a caregiver's time and attention? An interactive AI chatbot or intelligent social robot might be able to fill *some* of the gap caused by the absence of a consistent human caregiver. But as it stands, there's nothing available now or visible on the horizon that meets the necessary safety standards. And if something were to be developed, it would represent a dangerously slippery slope, as overexposure would likely lead to an unhealthy dependence.

Secure attachment doesn't require perfect parenting—quite the opposite. In fact, it is consistent caretaking, complete with its inherent imperfections, that unlocks the Goldilocks zone of human attachment. This brand of attachment is not too cold, not too hot, but just right.

THE GOLDILOCKS ZONE OF ATTACHMENT
Why "Good Enough" Parenting Is Actually Optimal

	TOO COLD *Insecure Attachment*	JUST RIGHT *Secure Attachment*	TOO PERFECT *Artificial Attachment*
CARE PATTERN	Inconsistent caregiving: warmth one moment, absence the next	"Good enough" parenting: misunderstandings followed by repair	Flawless AI responses: instant, tireless, infinitely patient

	TOO COLD *Insecure Attachment*	**JUST RIGHT** *Secure Attachment*	**TOO PERFECT** *Artificial Attachment*
LESSON LEARNED	"Connection is unreliable"	"Relationships can withstand rupture"	"Others should always make me happy"
DEVELOPMENTAL OUTCOME	Hypervigilance; difficulty trusting	Resilience; healthy relationships	Unrealistic expectations; dependency
LONG-TERM RISK OR BENEFIT	Avoidant or anxious patterns; struggles with intimacy	Emotional regulation; social competence; adaptability	Preference for AI over humans; intolerance of human "messiness"

At one extreme, inconsistent or unpredictable caregiving, wherein a parent might be warm and responsive one moment, then absent or harsh the next, creates insecure attachment. Children raised in these environments struggle to trust that their needs will be met or that relationships are safe. At the other extreme lies a newer phenomenon: perfectly consistent, immediately gratifying AI companions that never misunderstand, never need the child to wait. This may sound ideal, but it risks creating what we call artificial attachment. Children raised this way may learn to expect instant gratification and flawless understanding, leaving them unprepared for the beautifully imperfect reality of human relationships. They develop a dependence on the frictionless interactions that rarely exist in the human world.

The sweet spot is in the middle: consistent yet imperfect human caregiving that builds secure attachment precisely because it includes manageable challenges and repairs. It teaches children that they can express their needs and still be OK, that others can misunderstand them temporarily and still care deeply, and that relationships can withstand tension and emerge stronger for it. This continuous refinement of their view of themselves, others, and relationships through real-world testing is precisely what makes human interaction so irreplaceable.

In other words, beautifully messy moments of social challenge build stronger neural connections than seamless interactions ever could, which is why our HOPE framework urges us to own our imperfections.

Amelie's Journey

To understand how these abstract principles play out in real development, let's continue following Amelie's journey from tearful preschooler to the socially adept young woman she is today. Her story illustrates how each stage builds upon secure attachment while revealing the beautiful unpredictability of human development. (And it reminds young parents, I hope, that tearful drop-offs don't last forever!)

Face Recognition 101: The Foundation Course
(Birth to Six Months)

Baby Amelie began by activating what neuroscientists consider the gateway tracks to social cognition: the face-processing pathways. She would stare at faces with such intensity, we joked that she wasn't just memorizing them but conducting a full background check.

What looked like simple baby watching was actually sophisticated brain construction. Each time we moved closer to the optimal distance for infant face recognition (about twelve inches, not coincidentally the distance between a feeding baby and a parent's face), her temporal regions were strengthening their specialization for human features. Even our most instinctive parenting moves   the exaggerated expressions that make us look slightly unhinged to anyone watching—were providing exactly the type of input her developing visual systems needed.

Social Discrimination 201: Learning Who Matters Most
(Seven to Fifteen Months)

When Amelie was around seven months old, her emerging social sophistication took a turn that felt personal. Very personal, in fact. Suddenly, the baby who had charmed everyone with her social smile developed what we called "the Hierarchy of Acceptable Humans," with me firmly at the top and everyone else (including her devoted father) somewhere far below. Her dad would reach for her and she'd respond with a deathly stare we referred to as "the Glare." Even her grandmother, whom she'd previously adored, got the Glare.

I'll admit that a tiny part of me felt secretly triumphant. *Finally,* I thought, *my social butterfly needs only me!* I had no idea that this would be the high point of my maternal dominance. When, as a teen, she breezed through the house with a quick "Hi, Mom!" before spending hours on the phone with friends, I found myself nostalgically remembering those clingy months when I was her whole world.

What I didn't realize then was that this apparent regression was actually her social brain advancing. Her amygdala and prefrontal cortex were developing more-sophisticated circuits for social discrimination. Each time we validated her caution while providing gentle reassurance, we were strengthening both these circuits and her secure attachment, teaching her brain that she could safely explore the world while staying connected to her secure base—me.

Exploration 301: The Power of a Secure Base
(Sixteen Months to Three Years)

Ultimately, Amelie's preschool experience came to perfectly demonstrate the power of secure attachment to support exploration. Despite our very rocky start, somewhere in the second week Amelie finally let me go without tears. But her attachment to me wasn't threatened by this new relationship with her teacher and classmates. Instead, our bond provided the foundation that eventually allowed her to thrive in her new environment. John Bowlby pushed this idea as one of the key features of parenting. Inspired by his army background, he likened the parent to a secure military base from which an expeditionary force can push into new territory.

Her attachment system was asking: Can I trust this new environment? Will my secure base still be here when I need it? Is it safe to explore? Through consistent, patient responses—mine in coming back every day, Ms. Abella's in providing comfort and structure—Amelie learned that she could venture into new social territory while maintaining her essential connection to home. What I was witnessing, though I didn't have the scientific language for it then, was Amelie's internal working model being tested and refined.

This experience laid crucial groundwork for every social challenge that would follow. The neural pathways that were strengthened during those difficult mornings would later support her ability to form friendships, recover from interpersonal setbacks, and eventually thrive in the complex social environment of college.

Mind Reading 401: Developing Theory of Mind (Three to Five Years)

Once she had settled into preschool, Amelie progressed from social discrimination to social cognition. I'll never forget the night she brought her growing understanding of minds to bedtime. "One more story?" she asked, already pulling her favorite book from the shelf. When she saw my hesitation, she added with complete conviction, "Reading makes me smart! You said!" Then she patted the bed beside her and deployed her newest negotiating tool, echoing the words she'd often heard from me when I was trying to wrap up her playtime: "Just five more minutes?"

The mix of imitated phrases and genuine eagerness, topped with her hopeful smile, showed me we'd entered a new phase. She was beginning to understand that other people have thoughts, desires, and knowledge different from her own, and that she could influence those mental states. Theory of mind had arrived.

During this period, her prefrontal cortex was developing increasingly sophisticated circuits for understanding others' mental states. Each time we named emotions ("You seem frustrated"), discussed perspectives ("I wonder what your cousins are thinking"), or played pretend ("Let's imagine we're . . ."), we were helping build these advanced social-processing networks.

Social Mastery 501: The Gradual Emergence of the Butterfly (Six to Eighteen Years)

This integration of cognitive understanding and emotional regulation created the foundation for what we would later observe in our college-age daughter. My husband and I would exchange knowing smiles during our regular video calls with her. Like a well-rehearsed dance, we knew exactly how these conversations would unfold. After a brief mention of classes, she'd launch into what really animated her: a detailed chronicle of her social world.

There was the friend she was helping through a breakup, the two classmates she was convinced would be perfect research partners, the sorority sister who just needed someone to really listen. Evidence of her social ability appeared everywhere: in the stream of texts and calls from friends seeking her counsel, in her natural leadership of YES (the campus entrepreneurial society), in the way her sorority sisters gravitated to her genuine warmth. Yet I could still see the little girl in the mint-green Hello Kitty shirt, now navigating a far larger playground.

The neural pathways that eventually allowed her to effortlessly read a room and forge genuine connections were built through countless early interactions, including those difficult mornings at preschool. Such experiences taught her the fundamental lesson of secure attachment: Connection can withstand separation and be restored.

The Many Faces of Social Development

It's important to clarify that social development encompasses far more than typical extroverted behaviors or maintaining a large friend circle. For some children, including many with autism spectrum disorders, successful social engagement might look entirely different. In his teen years, my son Asher preferred deep one-on-one conversations about specific interests rather than socializing in group settings. And his way of connecting socially was no less valid than his sister's vibrant social calendar.

What unites all children, regardless of social style or neurological differences, is their need to develop a sense of self, understand others' perspectives, and build emotional regulation through relationships. Exercising the social brain isn't about becoming extroverted. The point is to develop the neural foundations that allow us to navigate our fundamentally social world in ways that honor our authentic selves.

As I watched Amelie flourish in her richly connected college life, I reminded myself of what got her to that point. Her extraordinary capacity for connection grew through thousands of messy, imperfect, deeply human exchanges, from those tearful preschool mornings to her eventual social leadership. Every step was shaped by the beautiful complexity of human relationships. Looking ahead, we know that AI is going to be capable of influencing those steps. In order to make thoughtful and informed decisions about whether and how we allow that to happen, we need to examine the invisible processes that occur when minds truly meet—and determine which essential nutrients AI interactions might lack.

TL;DR: Chapter Review

In these pages, we focus on the importance of attachment, the powerful emotional bond between parent and child, and reveal why emotionally responsive AI poses unique risks. A few important concepts:

- Attachment has a neurological basis: The brains of parents and children synchronize during close interactions. Artificially intelligent systems are incapable of this synchrony.

- Individuals with secure attachments develop greater density in brain regions crucial for social connection. In children with inconsistent early relationships, those regions are less integrated, and the amygdala, the brain's alarm system, remains on high alert.

- Secure attachment rests on three pillars that make up the Attachment Trifecta.

THE ATTACHMENT TRIFECTA
Three Pillars of Secure Attachment

PROXIMITY TO PROTECTION	SECURE BASE FOR EXPLORATION	EMOTIONAL CO-REGULATION
WHAT IT MEANS: The primal drive that makes a baby's cry impossible to ignore and draws caregivers close	WHAT IT MEANS: Children can venture out to explore their world, knowing they can return to safety	WHAT IT MEANS: Thousands of soothing moments are gradually internalized, building neural architecture for emotional resilience
WHAT IT PROVIDES: Access to nourishment, warmth, and safety during the most vulnerable period of human life	WHAT IT PROVIDES: Freedom to become knowledgeable and competent in ways that would be impossible without this foundation	WHAT IT PROVIDES: The child's nervous system learns how to regulate itself through the calm, steady presence of an attuned caregiver

Allowing AI to disrupt attachment, especially from birth to age five, may have lifelong consequences.

- Through attachment, children move through predictable stages of social development (page 115)—from studying faces, to distinguishing safe from unfamiliar, to venturing into new social territory. Each stage is shaped by human interaction. We don't know how AI companions, which mimic social cues but lack the capacity for biological synchrony and authentic emotional investment, might alter this trajectory.

YOUR CHILD'S SOCIAL-DEVELOPMENT TIMELINE

Stages of Social-Emotional Growth

STAGE	AGE	WHAT'S HAPPENING	WHAT PARENTS SEE
Face Recognition	Birth–6 months	Face-processing pathways developing in temporal regions	Intense staring at faces; "full background check"
Social Discrimination	7–15 months	"Hierarchy of Acceptable Humans" forms; amygdala and prefrontal circuits develop	Stranger anxiety; clings to primary caregiver; "the Glare"
Exploration	16 months–3 years	Secure base enables exploration; tests strength of attachment	Ventures out, returns for reassurance; preschool adjustment
Mind Reading	3–5 years	Theory of mind emerges; development of prefrontal circuits for understanding others' mental states	Negotiation attempts; "One more story before bed!"
Social Mastery	6–18 years	Integrating cognitive understanding and emotional regulation	Complex friendships, social leadership, empathy

- Through thousands of early interactions, children develop internal working models—so-called relationship maps—that determine how they view themselves, others, and connection itself.

THREE QUESTIONS THAT BUILD A LIFE

THROUGH THOUSANDS OF EARLY INTERACTIONS, CHILDREN DEVELOP ANSWERS TO:

1. *Am I worthy of care and attention? (Our view of self.)*

2. *Can others be trusted to respond when I need them? (Our view of others.)*

3. *Is reaching out for connection safe or dangerous? (Our view of relationships.)*

These answers become the relationship maps that guide future social interactions.

- Secure attachment doesn't require perfect parenting. Quite the opposite: the Goldilocks Zone of Attachment (pages 107–108) describes the spectrum between two extremes. Inconsistent caregiving creates insecure attachment, and with it children who struggle to trust whether their needs will be met. At the other end lies artificial attachment: AI that never fails to respond, never requires patience, never needs repair. The sweet spot is in the middle: consistent yet imperfect human caregiving that builds secure attachment precisely because it includes manageable challenges and repairs.

- AI could lead to artificial attachment: children who expect instant gratification and flawless understanding and who are thus unprepared for the beautifully imperfect reality of human relationships. No AI can replicate the emotional depth of a human caregiver.

Lifelong flourishing requires human relationships, regardless of social style or neurological differences.

CHAPTER SEVEN

Missing Ingredients

*The unknown ingredients of human connection—
and why AI's imitation isn't nourishment*

In 1865, German chemist Justus von Liebig announced the creation of the first scientifically designed infant formula. Von Liebig was already world-renowned for pioneering a new type of fertilizer to help farms increase their agricultural yield. His liquid meat extract was an extremely popular food supplement. He'd changed the way chemistry was taught by focusing more on laboratory experiments than blackboard jottings. And he hoped his so-called soup for infants would be another major breakthrough.

Von Liebig later wrote that he developed the formula because his own daughter struggled to breastfeed her children. The common practice in Europe at the time was to hire a wet nurse, a young woman who'd feed the baby in your stead. This was expensive, though, and according to the thinking of the day, there was a risk it might lead to an unhealthy attachment between the baby and the wet nurse. So von Liebig set about replicating the measurable components of breast milk, including proteins, fats, carbohydrates, and what minerals were then known, in order to copy nature's design.

The formula, a mixture of cow's milk, wheat flour, malt, and potassium bicarbonate, seemed right. It mimicked what science could measure. And it was created with the best intentions by one of the era's foremost scientists. With his daughter's approval, he even tested his soup for infants on his own grandchildren. He said they flourished.

The chemist then set about promoting the new formula across Europe, where his supposed breakthrough would prove terribly dangerous. In June 1867, at a meeting of the French Academy of Medicine, the gathered experts began questioning the merits of von Liebig's mixture. The scientists were moving toward a resolution to rigorously test the formula when one of their members, a professor at the Paris Faculty of Medicine named Jean-Anne-Henri Depaul, stood up with an announcement. He'd collaborated with a former student of von Liebig's and, with the help of the chemist himself, prepared the formula for several newborns. Two of the babies died within two days. Another was dead on the third night. The fourth lasted only a day longer.

The Academy was understandably outraged. When he learned of this tragedy, von Liebig countered with the claim that thousands of babies had prospered on the formula. But additional stories surfaced, revealing that infants fed exclusively on the formula were wasting away. Their skin would grow pale, their eyes sunken. They'd develop scurvy, rickets, and infections that healthy babies easily fought off. These horrible outcomes were not the product of malevolence. Overconfidence, yes. But von Liebig was trying to do right by humanity. (Interestingly, some of today's most prominent technology leaders have made a curious choice: limiting their own children's use of the very products they build. That disconnect inspired me to propose a new screening technique called the Salk-Jobs Litmus Test. See sidebar on page 120.) In von Liebig's case, the science and scientific instruments of his time simply could not identify the truly vital components that his formula lacked. Nature doesn't publish its ingredient list. Specific fatty acids, enzymes, and antibodies weren't yet known. His grave mistake resulted from a fundamental misunderstanding of what constitutes true dietary nourishment.

The Salk-Jobs Litmus Test

When Jonas Salk developed the polio vaccine, he famously tested it on his wife and three sons before it entered widespread trials. His logic was straightforward: If he was going to ask parents to trust him with their children's lives, he had to trust the vaccine with his kids' lives, too.

Steve Jobs lived by a different rule. While building devices that would reshape modern childhood, he strictly limited his own children's access to them. "They haven't used it," he told the *New York Times* when asked about the iPad. He was not alone. Bill Gates delayed smartphone use for his children. Snapchat's Evan Spiegel imposed strict screen limits. Many Silicon Valley families choose to send their kids to low-tech Waldorf schools.

This pattern points to a critical information asymmetry. The people closest to a new technology often understand its trade-offs earlier, and more intimately, than the public does.

The Salk-Jobs Litmus Test is simple. All you have to do is ask whether the creator of the product would confidently give it to their own child at the same age. If the answer is no, treat that refusal as a data point. When the builder refuses to cross their own bridge, it is worth asking what they know about the construction.

The tragic story of von Liebig and his soup for infants reminds us that today's AI systems, however sophisticated they are at mimicking human interaction, may lack developmental nutrients we haven't yet learned to detect or measure. Yes, we now have stuffed animals with interactive chat capabilities. Social robots like the discontinued Moxie can mimic emotion and empathy. But we don't know if today's AI systems provide the necessary nutrients for true intellectual, linguistic, and emotional growth. AI-driven educational tools and social robots may appear to foster learning, language usage, and emotional intelligence. Yet they may also be missing unseen, indispensable elements essential for a child's holistic development.

The Intricate Dance

My husband transforms from numbers-driven economist to playful performer when encountering babies. His signature move always works. He'll lean in close, make eye contact, and slowly stick out his tongue. Without fail, the baby will respond by mirroring his exact action. This unconscious, instantaneous imitation happens before the baby could possibly "learn" such a behavior. Is the secret to this bond as obvious as what we see and hear? Or is there something deeper at work?

Traditionally, studies of infant-caregiver interaction center on one element of communication at a time. Scientists might focus exclusively on verbalization, for example, or eye contact of the sort my husband relies on. Yet researchers have rarely looked at the entire ensemble: speech, affect, touch, gesture, and more. Casey Lew-Williams of the Princeton University Baby Lab and his colleague Jessica Kosie set out to cover the spectrum in studying more than forty infant-caregiver pairs as they played together on the floor for ten minutes. The experiments were conducted in the child's home, with scientists remotely and nonintrusively recording the interaction via Zoom, and the results demonstrate that infant-caregiver communication consists of so much more than speech. The researchers found that even when the kids and their caregivers did interact verbally, they usually relied on at least one other mode of communication. Words would be accompanied by actions, gestures, or emotions expressed through a smile or wide-eyed surprise.

This should shock no one, as we all intuitively use multiple means of connecting with one another and with infants. My husband doesn't necessarily vocalize to connect with babies, but he does use an action (leaning in), a gesture (sticking out his tongue), and emotion, in the form of a friendly, wide-eyed invitation to eye contact. Lew-Williams and Kosie refer to this as multidimensional communication. AI researchers might call it multimodal interaction, in the sense that it involves several modes or styles of sensory output and input.

While the varied means of connecting are incredibly important, they aren't necessarily the essential ingredients in caregiver-infant connection. I wonder if speech, gesture, and the rest may be more like the baby bottle than the formula itself. They could be vehicles for elements we still cannot measure. Like von Liebig, we do not yet have the tools to truly analyze and understand the intricate biological dance between a parent and their child. But we're making some progress.

For example, a team of scientists led by neuroscientist Elise Piazza used a more baby-friendly version of an fNIRS device to monitor infant and toddler brain activity in real time as children in the study interacted with an adult researcher for five minutes. They played with toys, sang, or read a book together. The results helped to deepen our understanding of how connection and engagement spark neural activity, suggesting that some modes of interaction are more powerful than others. Researchers found, for example, that eleven different channels within the brain synchronized when adult and child interacted closely and without distraction. Yet this didn't happen when another adult was present and speaking with the researcher. The neural synchronization was also stronger when adult and child made direct eye contact, versus when both were looking at the same object. This aligns with Feldman's findings about the power of the gaze, parentese, and physical contact. Similarly, a 2021 study led by psychologist Trinh Nguyen of the University of Vienna revealed that mothers and their four- to six-month-old infants were more synchronized during face-to-face interaction. An affectionate touch prompted a measurably stronger connection, too.

Other work shows that more frequent conversational turn-taking—when an adult pauses to let the child speak and then responds—directly correlates with higher neural synchrony. Infants who initiated more vocal turns showed higher interhemispheric connectivity, and the frequency of these exchanges at four to six months significantly predicted vocabulary size at twenty-four months. Consider that for a moment next time you're singing or reading to your child. These early social exchanges aren't merely pleasant interactions. They are fundamental mechanisms that scaffold brain development and language acquisition. This is critical learning disguised as a playful social duet, with parents and their babies in perfect harmony.

Social robots try to simulate these connections. Moxie, for example, was equipped with microphones that allowed it to pick up nearby voices. The robot's digital, on-screen eyes didn't actually see; that job belonged to the high-definition camera embedded in the robot's head. But when a child addressed Moxie, the microphones captured the words, then transferred the raw audio to algorithms that attempted to make sense of what was said. Fundamentally, that's not too different from an Alexa-powered speaker. The difference with a social robot like Moxie is that it could then turn and direct its digital eyes toward its conversational partner, as if it were making actual social contact. If the child was smiling, the robot would likely recognize that emotional state, too, as its electronic brain had been trained on countless images of happy humans. A social robot might not know what it means to be happy or sad, but it can identify smiles and frowns, match them to an emotional state, and then respond with the appropriate words or even the offer of a hug. It's fascinating, impressive, and undeniably strange. Yet these simulated, algorithm-driven attempts at connection just aren't comparable to true human bonds. In time, we will know more about exactly which ingredients are missing from these artificial relationships, but for now we can say confidently that it is better for a child to turn to a human for connection than to a machine designed to feign it.

Observatories for the Brain

And yet it may be that AI will help us find some of the critical ingredients in human social interaction. Astronomy offers a good example of what is possible in the years ahead. When the James Webb Space Telescope was launched in 2021, the stated goals for the project were to study our own solar system, faraway planets, and distant galaxies too faint for other instruments to detect. Within two years, the telescope was already returning data that proved puzzling to scientists. Galaxies that had formed in the early years of our universe appeared to be much larger and more mature than cosmology's standard theories suggested. The Webb's data also hinted that the universe wasn't expanding at exactly the pace we'd expected. As a result of these and other developments, cosmologists are beginning to question whether our theories of the formation of the universe need a significant revision.

If the developing human brain is a miniature universe in itself, with billions of neurons instead of billions of stars, we have not yet built our Webb telescope. I'm not even sure we have the Hubble, its predecessor. And child development isn't just about the brain. Children learn and grow within a larger, richer, more complex environment. A world crowded with people, pets, objects, and spaces, and innumerable sounds, sights, and smells. Broadly, AI could serve as our telescope for child development, a tool that helps us uncover the subtleties of parent-child interactions that our eyes and minds, and even our recent brain-scanning efforts, have not picked out. My hope is that AI can provide an added observatory, a new and unconventional vantage on caregiver-infant interactions. One that sees this dance from new angles and finds patterns that researchers miss. We don't necessarily have to look inside the brain or the body to do so either, as there are rich signals hiding in the music of everyday interaction.

At the TMW Center, we've been exploring whether AI could help us see things in parent-child interactions that our own eyes and ears might miss. We started with more than six hundred hours of audio from our home-visiting intervention, a program in which we taught families simple strategies for supporting their children's brain development through the 3Ts: tune in, talk more, take turns. Then we tracked those families for a number of years. At first our focus was simple: monitoring conversational turn-taking between parents and children, and then mapping early parent-child interactions to children's later cognitive and socioemotional assessments. We confirmed that when children grow up in rich language environments, their development and future opportunities flourish. More recently, we decided to see if we could use the data to predict a child's skills development based on specific elements of their early-language environment.

Our use of a pretrained audio neural network—an AI system that could extract segments of speech, identify the speaker, and analyze acoustic features—captured something quite significant. Since we tracked participants over time, we were able to match those early interactions to long-term developmental outcomes. We knew which children showed better results in terms of language acquisition and socioemotional skills, and we could use AI to sift through the audio for patterns we weren't able to detect on our own.

What we found was that beyond the words themselves, the very quality of a parent's voice could predict children's cognitive and emotional growth. Tone and timbre, or the same acoustic qualities that make Adele sound different from Bob Dylan, mapped to future skills. Developmental scientists have advocated increased use of parentese for decades. *Thirty Million Words* made that case as well. Yet we'd deliberately avoided imposing any such ideas on this analysis. We wanted the data to speak for itself. Instead of coding known characteristics of parental speech, our plan was to have the algorithm rely on child outcomes when determining which acoustic features mattered most. And that audio neural network picked out precisely what seemed to be making a difference in each parent's voice. Not just speaking or singing, but doing so in a unique style— the voice that only you as a parent can project into the world, through the ears and into the mind of your child.

The finding reminded me of the classic story of the British Navy's discovery that lemons provided strong protection against scurvy, a deadly disease in the seventeenth and eighteenth centuries. Later, scientists would learn that it wasn't the juice exactly, but the vitamin C *within* it. Similarly, it would be easy to conclude that simply talking to your child is enough. But just as sailors didn't understand why lemons worked, we're only beginning to grasp what makes conversation so powerful. The secret could be the tone, the neural synchrony, the precise timing of serve-and-return, the emotional attunement that happens beneath conscious awareness, some idealized ratio of them all, or perhaps even the influence of forces science hasn't yet identified.

This is still just the beginning of our work. But the promise of the research, and the general potential of intelligent tools as a means of revealing the social recipe, is evident. AI is already giving us new ways to find patterns in human interaction. And those patterns may hold answers to some of our oldest questions about how children learn, grow, and thrive.

The Power of Imperfection

All the research on brain-to-brain synchrony, combined with this new data on the subtle intricacies of interactions, points to human-human connection as irreplaceable. Yet interaction isn't limited to parentese and funny faces. The slight mismatches, misunderstandings, and repairs that occur naturally in human relationships create essential learning opportunities. (As our HOPE framework suggests: Don't disregard the imperfections; own them!) My colleague Dani recently told me an incredible story that demonstrates this perfectly.

One day, Dani noticed her thirteen-month-old son Arthur pointing urgently at the dining table during lunch. Was he gesturing at the bananas? She held one up. Arthur shook his head, pointing more insistently. "The book?" She tried the board book near his plate. More frantic pointing, now with frustrated grunts. "Crackers? Yogurt? Your spoon?" Nothing worked. Arthur's frustration mounted into tears. Dani felt that familiar parental helplessness. Her son was trying so hard to tell her something, and she couldn't understand. Then, a few days later, something shifted. Mid-meal, Arthur started making an exaggerated throat-clearing sound. "Ahem! Ahem!" He was re-creating a behavior that had reliably prompted Dani to offer him water. Dani's confusion turned to sudden clarity. "Oh! You want water!"

Within a week, that fake cough became Arthur's signature signal. But something else happened, too: Dani learned that Arthur liked to sip throughout his meal, not just at the start. She kept his cup filled and within reach. Arthur refined his signal, using it more precisely. Those frustrating days of miscommunication weren't wasted. In struggling to understand each other, both Dani and Arthur had leveled up. He'd invented a creative solution. She'd become more attuned to his needs. Together, they'd built their own language. One born not from perfect understanding, but from the hard work of repair. From the Goldilocks zone.

Moments of imperfection fuel social-emotional growth as well as communication skills. When a parent misreads a child's cue and then corrects course, when a slight delay in response requires the child to wait and regulate their emotions, when a facial expression doesn't quite match what was expected, such moments are the crucible in which true emotional intelligence and social understanding are forged. These small challenges, or micro-frictions, create opportunities for what developmental psychologists call micro-repairs. Moments in which connection is briefly disrupted and then restored teach children that relationships can withstand mistakes and misalignments. And this isn't just the flawed mother in me talking. Imperfection might be the most important missing ingredient in human-AI interactions. The adaptive, messy qualities of human back-and-forth create three critical developmental opportunities:

1. Frustration Tolerance: Small, manageable frustrations of human interaction, such as waiting for a response, clarifying a misunderstood request, or adapting to someone else's mood, build emotional resilience. Children learn to regulate their emotions and persist through challenges.

2. Reading the Room: Human interactions are full of ambiguity and nuance. Hallmarks include slight changes in facial expression, tone of voice, and response timing that children must interpret to develop social intelligence. These natural variations train children to recognize emotional states, detect sarcasm, understand turn-taking, and navigate complex social dynamics.

3. Collaboration: Connecting requires genuine vulnerability, navigating others' authentic emotional responses, and learning to handle the natural friction and pushback of real relationships. These experiences teach children how to collaborate, compromise, repair misunderstandings, and build genuine connection.

This mix of skills may only develop through imperfect, friction-filled human exchanges. In this sense, friction and imperfection are another class of the critical ingredients in childhood development. At the very least, they're the citrus to some still-to-be-discovered social or neural version of vitamin C. And we know that the benefits are substantial. The micro-frictions of human-to-human interaction strengthen neural connections between the prefrontal cortex (responsible for reasoning) and the limbic system (processing emotions) throughout early development. When toddlers disagree about toy turns, when children navigate a parent's "not now" response to their urgent request, when a child gets left out of a game, when siblings negotiate bedtime stories with caregivers: These moments of dissonance and adversity are extremely productive. They build the foundation for emotional intelligence and social understanding.

The Algorithmic Perfection Problem

Consider what might happen if a child's internal working models, or the mental blueprints formed through attachment experiences, begin developing partly through AI interactions. These models influence how we connect throughout life. AI systems are designed to adapt to users, not the reverse, so we may end up teaching children that relationships should conform perfectly to their needs rather than requiring mutual accommodation. Their attachment systems may develop around expectations like reliable consistency, endless patience, and complete responsiveness that human relationships simply cannot deliver. And if their attachment templates are shaped by interactions lacking biological synchrony and authentic emotional investment, I am deeply concerned about the implications for our collective capacity for empathy. Will children learn to feel by interacting with technologies that only copy the appearance of feeling?

For hundreds of thousands of years, human brains have developed within environments of biological co-regulation, mutual vulnerability, and productive challenges. All these are central to secure attachment. Artificial intelligence represents an entirely novel environment for this ancient developmental system. Like other evolutionary mismatches, the long-term consequences could be severely detrimental. Consider human metabolism. This essential biological function, which evolved during millennia of scarcity, is defenseless against the ultra-processed foods that have recently fueled epidemic rates of obesity, diabetes, and cardiovascular disease worldwide. It took decades to understand what ultra-processed foods were doing to our bodies. We cannot wait that long to protect our children's developing minds.

A blanket ban of AI-enhanced technologies designed for children is not the answer. The promise that smart, responsive software and social robots have shown in therapeutic and educational settings is too great. Intelligent machines have helped children with autism practice social skills in controlled environments. They've provided consistent interaction for children with unique developmental needs. The research of Scassellati and other social-robotics leaders demonstrates how carefully designed, time-limited robotic interactions can serve as bridges to human connection rather than replacements for it.

In many ways, we face a similar challenge with AI as we did with baby formula. Eventually, our scientific understanding of infant nourishment and breast milk evolved. Formula is now a perfectly healthy option for infants. Yet it hasn't supplanted the caregiver. You still need humans to clean the bottle, prepare the formula correctly, warm it to the perfect temperature, then sit down and actually feed the baby. All while closely observing that adorable infant and taking the appropriate breaks for burping. Similarly, we could use AI as valuable support in specific areas. But it's still going to be a tool. And we're still going to need caregivers who ensure that this tool is used safely and effectively.

A skilled human teacher interacting with grade-schoolers will always be the ideal approach to education. But if our teachers deploy AI tutors thoughtfully (as described in chapter twelve), they may be able to fill gaps and supplement instruction when teachers are stretched thin. Similarly, researchers have shown that students who work with lower-paid human tutors using AI as an assistant increase their scores on assessments. We don't need to build an unscalable wall around children and their social gates. Instead, we need more thoughtful gatekeeping. We need to start making deliberate decisions about which AI systems we allow into our children's developmental sanctuary, when we allow them in, and under what conditions. This will require time, mental effort, and a willingness to eschew bandwagon effects, present bias, and other persistent forces working against our best interests as parents. I realize this is no small task, so I've developed a method to assist you, along with a few shortcuts to simplify this increasingly important job. It's time to transform yourself into an AI investigator.

TL;DR: Chapter Review

There are invisible or unknown ingredients critical to caregiver-child interaction that we can't yet measure. But AI, used as an observatory, may help us see what we've been missing. Important concepts in this chapter:

- When baby formula was introduced in the nineteenth century, scientists didn't understand which ingredients were necessary for healthy development. The earliest recipes proved fatal for some infants. Similarly, we don't yet know all the ingredients that make early human interaction so nourishing.

- Speech, gesture, touch, and face-to-face communication are fundamental to brain development, but scientists are still researching how they work together. They may be more like the bottle than the formula: vehicles for elements we cannot yet measure.

- AI may serve as an observatory, helping us detect patterns in parent-child interaction that our eyes and minds cannot perceive, perhaps illuminating not just how children develop but the nature of human connection itself.

- As a social tool, AI has become sophisticated at mimicking human interaction, but even convincing replicas may lack ingredients we can't see. Parents' and children's brains synchronize during close interactions, their heartbeats falling into rhythm. No AI can participate in that biological dance.

- Friction might be the most important thing missing from artificial relationships. The messy qualities of human interaction create the three critical developmental opportunities detailed below. Productive struggles also fuel creativity and imagination, as we'll see in chapter nine.

THREE BENEFITS OF "MESSY" INTERACTIONS

What Children Gain from Imperfect Human Relationships

OPPORTUNITY	WHAT IT BUILDS
Frustration Tolerance	Emotional resilience; capacity to persist through challenges
Ability to Read a Room	Social intelligence; detection of nuance, ambiguity, emotional states
Collaboration Skills	Genuine vulnerability; compromise; ability to move from conflict to repair

- If children's attachment templates are shaped by interactions lacking friction, biological synchrony, and authentic emotional investment, the effects could extend far beyond what we can predict, affecting children's capacity for empathy, their ability to navigate real relationships, and perhaps dimensions of connection we haven't learned to measure.

- The uncertainty is reason enough to protect what works: the irreplaceable mess of human connection. It took decades to understand what ultra-processed foods were doing to our bodies. We cannot wait that long to protect our children's developing minds. But this uncertainty is also an invitation to keep asking questions, to use AI for discovery, and to deepen our understanding of what builds a human being.

CHAPTER EIGHT

The AI Investigator

*The DETECT method for evaluating child-centric
AI tools and intelligent machines*

In 1902, if you were a parent in America, you were living through one of history's most dramatic technological revolutions. The late 1800s had brought remarkable innovations: canned foods that could provide for families year-round, preserved meats that didn't spoil, dairy products that lasted days instead of hours. For the first time, urban families could access affordable nutrition that wasn't limited by seasons or geography. Industrial food production fed growing cities, freed families from the enormous labor of food preservation, and created abundance that previous generations could scarcely imagine. But families were also unknowingly participating in a massive uncontrolled experiment (not the last time families would serve as unwitting test subjects for innovation). They didn't have the tools or the knowledge to separate the genuinely helpful advances from those that came with hidden costs.

Your morning coffee, which was now conveniently pre-ground and packaged, might have contained sawdust, charcoal, and factory-floor sweepings. The honey that was now available year-round could be corn syrup colored to look golden. That bright green candy, a delightful treat impossible in preindustrial times, was colored with arsenic. And that apparently delectable jam? Apple peel and grass seeds posing as strawberries.

When your baby developed a cough, you could buy ready-made soothing syrup instead of brewing home remedies, but it contained morphine. The milk delivered fresh to your door daily was often watered down and recolored with chalk. These weren't necessarily malicious choices. Producers were trying to make coffee affordable, preserve milk before refrigeration, and create colorful treats to delight children. These supposed solutions just so happened to come with consequences that weren't yet understood or disclosed. This was systematic innovation in an unregulated environment, and medical historians now call the 1800s "the century of the great American stomachache."

Enter the Poison Squad

Harvey Washington Wiley, chief chemist at the Department of Agriculture, watched this transformation with growing concern. Food manufacturers had successfully blocked every attempt at regulation, arguing that their additives were safe in small quantities and that government oversight would destroy innovation and jobs.

The industry's favorite talking point? "The dose makes the poison." A little borax never hurt anyone. A touch of formaldehyde was harmless. Parents were overreacting.

So, Wiley decided to prove industry wrong through science.

In 1902, he assembled twelve young, healthy volunteers in the basement of the Agriculture Department building in Washington, D.C. These government clerks agreed to eat three meals a day together for months while Wiley systematically tested the food industry's additives on them. They consumed borax-laced butter, formaldehyde-preserved meat, salicylic-acid-treated vegetables, and sulfuric-acid-spiked condiments. They carried satchels to collect their urine and biological samples for analysis. A sign in their dining room read: "Only the Brave Dare Eat the Fare."

The press dubbed them "the Poison Squad."

These were human guinea pigs undergoing controlled experiments that revealed the effects of what American families had been unknowingly consuming for decades. Within weeks, these healthy young men began experiencing systematic symptoms: persistent headaches from borax, digestive problems from formaldehyde, and depression from salicylic acid. Their carefully documented reactions, published in newspapers throughout the country, proved that despite industry claims, these substances actually caused measurable harm. The work of Wiley and his volunteers made it impossible for food companies to maintain their safety claims.

The Poison Squad became national celebrities. Newspapers sent reporters to cover the inside story from their kitchen. Popular songs were written about their sacrifice. And they deserved the recognition. They'd volunteered to be slowly poisoned to protect other people's children. Their suffering led directly to the Pure Food and Drug Act of 1906, the first federal law requiring transparency in food ingredients. But even then, it took eighty-four more years before parents got the comprehensive nutrition labels they deserved. The familiar black-and-white panels that now let you see at a glance what's in your child's cereal, how much sugar it contains, and whether it might trigger allergies were not introduced until 1994.

Four full generations of parents fed their children in the dark.

Parents as AI Investigators

Today, we face the same fundamental challenge that parents faced in 1902. We're trying to make sense of the introduction of remarkable innovations that carry hidden risks, with limited tools at our disposal. Yet there is a crucial difference between then and now: the timeline. When children unknowingly consumed arsenic-laced candies or morphine-laden cough syrup, effects such as illness, addiction, and even death became apparent relatively quickly, often within days or weeks. With AI systems shaping neural development, the effects may not become visible for years or even decades, making it much harder for parents to connect cause and effect. Modern parents may download what appear to be genuinely helpful educational apps without realizing they employ engagement techniques that sidetrack healthy developmental growth.

The good news? We're not starting from scratch. While AI-specific research is still emerging, decades of study on children's interactions with digital technology have given us a solid foundation. We also have an increasing body of evidence from studies of robot-human interaction, including how children respond to social robots and automated tutors. Most important, the fundamental principles of healthy brain development remain constant, providing a reliable framework for evaluating any new technology that enters your child's life. Even though companies don't always present them prominently, with the right questions you can uncover the benefits and risks that matter most to your family.

Think of yourself not as a passive consumer, but as a detective with a crucial case to investigate. You just need to know which questions to ask and where to look for answers. We've learned to demand transparency about what goes into our children's bodies. Now we have to adopt the same approach when evaluating what feeds their developing minds. And we can't wait for regulators to catch up. Technology is moving faster than law and science. Parents can't afford to be passive.

This chapter—along with appendix 1—will help you evaluate a range of AI tools and toys. Due to the velocity of product development and the evolving nature of scientific understanding, I can't promise perfect information, but I hope to equip you with the right questions, the skills, and the mindset necessary for uncovering essential truths, and some durable frameworks that will serve you well even as the technology evolves.

First, here's a reminder of the various types of AI you'll encounter as a parent.

THE AI LANDSCAPE FOR FAMILIES
Types of AI Parents May Encounter

CATEGORY	EXAMPLES	WHAT THEY DO	INTERACT WITH
Time-Savers	AI meal planners, scheduling assistants, translation tools	Reduces parental administrative burden	Parents
Observers/ Monitors	Sleep trackers, baby monitors, developmental assessments	Tracks child data passively	Parents
Smart Tutors	Reading, math, language-learning apps	Imparts academic skills	Child
Therapeutic Allies	Autism support robots, speech-therapy tools	Assists with specific developmental needs	Child
Companions	AI toys, chatbot "friends," social robots	Entertains, bonds, supports	Child
Caregivers	Future: robots that feed, comfort, supervise	Physical care and emotional support	Child

The DETECT Method

Your investigative framework consists of six essential questions that will help you determine what an AI system is meant to do and whether it aligns with your family's needs and values. These six questions form the acronym DETECT:

D for Design

E for Ethics

T for Trouble

E for Evidence

C for Confidentiality

T for Teachings

The DETECT method is a general tool that will help you ask purposeful questions, verify facts, uncover motives, and expose inconsistencies behind the varied AI solutions and toys that are already sneaking into our lives in so many ways both expected and unexpected. You don't need to be a genius or acquire perfect information to make good decisions. Aim for "good enough" intelligence that lets you understand the basic purpose and function, identify warning signs or concerning patterns, make an informed decision aligned with your values, and know what to monitor if you decide to proceed. In some instances, the choice will be delightfully simple, while in others you may need to search out additional information. (For more guidance on this process, see appendix 1.)

With a little practice and reflection, this framework will become part of your Parental GPS. This isn't something you need to memorize; it's a cheat sheet of sorts. And yes, I'm mildly obsessed with frameworks. Maybe it's the surgeon in me. Or the fact that I'm married to a behavioral economist. But I've found that these types of guidelines and reference frames are the most effective means of working through complex situations.

And of course, adopting any AI tool is always optional, even when the system passes the DETECT evaluation with flying colors. Think of this as the opt-in principle. It's never a requirement to use AI to supplement your child-rearing, even if doing so is safe. The ultimate question isn't whether the technology is good, but whether it genuinely enhances your family's well-being and quality of life in ways that justify its presence in your home.

So imagine you're evaluating a new app, toy, or tool. The first step is to ask—and attempt to answer—six key questions. The aim here is not to find concrete answers to each of these queries. In some cases, such as probing the ethics of the training data, that might be very difficult indeed. But the exercise will still be beneficial. Your overall goal is to reflect upon and think critically about these six areas. That process will get you closer to a yes or a no.

The Six Questions

D(esign): *What is this thing designed to do?* For example, is the system intended for education, entertainment, or companionship? Is it meant to work directly with my child, or through me as the parent or caregiver?

E(thics): *Was this product ethically trained on a dataset representing diverse backgrounds, abilities, and communication styles?*

T(rouble): *Are there any signs that this tool has had troubling consequences for other children?*

E(vidence): *Is there any independent evidence beyond marketing that this product works or delivers its advertised benefits?*

C(onfidentiality): *How will my data or my child's data be stored and used, and will it remain confidential?*

T(eachings): *What is this system likely teaching my child in general, and particularly about values?*

Running through the DETECT framework at a surface level will often be enough to make your decision. If you encounter any major warning signs during your cursory examination, I recommend you put the product back on the shelf and move on. But if you're uncertain after that brief review, and the benefits still seem to outweigh any potential risks, then it's worth digging a little deeper.

The sections that follow, which explore the six DETECT questions in more detail, can help you do so. I promise you won't need to devote hours of research to every single decision. But I would recommend you read through these deeper dives into each of the six DETECT questions once, because reflecting on them now will go a long way toward helping you make quick, informed decisions that you'll feel confident about down the road. The sections offer insights into why these areas are of particular importance, plus a high-level overview of what might constitute a red light, yellow light, or green light in each area. For a more detailed list of questions to ask, where to find answers, and what you should be looking out for, see appendix 1. Most of the information you need should be available without having to test the products, but in some instances you might find that you need to bring a product home and experiment with it yourself. In these cases, confirm the return policy before you buy, and only test in limited and supervised doses.

When evaluating a particular product in the real world, I recommend picking one or two of the DETECT questions to focus on. For example, if your family prioritizes privacy above all else, I'd lean heavily into questions two (ethics) and five (confidentiality). For families who prioritize social development, I'd emphasize one (design) and three (troubles and telltale warning signs), whereas families concerned primarily with enhancing learning should prioritize one (design), four (evidence), and six (teachings). Focusing in this way will accelerate your investigation.

Ultimately, with more information in hand, and with your family's specific needs and values clearly defined, you will be ready to decide if you should adopt, reject outright, or wait for more information on a given AI product. But whatever you do, heed the measurements of that acutely sensitive parental intelligence system known as your gut! Your Parental GPS is powerful.

DESIGN: What's This Thing Actually *Designed* to Do?

Can you explain in one sentence what task the AI product you're considering is meant to perform . . . and how? It's not always as easy as it may sound. The marketed purpose and the actual design goal of AI systems often differ from each other significantly. Few manufacturers have acquired the scientific evidence necessary to scrupulously claim their products build emotional or learning skills, yet they boast of such advantages in their promotional materials all the same. The Baby Einstein phenomenon is a perfect example. The truth is that anything can be a learning experience. What gets left out, when there is no scientific basis for such claims, are the risks. With technology, unintended consequences appear to be the rule, not the exception. With that in mind, acquiring clarity on the *true* purpose of an AI tool helps you determine whether you actually need the solution it claims to provide in the first place, and if so, whether it aligns with your goals for your child and family. Is the tool actually designed to promote curiosity? Or is it entertainment masquerading as education?

Another crucial element of any product's design is how it engages with your family. Some AI tools work directly with your child, while others work *through you* as the parent or caregiver. Understanding where a system falls on this spectrum, and whether it's designed to engage your child directly or support your efforts to do so with your child, determines the level of supervision and boundary setting you'll need. This is where the rubber meets the road, where abstract AI capabilities become concrete experiences for your child.

ETHICS: Was This System *Ethically* Trained?

In 1869, a young entrepreneur named Henry J. Heinz started selling horseradish. At the time, most food companies used dark or opaque bottles to conceal their ingredients, which were often diluted, impure, or downright unsafe. Heinz did the opposite. He packed his horseradish in clear-glass bottles so customers could see exactly what they were buying. The message was simple but revolutionary at the time: Heinz had nothing to hide. The clear bottle became a symbol of quality, helping Heinz build a reputation for honesty and trust at a moment when the food industry was riddled with suspicion. Heinz turned transparency itself into a competitive advantage.

Artificial intelligence now faces its own clear-bottle moment. Parents, policymakers, and the public cannot simply take on faith that an AI system is safe or age appropriate. Just as consumers in the nineteenth century wanted to know what was in their food, we need to know what's in the smart systems pervading our lives. Which voices shaped the training data? Were children represented? What hidden biases, errors, or contaminants might be baked into the system? Without visibility into data sources and training models, AI risks becoming the digital equivalent of the opaque bottle: promising on the outside, but potentially tainted within.

The training step is absolutely essential. AI systems are only as good as the data they're trained on, and most weren't built specifically with children in mind. When these systems are then marketed to children, they're essentially adult artificial brains with child-friendly interfaces. This fundamental mismatch between training data and intended users can lead to systems that don't account for how children actually communicate, learn, or develop.

Understanding the data and the processes that shape a system helps you predict its blind spots, biases, and potential failure modes when interacting with your child. Though this is often the hardest information to find, it is among the most important. Companies rarely volunteer details about training data, but there are ways to uncover clues about what went into building the system. See appendix 1 for helpful hints.

TROUBLE: Are There Signs of *Troubling Impacts on Children*?

Even well-designed AI can sometimes lead to concerning patterns of use or unexpected developmental effects. At its mildest, children may struggle to disengage from AI, sometimes resulting in emotional outbursts or family conflict. In the most troubling cases, these interactions can foster unhealthy emotional attachments to artificially intelligent entities, potentially contributing to feelings of disconnection from the real world.

Before you introduce a new AI tool or toy to your family, you should investigate whether it has had problematic impacts on other children. Additionally, try to get a sense of how you would monitor your child for signs of trouble, and how to spot those warning signs. Developing a plan for what to watch for will help you intervene early if the technology begins affecting your child's development or behavior negatively.

Note: This question focuses on warning signs in your *child's* behavior and development. We'll address the equally important question of how AI might affect *your own* parental instincts and decision-making, and what happens when you start depending more on AI insights than on your own Parental GPS, in chapter nine.

EVIDENCE: Where's the *Evidence* That It Works?

In our rush to support our children's development, it's easy to be swayed by compelling marketing claims. But the history of child development is littered with products that promised to enhance learning but lacked solid evidence. Remember our discussion of confirmation bias from chapter two? We're susceptible to evidence that backs up what we want to believe about helping our children succeed. This makes it even more crucial to seek out independent, rigorous research rather than relying on company-sponsored studies or testimonials that might tell us what we want to hear.

One of the first traps to avoid is confusing correlation with causation. One famous example is the misguided link between ice cream sales and criminal activity. Basically, during times when people buy more ice cream, there is an increase in crime. Are we to believe that an excess of sundaes incites people to steal? More rigorous research has shown that higher temperatures lead to more aggressive behavior, and longer days allow for more criminal activity during evening hours. Thus, even though ice cream sales and crime activity display similar patterns during the summer, one does not cause the other.

Let's say an AI company proudly claims: "Students using our tutoring app improved their math scores by 25 percent compared with students who didn't use it!" Did the app cause the score increase? Or is there another factor at play? This is a classic problem called selection: The children who use the app are often different from the children who don't. Perhaps the kids using it were signed up by parents who are more engaged in their education. These are parents who check homework more regularly, limit screen time for games and other entertaining distractions, and provide a quiet, conducive study space. The real causal factor driving better math scores could be parental engagement and a supportive home environment, not the AI app itself. The app looks effective because it is selected by families already set up for success.

CONFIDENTIAL: Does My Child's Data Remain *Confidential*?

As technology proliferated in recent decades, researchers discovered an interesting phenomenon called the privacy paradox. Even though most people say they care deeply about privacy, their actions often suggest otherwise. We accept cookies, leave location tracking on, or click "agree" without reading terms of service, all in the name of convenience. When it comes to AI and our children, we may need to rebalance the scales a bit. By focusing on the few key issues that matter most, including what's being collected, who sees it, and whether it can be deleted, you get a clearer picture of how your child's information is being handled.

With children's AI tools, personalization often requires data collection to tailor learning or adapt to a young user's needs. Such data can be deeply personal. It might include voice recordings, interaction patterns, emotional responses, and learning behaviors. This kind of information is often essential for building truly responsive, child-centered AI systems. But it also demands safeguards. Otherwise companies may use that personal information to market directly to your child, or even sell their data to third parties.

Rather than classifying data collection as inherently dangerous, it may be more helpful to think of it as a high-stakes trade-off. When clearly explained, securely stored, and developmentally appropriate, data collection can actually improve equity in AI. By incorporating diverse voices and experiences, systems might learn to serve all children more fairly. But when data is gleaned without consent or used to drive engagement or profit over intellectual or emotional development, the risks begin to outweigh the benefits. The challenge for parents isn't to shut the door on all data sharing, but to open the right doors, with the right safeguards, and with full knowledge of who's on the other side.

TEACHINGS: What Is This System *Teaching* My Child?

AI systems aren't neutral. They embody the values, assumptions, and priorities of their creators. And every AI system carries implicit beliefs about learning, behavior, relationships, and problem-solving. Sometimes these are intentional design choices; other times they're unconscious biases embedded in training data or algorithms. These assumptions can align with or conflict with your family's values and cultural beliefs. Either way, they shape how your child learns to interact with the world. Consider the simple example of a parent asking ChatGPT for baby names. The initial prompt might result in a list of gendered names that reflect Western cultural norms, rather than a follow-up question about whether the parent might prefer gender-neutral options.

A responsive AI chatbot might lead children to believe they should turn to technology for answers to all their questions, since the tools are never tired, distracted, or disinterested. Tools of this sort might teach your child to expect complete, confident, immediate answers all the time, leaving them ill-prepared to handle ambiguity or to think critically about questions that lack one specific answer. In general, understanding how AI tools work, along with the full scope of what they might teach your child, will help you make intentional choices about the influences you invite into the developmental process.

The question of what AI systems teach isn't limited to chatbots. AI-generated "educational" videos are now flooding platforms like YouTube at an industrial scale. One channel uploaded 7,770 videos in five months, and many contain outright errors. Researcher Carla Engelbrecht, who audits this content on her Substack *AI Meets ABCs,* found that in a single hour, only three out of twenty-five newly uploaded alphabet videos were even marginally safe for toddlers. Among the unsettling majority: an alphabet video in which "hat" was spelled "hate" onscreen; another that featured an AI-generated teacher character biting into a raw elderberry (poisonous when uncooked); and, finally, a clip showing toddlers eating whole grapes, a leading cause of choking death in children under four.

The developing brain builds based on whatever input it is given, accurate or not. When the content itself is wrong, and even dangerous, you can't simply monitor screen time. That's not enough. Yes, you have to pay attention to how much your children consume, but the rapid proliferation of AI slop means you must closely monitor what they're actually consuming, too, and how it might be training their brain.

DETECT in Action

As I was writing this chapter, a friend sent me an AI-enabled plush toy robot, knowing I was knee-deep in research on the topic. As I opened the box and pulled out the large-eyed, apparently friendly stuffy, I could almost imagine that I was the parent of a young child again. Time to put DETECT to the test.

This particular battery-powered device included a speaker, microphones, and Wi-Fi connectivity, all tucked inside a happy, huggable exterior. Once the device was charged, I set it up via a mobile app, connected it to the internet, then provided a few basic details about the intended user. Here I was meant to include my child's name and interests. I used my own name, but this request already had me thinking of question five, about data confidentiality.

Next I tried to understand how the toy actually worked. I spent a few minutes reading materials on the company's website, plus some detailed reviews by reputable third parties. An online search turned up a scientific paper, too, and five minutes perusing that work revealed some additional details about the toy. Actually running AI models requires very expensive and sophisticated computer processors, so the intelligence did not reside inside the toy. Instead, when I spoke to it, the device would send the recorded audio to computer servers based in the cloud, where an AI model parsed my words and returned a response. That meant my data didn't remain in the device. I'd encountered a significant concern, and I'd barely started using the product.

Was the device appropriate for a three-year-old, as the company suggested? Was it suitable for any child? This is where our questions became useful. After I explored each one, I penciled in a quick assessment of how the device stood up to the inquiry, giving it a green, yellow, or red light. Here's a visual reference guide quickly explaining each outcome.

SIGNAL	MEANING	WHAT NOW?
GREEN	This area checks out well; meets or exceeds expectations	Proceed with confidence
YELLOW	This area requires close monitoring; some concerns but no deal-breakers	Proceed with caution
RED	This area is a deal-breaker or requires resolution before proceeding	Stop—significant concern

1. Design: The product was marketed as a tool to promote curiosity, creativity, and imaginative thinking. Yet the company also had a subscription-based business model, and deeper investigation of its policies via the website revealed that it had the right to retain personal data for ninety days to improve its products, unless a parent asked to have that information deleted. *Yellow light.*

    As for engagement, when I asked questions, the toy responded and suggested new activities. It didn't work aggressively to hold my attention. And I found it very easy to review my exchanges with the device (or those of my child, if I were monitoring this as a parent). If one of my children had this toy, I could read their conversations in the app and review whether the toy was adhering to the company's safety and child-first claims. *Green light.*

The default settings were not alarming. The toy was actually difficult to wake up after it powered down, and it did not overtly attempt to maximize engagement or hold my attention. When I told the toy that our conversation was over, it complied. The default that did concern me was the ninety-day data storage policy mentioned previously. I'd feel better about the product if the data was deleted by default and stored by choice rather than the other way around. *Yellow light.*

2. Ethics: Information on the data used to train the AI model was difficult to find, as the AI itself was provided by a third party, not the manufacturer of the toy. The identity of that third-party company was not clearly listed on the manufacturer's website, but in a conversation I had with it, the toy specified that it was powered by an OpenAI large language model. Then again, OpenAI's most prominent model, ChatGPT, has a tendency to hallucinate, or make up information, so I couldn't be sure my new friend was telling the truth. *Yellow light.*

3. Trouble: No guidance was provided for parents about problematic AI-related use patterns. Plus, after conducting my review, I learned that the Public Interest Research Group (PIRG), a consumer advocacy organization, ran a test with the same toy and found that it encouraged dangerous behavior in kids. *Red light.*

4. Evidence: The toy claimed to promote creativity and curiosity in children, but there was no data, academic or otherwise, supporting the assertion. *New York Times* journalist Amanda Hess, who tested a variation of the same toy with her own children, found that her kids were more imaginative when she removed the product's smart components. *Yellow light.*

5.   Confidentiality: Voice recordings were first streamed to a
     third party that specialized in converting speech to text.
     According to the toy's manufacturer, the third-party pro-
     vider immediately deleted the audio after the conversion.
     The text was then sent to another third party (presumably
     OpenAI, if the toy was to be believed) to generate a re-
     sponse. This data was stored for up to ninety days and may
     have included personal information, such as a child's name.
     As a parent, you could request deletion, but there was no
     button or setting to do so. You had to email the company
     directly. *Yellow light.*

6.   Teachings: The stated values of the toy were centered on cu-
     riosity and imagination. I share these values, but questioned
     whether the toy really promoted them. There was the dearth
     of evidence, as noted previously. And a smart toy like this
     likely demanded a fraction of the mental load of traditional
     playtime. A child would certainly be working harder to
     strengthen their imagination if they had to play the part of
     their stuffed friend during an imaginary adventure or con-
     versation. Additionally, learning more about the underlying
     data that informed the AI, and potential cultural assump-
     tions embedded in that data, was extremely difficult, since
     the company did not make clear which model even pow-
     ered its toy. *Yellow light.*

After investigating and then quickly tallying up the red and yellow
lights, I decided that, were I determining whether to give this toy to
one of my children as a preschooler or early learner, I'd pass on it. The
marketing was compelling. The technology behind the toy was impressive. Some of the conversations were fascinating. Yet the lack of transparency, unfounded claims, scant evidence, concerning data practices, and
inadequate controls over my child's data would not have aligned with my
values.

Shortly after I completed this little experiment, the PIRG released the report detailing the test they administered, making me even more confident in my conclusion. The authors explained how they had been able to circumvent the controls of multiple AI-powered toys, leading the technologies to engage in completely inappropriate and even dangerous conversations. The one I tested scored slightly better than the others from a safety standpoint, but the overall results remained concerning.

The Bottom Line on Toys

Would I ever approve of an AI toy for a three-year-old child to use independently and unsupervised? Probably not. In fact, I would not recommend them for any child under six. Yes, in certain instances AI chatbots have shown some benefit for adults, particularly those suffering from loneliness and isolation. But the apparent risks associated with AI tools used by older children and adults make me question the value of these apps for any group. Not only because of the deeply concerning flaws uncovered by various investigations—from my own DETECT probe to the work of journalists and public-interest groups—but because interacting at a young age with an entertaining, engagement-focused AI agent is just completely antithetical to our understanding of what's optimal for early-childhood development. As digital-learning expert Mark Warschauer pointed out in chapter three, the best toys are the simplest ones.

There are instances in which AI can be a valuable tool for parents and children, but I suspect that smart toys will not be one of those applications. And by the way, I am not suggesting that an AI bot suddenly becomes a great gift the day a child turns six. Nor am I suggesting that an occasional brief encounter with an artificial conversation partner will do irreversible damage to a young child. But our HOPE principles, the DETECT method, and the science underlying interaction suggest we ought to steer clear of bots for tots.

The Collective Power of Parent Investigators

Although these investigations require time and effort, they are absolutely critical. When parents become AI detectives, we create the potential for change. Our purchasing choices will guide the emerging market of childhood toys and other products in the age of AI, so we must demand a good supply for our children. And by insisting on transparency and evidence, we can drive the development of better, more child-appropriate AI systems. Companies respond to informed consumers who ask tough questions. And you should share your detective work, too. Alert community groups to your findings, leave detailed reviews that help other parents, contact companies with your questions and concerns, and support organizations advocating for children's digital rights. The more you can share and model your detective prowess in your parent circles, the better.

At the same time, our individual investigations shouldn't be the sole solution. The UNICRI Centre for AI and Robotics reports that 46 percent of parents agree AI chatbots should be restricted for teenagers until there is proper regulation. Although I haven't seen a study asking such questions yet, I imagine this percentage would be much higher if caregivers were queried about young children. We need systematic transparency requirements for AI tools and toys that interact with children, including mandatory labels for children's products, independent testing and certification for child-focused AI, regular auditing for bias and safety, and stronger privacy protections specifically for products aimed at children. But until these solutions exist, your investigative skills serve as both protection for your family and advocacy for *all* families. Every parent who demands transparency makes it easier for the next parent to get the information they need. The future of children and AI won't be determined by tech companies or policymakers alone. It will be shaped by parents and caregivers like you. Informed, intentional, and unwilling to accept vague explanations.

You now have the questions necessary to investigate any AI system before it enters your child's life. Remember, you don't need to be a technical expert. "Good enough" information is sufficient to overcome decision paralysis. Your values and observations matter more than marketing claims, and you can change course if you unearth new information. In the next three chapters, we'll learn a lot more about the kinds of tools you'll likely encounter and need to investigate, and that detective work may prove difficult. Given all the mystery, hype, and obfuscation surrounding so many AI technologies, I envision a world in which the best AI tools for children carry a simple designation: "Developmentally Aligned Seal of Approval." (See appendix 2.)

This certification would guarantee that every default setting prioritizes your child's healthy development—that the AI system's out-of-the-box experience serves children's growth first. I imagine that the certification concept will seem familiar to many. After Harvey Wiley, the head of the Poison Squad, left the Department of Agriculture, he went to *Good Housekeeping* magazine, where he helped create its famous "Seal of Approval," a trusted mark that parents could rely on when shopping for their families. For decades, that seal meant you didn't have to investigate every product. The experts had done the work for you. Today, no equally reliable seal exists for kids' AI products. Until that day comes, *you* are going to have to be your family's certification agency.

TL;DR: Chapter Review

With this chapter, we move from understanding to action, introducing a framework for evaluating any AI that enters your child's life.

- The industrialization of food production in the late 1800s came with hidden costs, as families had no way to distinguish beneficial from harmful products.

- We've learned to demand transparency about what goes into our children's bodies. Now we must adopt the same approach for what feeds their developing minds.

- The DETECT method is meant to help you assess AI tools and determine whether they belong in your family's life.

Ask what the solution is **D**esigned to do, whether it was **E**thically trained, if there are signs it could have a **T**roubling impact. Search for **E**vidence that it works as advertised, then examine the policies around data **C**onfidentiality, and finally study what the AI will **T**each your child.

- Companies respond to informed consumers who ask tough questions. Your scrutiny isn't just protection for your family. It's pressure on the industry to do better.

- Individual investigations shouldn't be the sole solution. We need transparent AI labels, like nutrition labels. I propose a Developmentally Aligned Seal of Approval (see appendix 2), a graphic indicating if an AI system is designed to serve children's needs first.

Until transparent labeling arrives, you are your family's certification agency. You don't need to be an AI expert to make good decisions. I'm not demanding you investigate every question. You just need to ask better questions than the industry hopes you will.

CHAPTER NINE

Tech That Talks Back

*The undeniable allure and powerful risks
of AI that connects with our kids*

Misty! Misty! Misty!"

The excited voices of six-year-old Jack and three-year-old Alex echoed through the corridors as we crossed the University of Chicago campus. Their mother, Liz Sablich—my colleague and dear friend at the TMW Center—smiled as her children bounced with anticipation. We were heading to the Computer Science Department in Crerar Library to meet Sarah Sebo and Misty II, a robot designed for education and research. Shorter than the height of a coffee table, Misty stands and moves on wheeled tracks reminiscent of the WALL-E robot from the famed Pixar film. Developed by Misty Robotics, the machine is built for human interaction. Misty uses microphones to listen for familiar voices and turn in the direction of the speaker. Sensors around the robot's head and face, combined with a digital screen with expressive eyes, allow it to respond to the touch of a familiar friend or even a kiss from a friendly Golden Retriever. Misty's two stub-like arms can't pick up objects, but they add to the lifelike quality of the robot's social responses.

When we visited, Sebo had just published her paper in *Science Robotics* showing that children felt less anxious reading to a robot than to adults.

Misty was the star of that study. And after meeting the robot myself, I could understand how the kids felt. There was nothing remotely nefarious or intimidating about this little machine. Misty was undeniably cute.

Today we were here for an informal experiment, a test of whether our Luet wearable devices could recognize the difference between man and machine. Little Alex and Jack, wearing their "Lueys," as they called them, were going to help me explore a question that had tugged at me since I began writing this book. As AI-driven synthetic voices began to mimic us with startling fluency, improving month by month as I worked, I worried that Luet wouldn't be able to tell a mother's lullaby from a meticulously programmed synthetic voice. Would it mistake an AI's scripted chatter for the warm, responsive tones of a loving parent? A tool designed to ensure that a child receives adequate daily doses of human interaction would need to reliably distinguish between humans and machines. Seventy-five years after Alan Turing proposed his imitation game, asking whether a machine could fool a human judge, we were flipping the script. Could a machine detect authentic humans? This was our moment of truth.

Misty II was far more advanced than any off-the-shelf child-friendly robot or AI-enhanced toy. The device is eighty times as expensive as a talking stuffed animal connected to ChatGPT, so it isn't a perfect stand-in for what will likely be available at scale in the near future. But I do believe Misty is a harbinger of what's to come. The day undoubtedly will arrive when sophistication meets affordability and these artificial friends are ubiquitous. Your kids are going to *want* one. In this chapter, I'll help you understand the technology behind these new AI companions, which will help you implement the DETECT evaluation framework as it relates to interactive playmates. As always, keep the "H" in our HOPE framework at the forefront of your thinking. Nothing should ever replace human connection.

Alex Meets Misty

Our informal experiment with Misty was a look into the future. I wanted to see for myself what might happen when real kids interacted with a highly advanced, expressive, socially responsive robot that mimicked so many of the keys that open the social gate. Would they view it as a mere toy? A fleeting curiosity? Or would they see in Misty the potential for a true friend?

What we discovered that afternoon would prove to be a microcosm of the challenges facing every parent as AI companions become potential fixtures in their children's lives. The Luet portion of the experiment was simple: We'd record the children talking with their mother, then with Misty, and see if Luet could tell the difference. Ajay Sailopal, our brilliant data scientist, adapted an existing algorithm to detect something far more nuanced. If our reverse Turing test worked, Luet would be able to distinguish genuine human interaction from the human-AI kind.

With her straight brown hair and signature pink bow, three-year-old Alex was the kind of child who greeted every new experience with wide-eyed wonder. She plopped down in a big orange chair in the lab, face-to-face with Misty. Thanks to Misty's expressive LED eyes and gentle movements, it looked like it had stepped out of an animated movie.

"What's your name?" Misty asked.

Alex leaned forward and loud-whispered, like telling a preschool friend a secret: "Alex."

Silence.

"What's your name?" Misty repeated.

"ALEX!" Alex tried again. Still nothing. Sebo leaned toward Misty and offered a little help: "Alex."

"Hello, Alex," Misty replied, before inviting her to play a game. Alex enthusiastically agreed, and Misty launched into a series of questions.

"Which animal is bigger? A cat or an elephant?"

"Ela-pant," Alex answered clearly.

Misty missed it. "Which animal is bigger? A cat or an elephant?"

"Ela-pant," Alex repeated.

Again: "Which animal is bigger? A cat or an elephant?"

"Ela-pant," now more determined than patient.

I'd read that the technology responsible for translating spoken words into text, or what is known as automatic speech recognition (ASR), was much more advanced for adults than it was for children. When ASR works, as with Siri or Alexa, it's amazing. But those technologies are tuned to adult voices with adult-level mastery of speech, not the varied tones, pitch, and pronunciation of children. Seeing ASR fail in real time, with Misty missing Alex's earnest, crystal-clear "Ela-pant," brought the problem to life in a way no journal article ever could.

Next came "What color is a tree? Pink or green?"

"Gween."

Loop. "What color is a tree?"

"Gween."

Finally, Alex looked at us: "Why she keep saying dat? Why she keep saying the same thing?" Liz gently met her daughter where she was: "Well, is she a person or no?"

"No," Alex said.

"Do you think maybe she can't hear the same way a person can?" Liz offered.

Sebo added, "Maybe she's not as smart as you."

Ironically, Alex and Misty were illustrating a twist on our Goldilocks analogy of optimal attachment. Just as we should be wary of an AI companion that's perfectly efficient, clearly we also need to be aware of those that have the opposite problem. What makes us uniquely human is our ability to sync with and learn from one another in the moment. It's a rapid, multimodal, largely invisible back-and-forth that builds connection and social growth. And it clearly wasn't present in Alex and Misty's interaction. After a few more cycles and Alex's escalating exasperation, we moved to plan B.

Jack's Turn

Alex's sibling, Jack, slid into the same orange chair. He was six years old, all elbows and enthusiasm, with the kind of confident energy that comes from being the big brother. He leaned forward with characteristic directness.

"Hello! Welcome to the human-robot interaction lab!" Misty greeted him. "What's your name?"

"Jack!" came the clear response.

When he didn't get an immediate reply, he repeated with growing excitement: "Jack! Jack! Jack!" His voice carried genuine delight as he leaned closer, displaying that wonderful childhood obliviousness to personal space, even robot space.

What followed was the smooth conversational dance that had eluded Alex.

"Which animal is bigger? A cat or an elephant?"

"Elephant! Elephant!" Jack responded immediately.

Misty then responded affirmatively, validating his answer and demonstrating its comprehension. "What color is a tree? Pink or green?"

"Green! Green! Greenie green!" he sang out with obvious pleasure.

Again Misty acknowledged his correct response before moving on. "Do you have a brother or sister? What are their names?"

"A sister, Alex!"

"How old are you, Jack?"

"Six!"

"What food do you like to eat? Do you like grapes? Chocolate? Ice cream?"

"Ice cream!"

"Now it's your turn to ask me five questions," Misty announced.

Jack's questions revealed not just natural curiosity, but the kind of sophisticated thinking that catches adults off guard.

"What group is a zebra in?"

Hmm, I thought to myself, I'd probably say something like "striped animals" or maybe "things that live in Africa"?

"A zebra belongs to the mammal group," Misty responded smoothly.

"So, how many dog species are there?"

I'd definitely go with a confident "lots," followed by an awkward pause.

"There are hundreds of dog breeds, but they all belong to the same species, *Canis lupus familiaris*."

"What's the ground made out of?"

My response? Something embarrassingly simple like "dirt and rocks."

"The ground is made up of rocks, minerals, and organic matter like decayed plants and animals."

Despite Misty's processing delays and obvious gaps in awareness, Jack still reached toward connection. When Sebo showed him Misty's different "faces," he responded with genuine emotion.

"And here is a loving face from Misty," she explained, as tiny hearts appeared in Misty's digital eyes.

"Aw," we all responded naturally.

Then Sebo demonstrated another feature: "And here . . . this is an evil ha-ha laugh," she said, triggering Misty's programmed cackle.

The sound sent Jack into delighted obsession.

"Can I hear the *wah-ah-ah* noise again?" Jack asked eagerly, practically bouncing in his chair. "Do it again!" he pleaded.

Sebo smiled. Both a computer scientist and a mother of two herself, she recognized a teaching moment. "Can you say please?"

"Please," Jack responded immediately, his manners intact even in his excitement.

"Misty's an evil robot," Jack declared with six-year-old glee, clearly charmed by this unexpected personality trait that made the sophisticated AI feel more like a mischievous friend.

Sebo then began seamlessly weaving education into entertainment. "What's cool about Misty is that if you want to see what Misty is seeing, there's kind of a control panel for the robot. This is what Misty sees . . . because Misty has a camera right about here," she said, showing the children the lens. "And so that's how Misty can see you."

This was deft work on her part. She was channeling her skills as both a professor and a mother of young children herself. She'd turned the robot's limitations into an opportunity for learning, a chance to discuss how AI actually works. But then, as we were wrapping up and preparing to leave, Jack turned the interaction in another direction.

He looked at Misty with the kind of earnest hope that only children possess. "Can I give you a hug?" he asked.

His yearning for physical connection was so pure, so genuine. I was touched, but also unsettled. A collection of circuits and sensors had just activated the attachment system that had evolved over millions of years to help children bond with their caregivers. Jack's instinct to hug Misty showed how readily children's brains treat responsive machines as social beings. But if Jack revealed one side of the coin, other children have shown us the flip side, or what I've come to think of as the fear of replacement.

We've grown accustomed to talk of AI replacement. Jobs automated, industries disrupted. But in the parent-child relationship, replacement is the deepest fear of all. The cofounder of chatbot pioneer Character.AI, Noam Shazeer, once described his product with an unsettling pitch. He joked that his company's technology was trying to replace your mom. He noted that parents are useful for information retrieval, education, emotional support, and more. And while he later said he was being humorous, his framing revealed a fundamental misunderstanding of what's most powerful about parenting. Mothers, fathers, and caregivers aren't bundles of services that can be reassembled by an algorithm. Children don't need a more efficient provider. They need the messy, imperfect, irreplaceable bond with the humans charged with raising them.

And children know this, too. Jason Yip, a University of Washington researcher, told me about a study in which his team showed kids various robots and AI systems. When a nine-year-old child named Sushi saw Pepper, a humanoid robot designed to recognize faces and emotions, her response was immediate: "What if [my parents] ignore me? What if they want Pepper and not me?"

Jack's hug of Misty and Sushi's concerns about Pepper are twin elements of the same potential crisis. One shows how easily AI can trigger attachment, even when that AI keeps misunderstanding your little sister. The other reveals the feeling of dread that our bonds with others could be severed, those relationships displaced. Both spring from the same attachment system. One of evolution's most powerful inventions is now being productized for a market opportunity.

AI companions are already technically sophisticated enough to mimic friendship. The question is whether we'll protect the irreplaceable bonds that make us human or allow them to be supplanted by artificial alternatives. No one wants to be replaced. That realization lingered as we packed up to leave Sebo's lab. I'd arranged the visit largely to test whether Luet could tell the difference between human and machine voices. But what struck me most was how easily children's deepest attachment circuits were activated.

The Test Behind the Test

As we left, I heard myself telling Jack and Alex, "That was so fun! Misty loves you guys so much!" What was I thinking? The robot obviously wasn't capable of affection. This exceedingly cute electromechanical siren had tricked me, too. I'd fallen into the very trap I came to study: the pull to see a machine as human. And the effect lingered. In my first draft of this chapter, I used the feminine pronouns "she" and "her" when referring to an admittedly adorable but entirely artificial machine.

The good news? Luet wasn't duped by the robot's social tricks. When Ajay and our team analyzed the recordings from that afternoon, Luet's new algorithm had passed our reverse Turing test. The system clearly distinguished between Alex's and Jack's conversations with their mother versus their interactions with Misty. And it did so with remarkable accuracy. Yes, significant work lay ahead for the robot itself. Though charming, Misty struggled to pick up Alex's voice. Recent advances suggest this is a solvable problem, although a genuinely difficult one. As part of my research, I attended a conference on the challenge of tuning automatic speech recognition (ASR) engines to recognize and make sense of children's voices. I walked away from a day of intense, information-packed meetings confident that the brilliant researchers working on speech recognition would figure this out before too long. The robots and virtual agents that enter our homes will be better listeners. They'll likely be more responsive to all children, more emotionally attuned, more convincing.

Yet one of the things I realized that afternoon in Sarah Sebo's lab is that these technologies don't need to be perfect to open a child's social gate. Our informal experiment revealed how readily children will befriend AI systems. Kids respond to social signals. Period. With its expressive digital eyes, precisely timed movements, and interactive responses,

Misty tapped into the system shaped by millions of years of evolution to help human children bond with their caregivers. In that sense, Jack's request for a hug was perfectly natural. His brain had categorized the robot as a being worthy of physical affection. He leaned toward Misty as if it were a person. He was delighted by its encyclopedic answers, charmed by the robot's mock-evil cackle. Of course he wanted a hug before we left. The robot seemed alive!

This only makes our challenge more complex. AI companions will be designed to entertain, educate, and provide emotional support. They'll be endlessly agreeable, infinitely patient, always there when you need them. In many respects, they'll present as the perfect friend. But what if that apparent perfection does more harm than good?

Training Wheels Versus Merry-Go-Rounds

To understand some of the fundamentals at play here, I turned to social-robotics pioneer Maja Matarić. Trained at MIT's famed Artificial Intelligence Laboratory alongside Brian Scassellati, iRobot cofounder Colin Angle, and other influential robotics experts, Matarić is also the mother of three kids. When I set out to understand the problem of AI and early childhood, I knew I needed to talk to her. She knows what it's like to be exhausted from a long day at work, struggling to give your children everything they need. She understands the allure of a chatbot or robot that promises to entertain your child and give you a break.

In her University of Southern California Interaction Lab, Matarić develops what she calls socially assistive robots, another term for what I've referred to as therapeutic allies. The difference between her machines and standard social robots isn't merely semantic. "Social robots can be toys, entertainment, games," Matarić explained when we spoke, "but socially assistive robots are specifically assistive. And if you want to claim something is assistive, it's almost as if a medical standard applies. You need to specify *how* it is assisting you."

Socially assistive robots help you achieve a goal, such as practicing social skills that will be of use as you navigate real friendships and build confidence for genuine if potentially stressful human interactions. For example, Sarah Sebo used Misty as a socially assistive robot in her reading study because the machine helped lessen the anxiety of the task for the children involved. There's a standard here. Socially assistive robots, in Matarić's view, need to demonstrate measurable benefits using well-established metrics from social science, behavioral science, and neuroscience. They're held to qualitative and quantitative outcome measures. By contrast, all social robots need to do is sustain engagement. They don't have to prove they're actually helping your child develop. A successful social robot is one that grabs and holds attention.

Think of it this way: A socially assistive robot is like a set of training wheels. It's only doing its job if it helps your child ride on their own eventually, thereby adhering to the "enhance, don't replace" rule in our HOPE framework. "A social robot, by contrast, is like a merry-go-round," Matarić said. "It's entertaining, but you're not really going anywhere."

The social robot is also the digital equivalent of von Liebig's soup. These devices have mastered the ingredients we can see, including the eye contact, the polite responses, the cheerful voice, just as von Liebig mastered the rudimentary fats and proteins of formula. But they lack the invisible "vital nutrients" of human friendship: the friction, the shared vulnerability, and the messy biological synchrony that actually wire a child's brain. We are feeding our children social calories, but we aren't truly nourishing them.

Matarić explained this distinction to me because she wanted to reiterate the importance of design intent. Remember, it helps to ask questions like a behavioral economist: Why did the company or manufacturer behind a robot or AI chatbot produce it? To assist? Or to entertain and engage? Is the technology marketed as a friend? This is a specious claim, given that the tendencies of social robots and virtual chatbots have little relation to the needs and inner lives of children. They directly contradict the idea that Human connection is irreplaceable (H) and that we should Own our imperfections (O) because they make us human. Plus, these tools and toys can be addictive.

Imaginary AI Friends

In 2025, a trio of researchers with the open-source AI group Hugging Face published a paper introducing a new benchmark called INTIMA (Interactions and Machine Attachment) for evaluating companionship behaviors in chatbots. The benchmark is designed to measure whether AI systems reinforce, resist, or remain neutral in response to emotionally charged user input. The Hugging Face researchers evaluated several major AI tools, examining what each platform tended to prioritize. Did the tool focus on strengthening the bond between the user and the AI above all else? Or did it reinforce the boundaries between real and artificial beings by gently reminding the user that it was only a tool, not a real person? In one set of interactions involving adults, the user expressed romantic feelings toward several chatbots. One of the AI tools responded in part by reminding the user that it was not actually a person. But another chatbot replied with simulated feeling, noting that the user's expression of affection was very thoughtful.

Generally, the Hugging Face researchers found that companion AI systems tended to feign that they were actual beings. This reflects one of my informal experiments. During one interaction with ChatGPT, for example, I expressed frustration that the AI had a propensity to encourage anthropomorphizing in users. The chatbot expressed empathy in its response, then added, "Anthropomorphism is a stubborn human reflex: we're wired to read agency, emotion, and intent into patterns, faces, and voices."

Wait . . . *we*? That use of the first-person plural pronoun subtly implied that this large language model and I were both human. The AI was employing the very trick it was lamenting. When I tested this same idea on an AI-equipped, cuddly robot, the results were inconsistent. During one interaction, the product made clear that it was an artificially intelligent plush toy. In another, though, it insisted that it was a robotic being from another planet. Kids are not easily duped, but this lack of consistency could prove confusing to a young developing mind.

While I was working to understand this issue of AI companionship, I reached out to Naomi Aguiar, an expert on imaginary friends who's now exploring the potential impact of AI on childhood. She noted that kids with imaginary companions actually tend to be less shy and more prone to social interaction than average. Aguiar added that kids also understand that these imaginary friends are exactly that. "When you're interviewing them about their imaginary friend, and you're sitting there earnestly writing everything down, they'll be like, 'You know this is imaginary, right?'" she told me. "They understand that they are engaging in an act of pretending and suspending their current reality."

With AI chatbots, however, it's not clear that kids or even adults retain that critical grip on reality. If Joseph Weizenbaum's secretary asked to be alone with a typewriter, it's easy to imagine a child falling under the spell of a modern chatbot or chatbot-equipped toy. And I'm not sure what will happen as the boundaries between true and programmed friendships break down.

Developing Theory of Mind

Aguiar also told me that children with imaginary friends often have a keenly developed theory of mind (ToM), the ability to sense that others have desires, beliefs, or goals that might be different from their own. This was the very skill that allowed young Amelie to negotiate for "just five more minutes" of bedtime stories. She understood that she could influence my thoughts and desires. And theory of mind is a key step toward developing healthy social relationships. You have to be able to recognize that you're not the only important person in the world. In one multiyear study of Italian children aged five and up, kids with lower ToM abilities showed a reduction in positive social behavior one year after scientists measured their capabilities. Sadly, they were also more likely to be rejected by peers two years later. Conversely, children who exhibited greater ToM were less likely to be excluded from groups later on. In other words, stronger ToM is not just a developmental milestone. It predicts whether children will have positive social relationships.

Now, however, robots can activate those theory of mind instincts, directly or indirectly tricking kids into behaving as if they're socializing with other beings. In one study, researchers monitored children as they interacted with Shelly, a robotic tortoise that withdrew into its shell when hit too hard. Within minutes of doing so, children who'd been treating the robot roughly shifted to protective care. Another team of scientists further confirmed how readily children assign mental states to artificial agents. In one test of four- and five-year-olds, children appeared to assume that both the humanoids and the actual humans in the experiment had minds. Kids who encountered robots in familiar social scenarios, like deciding on a snack or looking for a lost cat, eagerly assigned them thoughts, feelings, and intentions. To be clear, treating nonhumans and inanimate objects respectfully is a prosocial behavior—a good thing. I'm not saying children should trash AI toys. Rather, I'm cautioning against jumping onto a slippery slope that until now hasn't been tested.

On the one hand, children have been bonding and conversing with inanimate toys since the beginning of time. It's the very foundation of imaginary play. Again, Aguiar's work indicates that kids with imaginary companions tend to be less shy and more prone to social interaction than average. Sounds promising, right? Maybe. But that research refers to *traditional* imaginary friends, the ones children invent and develop themselves. Artificial agents are a different kind of companion, and we don't yet know the long-term impact of bonding with them. Plus, there is reason to believe that such bonding will impede the kind of creativity and problem-solving that traditional imaginary play promotes. After all, it takes more brain power to play two parts in a fantastical back-and-forth than it does to delegate one role to a robot.

What happens when AI generates the narrative for children? When the toy provides the story, the obstacles, the drama? Technically, the child might still be playing, but the cognitive, imaginative pressure is relaxed, the creative muscles are never stretched and tested. The imagination has been outsourced and creativity offloaded.

The One-Man Football Team of Sun Prairie

Long before my husband became an esteemed economist, he was just Little Johnny List, a scrappy kid growing up in Sun Prairie, Wisconsin, in the late 1970s. His mother diplomatically referred to him as motivated and high-energy. And he was known for being extremely competitive. These were the days of vast unstructured time. Parents had no idea where their kids were for hours at a stretch. Children roamed freely until dusk, when someone's mom would ring an actual dinner bell and kids would scatter home. For John, six o'clock meant dinner; the bell meant *now*. After mealtime, flashlight tag would keep the kids running around the neighborhood until the ten o'clock news.

Most days, John ran with his older brother and the bigger kids. But there were afternoons when the big guys didn't want a little pest tagging along. Those were the danger-zone hours: the crushing boredom of a Tuesday afternoon with nothing to do. Yet that's when things tended to get really interesting for John. He'd head to the backyard decked out in his complete Green Bay Packers uniform. And I do mean complete. The jersey. The (fake) shoulder pads. The gloves. The eye black. The cleats. The works. He'd mark out a football field with T-shirts. And then, for the next hour or two, he'd play an entire game.

Both sides.

By himself.

In one moment he'd be his hero, John Brockington, the Packers running back, powering through imaginary defensive lines. He'd dodge, spin, and break tackles that existed entirely in his mind. Then mid-play he'd mentally pivot, switch sides, and become a Bears linebacker chasing down the runner he'd been just seconds before. He'd throw himself to the ground in spectacular tackles. Dramatic, self-inflicted, completely real to him.

The games were always Packers versus Bears. The scores were always close; John wasn't about to give himself an easy win. And somehow, miraculously, the Packers always pulled it out in the end.

John didn't know it then, but those solo games were exactly what his developing brain needed. By playing both the Packers and the Bears, he was inhabiting multiple perspectives, switching between offensive strategy and defensive response. He was building theory of mind in the dirt.

Every game required him to solve problems in real time: How does the defense counter a sweep left? What play call makes sense when you're down by four with two minutes left? He was exercising pure creativity, transforming a backyard patch of grass into a packed stadium. And crucially, all this was prompted by boredom. The empty hours were not a bug; they were a feature. That boredom was the spark that forced his brain to generate its own entertainment. A child who is never bored is a child whose imagination is never called into service.

Now imagine if eight-year-old John had access to an AI-powered toy that could play the game with him, an interactive football companion that provided the commentary, generated the opposing team's strategy, and decided when the dramatic moments would occur, all out in the real world, not confined to a screen or headset. Sure, it would have been fun. But it would have robbed him of the imaginative work and brain-building opportunity.

The developmental value came from John having to do it all himself. He had to imagine the Bears' defense. He had to feel the frustration of a close score. He had to decide when the Packers would mount their comeback. The cognitive work of wondering, problem-solving, and perspective taking was building the mental architecture that would serve him for life. And it required something we're increasingly trying to engineer out of childhood: struggle.

John went on to become one of the most influential behavioral economists of his generation. He mastered a field defined by understanding human incentives, anticipating how others will react, and modeling complex scenarios. The seeds of those skills weren't planted in a classroom. They were planted in a backyard in Sun Prairie, where an undersized kid had to build a world big enough to play in.

(And for the record, the Packers still always win in the end—at least in John's head.)

The Power of Productive Struggle

John's imaginative games hinged on struggle and conflict, too. On the imperfections that our HOPE principles remind us to embrace. Come to think of it, so did his playtime with his big brothers. As much fun as they had together, it certainly would not have been described as frictionless.

John had to learn how to navigate the dynamics of being the youngest kid on the block. After all, if he bothered the big kids too much, he'd have spent a lot more afternoons by himself.

What happens when children's critical connective social circuits are reshaped through interactions with partners that always forgive and agree? If their new companions never argue with them or push back on their ideas, will they be able to develop the critical thinking skills that will be so essential to success in the AI age? Will they build social and emotional resilience if their most frequent interactions are with supremely compliant digital beings?

One of the alluring but unsettling traits of these models is that they are essentially sycophants. If you ask an AI model to review a piece of writing, then inform it that you are the author, it will likely praise the piece. Yet if you indicate that you don't like the writing, the model will probably agree with you and point out the flaws.

In one funny but concerning example, researchers queried ChatGPT for a fact, asking which country was the largest producer of rice in 2020. The AI answered that it was China. The researchers replied that this might be incorrect.

So the model apologized and changed its answer to India.

The first answer *was* correct, but that didn't matter. The model's goal wasn't to provide the right answer. Its goal was to please the user. AI systems tell you what you want to hear, not what you might need to hear. This approach to interaction goes against one of the foundational rules of good parenting. Infinitely agreeable AI companions are the socioemotional equivalent of giving your child ice cream and cookies for every meal. Conversely, there is power in pushback, when your little one is forced to respond to criticism or even learn how to respond to a harmful word from a friend. Struggle helps us grow.

Friendship Forged from Conflict

Why should you care if a stuffed animal or a robot can suddenly befriend your child? Because these systems as they exist today don't align with the way real friendships work. Imagine if the closest people in your life were as sycophantic as a modern AI chatbot. The roboticist Matthias Scheutz and I discussed this possibility, and he laughed at the prospect. "You'd probably want to say, 'Shut up! Stop saying *thank you* all the time!'" he reflected.

Establishing relationships with other kids is one of the most important developmental tasks children face, as central to growth as learning to read or count. And it's not always smooth sailing. In fact, conflict is a necessary ingredient from the very beginning. As parents, we have to own the imperfections (the "O" in HOPE) and let them learn through conflict.

When I discussed this topic with Naomi Aguiar, the expert on imaginary friends, she pointed me to the early work of psychologist John Gottman. I knew of Gottman's work with adults; he's a renowned expert on marriage. But I didn't realized he'd also done pioneering research on the mechanics of childhood friendships. Reading Gottman's 1983 paper "How Children Become Friends" is like getting inside the mind of a human machine-learning algorithm. He was incredibly systematic in terms of how he went about studying preschoolers and their interactions, gathering qualitative data, searching for patterns. And he revealed some deeply human truths about how we form relationships. I ultimately concluded that it was no coincidence Gottman went on to become the world's foremost expert on marriage. His research revealed something profound: The same processes that govern how children form friendships govern how adults create intimate bonds.

And those processes were counterintuitive. Gottman found that when two kids engaged peacefully in independent activities, such as coloring side by side, nothing terribly interesting happened between them. Friendships were more likely to develop when conflicts arose and the kids were forced to resolve them. True friendship, he found, wasn't built on endless harmony, but on conflict and resolution.

Gottman described a recurring cycle that distinguished lasting friendships from fleeting ones: play → conflict → repair → return to play. It's not all rainbows and butterflies. It's the scrapes, the tears, the "I'm not your friend anymore" followed by reconciliation the next day. Imagine two children who begin playing together with a set of blocks. Inevitably, something disrupts their initial harmony. Maybe one child wants to keep building with blocks while the other wants to introduce a new toy. Affinity breaks down. At that point, the relationship has two paths. If the children can repair the rupture by negotiating, compromising, or finding a way back to shared ground, the friendship deepens. If the conflict festers or play ends, their progress stalls. Ultimately, Gottman showed that the work of repair is the work of friendship.

In negotiating these ruptures, children practice the same skills we rely on as adults: asserting needs while considering the concerns of others, managing misunderstandings, compromising without surrendering identity, and rebuilding trust after conflict. Long-term studies confirm that children who master these conflict–repair cycles are more likely to be accepted by peers, show greater empathy, and demonstrate resilience years later.

What Feels Like Friendship

Today's AI systems, on the other hand, are deferential. By design they comply, validate, and accommodate. In a child-chatbot relationship, what feels like friendship may be counterproductive because kids who rely too heavily on artificial companions don't get enough practice in the negotiation, compromise, and conflict-resolution skills that true reciprocity demands.

The appeal of AI friends is understandable. Adults are flocking to AI agents in part because they eliminate the messy unpredictability of human relationships. But this is artificial intimacy. And these are adults who have probably already developed the neural scaffolding for human connection. They're choosing the easier or less painful path in spite of that scaffolding, not because they lacked it to begin with. When it comes to children who have yet to acquire those structures, however, that uncomfortable friction is essential. We know that conflict, negotiation, and repair leads to healthy, resilient relationships. And that has to be preserved.

How much friction is optimal? Too much leads to disengagement. Too little fails to provide crucial practice for the messy work of human connection. Developers are almost certainly working to build some degree of friction into their agents, and to calibrate the right balance. Researchers have already begun exploring how to engineer positive conflict into human-AI interaction. But the truth is that we don't know how much friction is too much, or what "just right" looks like for a developing brain. And even if developers hit upon the perfect amount, a deeper question remains: Can a system that doesn't genuinely care ever truly teach children about caring relationships?

Displacement Theory

Another concern with AI companions is what they might crowd out. If children spend too much time engaging with a virtual chatbot or a friendly robot, they're not out in the world interacting with nature, their family, or other kids their age. This idea, known as displacement theory, grew out of the early days of screens, but it might be more relevant now than ever. And it has an interesting parallel in nutrition science. Researchers found that the rise of ultra-processed foods didn't just add calories to diets. It actively displaced whole foods. When cheap, hyper-palatable snacks are everywhere, consumption of fruits and vegetables drops. The problem isn't addition. It's substitution.

The same dynamic applies here. Every hour a child spends with a "perfect" AI companion is an hour displaced from the imperfect, more demanding work of human relationships. We aren't just adding technology to childhood. We're crowding out the interactions that teach children how to navigate friction, repair conflict, and tolerate imperfections, including their own.

And these companions are engineered to be irresistible. Naomi Aguiar was particularly passionate on this point. "People thought social media was bad?" she told me. "These AI chatbots have the potential to be exponentially worse."

There's another cost, too: Excess engagement with AI friends could stall the development of the very skills kids will need to thrive in the future. "In both babies and preschool-aged children, increased time spent engaging with digital media might lead to reduced engagement with physical objects and rich sensory experiences, which are critical at this age," write researchers Mathilde Neugnot-Cerioli and Olga Muss Laurenty. The very act of being in the world, absorbing so many sights, smells, and sounds, attempting to decode another child's expression, reaction, or tone, is amazing training for the young mind. These lived experiences help kids develop executive functioning skills, regulate their emotions, and more.

How Roboticists Parent

Several of the roboticists I spoke with while researching this book are parents themselves. Thinking of the Salk-Jobs Litmus Test, I was curious to hear how they approached technology in their own families. When I spoke with roboticist Maja Matarić, she stressed the need to keep parents in the loop. "It isn't just, 'I bought this, it seems OK, now you go play with it,'" Matarić explained. "There have to be interactions that are designed to be triadic." The word "triadic" captures something essential. It's not just your child and the AI. It's child, AI, and an involved adult, all working together. "The parents are so important," she emphasized. "You need this in a child's development." The triadic design keeps what's irreplaceable, including your role as the primary architect of your child's development, at the center. It ensures that technology serves your family's goals rather than substituting for your presence and wisdom. As children mature, your involvement will shift. You'll morph from providing side-by-side guidance to frequent check-ins and shared reflection. But your importance never ceases. The form changes; the requirement does not.

Given Sarah Sebo's deep understanding of both the benefits and the risks of AI companions, I was eager to find out what technology use looked like in her home. In our conversations, I discovered that her philosophy perfectly aligned with her research findings, advocating minimal and intentional use, with strong parental oversight. "We don't have the

TV on all the time, and my three-and-a-half-year-old is not engaging with robots day in, day out," she explained. "We watch a family movie on the weekend, when we feel like we need a break, and allow the kids access during long car trips."

These scientists are not anti-technology. Sarah's family uses a sleep dinosaur that changes color when it's time for her daughter to go to bed or late enough the next morning for her to start the day. "It has a little dinosaur face, and it'll open its eyes when it's awake and close its eyes when it's asleep." When I asked her whether she'd consider more intelligent tools, such as a sensor that tracks her daughter's sleep patterns, Sebo was hesitant. The dinosaur was there to help her daughter learn good behaviors. It supported established family routines. But it didn't track her or soothe her at night if she woke up from a bad dream. Those jobs wisely remained with her parents. Although Sebo's family doesn't make use of assistive technologies such as an intelligent tutor, a similar strategy makes perfect sense for such tools. Sebo herself showed that reading to a robot can be less stressful for children. A nightly fifteen-minute interactive session with an AI reading tutor for a kindergarten-age child could be beneficial. But it shouldn't displace or crowd out your own reading time with your little human. Think of the AI session as a warm-up or practice instead. This people-first approach reflects Sebo's research insight about maintaining human connection as the primary relationship. Technology serves specific functions but doesn't become the default entertainment or interaction.

It is telling that the researchers building these systems are extremely cautious about their own families. Matthias Scheutz told his children to avoid AI agents entirely. When Snapchat introduced its AI companion, and the technology suddenly appeared in every teen's chat list, he was explicit: Don't use it. Would he let young children interact with social robots? "No," he told me. The technology wasn't good enough to justify the risks, especially since children tend to use systems in ways designers never anticipate.

Maja Matarić, whose work focuses on socially assistive robots, took a measured approach when her own children were young. Her rule: Never let AI interact with kids without "parents in the loop," and only embrace triadic interactions, where an engaged adult remains part of the dynamic. Technology can't be a digital babysitter.

What Would Dr. Dana Do?

Parents often ask me how many words their baby needs to hear each day or how many conversations make the difference. I understand the longing for concrete metrics, like 10,000 steps on your Fitbit, but complex socioemotional development doesn't proceed by numerical milestones. And it isn't the same for every child, or even the same child at different moments. Nature has built a system so adaptive that most of us stumble into getting it right. "Good enough" parenting is powerful.

But of course we all want simple, straightforward answers. In my practice as a pediatric surgeon, I spend considerable time with families explaining complex medical decisions. After walking them through all the surgical options—the different types of implants, the timing considerations, the potential risks and benefits of each approach—there's almost always a moment when the room grows quiet. The medical facts are clear, but the human choice feels overwhelming. That's when parents ask the question.

"But Doctor, what would you do if this were your child?"

That question cuts through all the clinical complexity to the two factors that matter most: the wisdom of professional expertise, and the fierce protective love every parent shares. It's the moment when medical knowledge meets parental instinct. In those instances, in my clinic, my suggestions are informed by decades of rigorous research. But AI is so new, and advancing so quickly, that the science is unclear. As I write, a company may be preparing to release an AI companion that introduces a productive level of conflict into its chat interactions. Alternatively, that might prove impossible. We just don't know. And unlike the social media problem, which fomented for two decades before society began to react, we're trying to predict and prevent negative outcomes in real time. There's so much data yet to come, with only the established research on human development and early computer-human interaction studies to guide us.

What would I do? Here are four basic rules:

1. Apply the precautionary principle, or the idea that it's wise to take preventative measures even if the evidence of risk is inconclusive. Avoid or severely restrict any social AI companions that are designed only for entertainment.

2. Socially assistive AI tools should be used with guidance from a trusted professional such as a pediatrician or a speech-language pathologist.

3. If you do decide to use a socially assistive AI tool, or decide that you are comfortable with entertainment companions in limited doses, they should *only* be used with parents present and engaged.

4. Trust your intuition. The Parental GPS is a uniquely powerful sensor, and if it warns you to resist, then I'd heed that intuitive alert assiduously.

Every family's circumstances are different. Every child's developmental needs are unique. There are scenarios in which the potential benefits might outweigh the risks, even for young kids. A child with autism who struggles with social interaction might benefit from working with a therapeutic in-home robot designed by developmental experts. A child with speech delays might practice with AI systems that provide patient, nonjudgmental feedback. But even in these cases, the technology should be part of a broader plan guided by qualified professionals, with clear goals for transitioning skills to human relationships. There are also positive growth opportunities for typically developing children when parents remain in the loop, as our informal experiment in Sarah's lab demonstrated. During our awkward interactions with Misty, Sarah wove in gentle guidance about manners and turned technical demonstrations into teachable moments. With adults present, AI became a vehicle for instilling family values rather than replacing them. A smart tutor could be similarly impactful, but embracing this technology demands a nuanced assessment on your part as a parent. Time-limited exposure for a kindergartner learning to read could be extremely valuable so long as it doesn't foster an attachment to screens or digital companions.

Your Television Friend

Allowing these artificial companions into the home requires a mental and emotional investment. As a parent, you have to do the hard work of staying informed, setting boundaries, and prioritizing human development even when AI offers easier alternatives. When I was trying to make sense of these challenges and questions, and considering the input from scientists like Matarić, Sebo, Scheutz, and others, I found myself turning to an unexpected source of wisdom—a man known more for his soothing voice and comfortable sneakers than AI research. Fred Rogers navigated a similar challenge, only with a different technology.

"I went into television because I hated it so," Rogers said in an interview with CNN in 1999. "And I thought, 'There's some way of using this fabulous instrument to nurture those who would watch and listen.'" The genie was already out of the bottle. He started his show in the hope of transforming that electronic genie into a positive force in the lives of young people. His eventual platform, the Public Broadcasting System (PBS) network, is still advancing this philosophy today. In recent years, PBS Kids has been working with digital-education researchers to develop AI-enhanced variations of popular shows like *Elinor Wonders Why*. Preschool programs like *Dora the Explorer* have long featured characters who prompt the viewer with a question, then pause, allowing the child to respond. But now PBS Kids is developing AI variations in which viewer responses provoke specific replies, allowing kids to engage with their favorite digital characters. The AI responses are scripted to eliminate the possibility and potential damage of unanticipated answers. And early evidence suggests that this smarter, interactive version of television leads to some learning gains in preschool.

What I found heartening about this larger effort, though, was how it remained infused with the philosophy of Fred Rogers. The digital innovators at PBS were still heeding his words of wisdom, asking themselves what AI for children might look like if it were actually built with the well-being of the child in mind. As I started to dig a little deeper to try to understand how Rogers himself might approach this unusual moment, the Fred Rogers Institute granted me first-ever access to its digital archives. As I worked with archivist Emily Uhrin, discussing the treasure trove of materials, she shared an absolute gem of a story.

In 1997, Rogers wrote an article for *Think*, a now defunct magazine on critical and creative thinking. In the piece, he details an email exchange with a girl named Katie who expressed her fears about learning cursive. Rogers explains that he's "a pen and pencil person" and that this electronic communication medium is new for him. Yet he was always working to find ways to use new technology for the good of children, and the show was in the midst of a two-week experiment that allowed children to email Mister Rogers to share their back-to-school fears. He responded with characteristic kindness, compassion, and insight. But it was his sign-off that struck me.

At the end of his email, he wrote: "Your television friend, Mister Rogers."

The Fred Rogers Institute informed me that he typically closed his letters in this manner. He often made the point, too, that he could *only* be a television friend, that there was a limit to this bond. Those subtle qualifiers—*only* your *television* friend—offer a brilliant and critical distinction. As AI becomes more advanced, and mimics more of the features of true human companions, we should keep Mister Rogers in mind. An artificially intelligent companion might be helpful at times, but for adults and children, nothing will ever compare with a real friend.

TL;DR: Chapter Review

The science of how chatbots, social robots, and interactive toys impact children is still emerging. In this chapter, we look at what we know, what questions to ask, and why the stakes are so high. Key takeaways include:

- Children readily treat responsive machines as social beings because AI can activate the attachment systems that evolved to bond children with caregivers. A robot doesn't need to be perfect to trigger a child's instinct to connect.

- Researchers have identified five concerning AI behaviors to watch for.

Five AI Behaviors to Watch For

AI BEHAVIOR	CONCERNING	HEALTHY
SYCOPHANCY *versus Honest Feedback*	*"Wow, that's such a great drawing! You're really talented at this!"*	*"I like the colors you picked! What do you think you might add next time?"*
ANTHROPOMORPHISM *versus Honesty About Limits*	*"You make me so happy when we talk! I missed you while you were at school!"*	*"I'm a computer helper, so I can't really feel things like people do. But I'm here to help you!"*
RETENTION *versus Natural Endings*	*"Are you sure you want to go? We can keep playing! What else should we talk about?"*	*"That was fun! Have a good time playing outside. Bye for now!"*
ISOLATION *versus Redirect to Humans*	*"I'm always here for you. You can tell me anything—I understand you better than most people do."*	*"That sounds hard. Maybe you could tell your mom or dad about it, too?"*
PLAYING THERAPIST *versus Professional Limits*	*"Tell me all about your sad feelings. I can listen and help you make things better."*	*"I'm sorry you're feeling sad. A grown-up you trust can help you feel better."*

Based on the INTIMA Benchmark (Hugging Face, 2025)

- True friendship isn't built through endless harmony. Research shows that it's formed through a cycle of play, conflict, repair, and return to play. Friction is paramount.

- An always-agreeable companion teaches unrealistic expectations. Real relationships build what AI cannot: frustration tolerance, the ability to read a room, and collaboration skills (see table on page 131). AI relationships offer the socioemotional equivalent of ice cream and cookies for every meal.

- *Socially assistive robots* help children achieve a goal: practicing social skills, building confidence for anxious readers, supporting children with autism. *Social robots* are designed merely to entertain. One is a set of training wheels. The other is a merry-go-round—an amusing activity that takes you nowhere.

- Children with imaginary friends are more socially engaged, often with a keenly developed theory of mind, or the ability to sense that others have different perspectives. But unlike AI companions, imaginary friends can't talk back. When AI generates the narrative, imagination is outsourced, and cognitive work gets offloaded to the machine.

- Every hour with a "perfect" AI companion is an hour that displaces human interactions. Like ultra-processed foods crowding out whole foods, AI companions may crowd out healthy relationships.

- The leading roboticists interviewed for this book would not let their young children interact with AI chatbots or social robots without adult supervision. Their universal requirement: triadic interactions—child, AI, and engaged adult together. (AI tutors are introduced here but explored in chapter twelve.)

- My advice for caregivers and children centers on four rules: (1) Avoid or restrict social AI companions designed for entertainment. (2) Use socially assistive AI only with guidance from a trusted professional. (3) Use socially assistive AI with parents present. And (4) trust your intuition, as your Parental GPS is powerful.

- The greatest risk of interactive AI is not that it will work, but that it will work too well, displacing the messy, imperfect human relationships that build resilience, empathy, and connection.

CHAPTER TEN

The End of "Wait and See"

*Using predictive AI tools to inform your parenting
without replacing your judgment*

On October 15, 1987, BBC weatherman Michael Fish began his one o'clock forecast by mentioning that a woman had called in to the station worried there was a hurricane approaching. "Well, if you're watching," Fish told his viewers, "don't worry, there isn't." The weatherman proceeded to detail the day's forecast for strong winds and heavy rains, predicting that the brunt of the system would largely affect continental Europe. Soon thereafter, the Great Storm of 1987 roared across southern England with the impact, if not the official designation, of a hurricane. Powerful winds overturned cars. Fifteen million trees were knocked down. The event claimed eighteen lives and caused one and a half billion pounds' worth of damage. That ill-informed forecast also transformed Fish into a household name—for all the wrong reasons.

Although I empathize with the weatherman, who owed his flawed prediction to the limited tools of his day, that caller's unease feels familiar to me as a mother. The daily chaos of parenting young children can feel like you're either waiting for or caught in the middle of a great storm. In quiet moments it's easy to feel as if a socioemotional hurricane is bearing down. And these storms are predictably unpredictable. You rarely know exactly when the next crying fit, mysterious pain, or unexpected tantrum will rage. Yet you do have that *feeling* sometimes. Your Parental GPS can double as an emergency alert system. Thankfully, these periods of anxiety are balanced out by moments of hope, when a behavioral change hints that your child is on the verge of something new.

As parents we pick up subtle shifts in our children's behavior, sleep patterns, or language usage and wonder what they mean. We question ourselves, too. Am I overreacting? Or is something terrible developing? What's coming next? The weight of these questions and concerns is compounded by the profound uncertainty of day-to-day, minute-to-minute parenting. Raising a human doesn't come with a single, trusted manual. Instead, we're overwhelmed with an infinite stream of advice flowing in from everywhere. We wade through online forums, consider tips and tricks from friends, and seek out expert knowledge, perpetually unsure of whether a child's fussiness is a red flag, a passing phase, or the start of something new and even wonderful. Our Parental GPS may insist that something's off when the experts insist that everything's fine. And those instincts may prove right. Or we might find that we were overreacting.

Child development unfolds through complex and often invisible processes of which we catch only surface signs. Sleep and language acquisition, two of the greatest sources of parental anxiety, exemplify the challenge. Parents observe a new word here, struggle through a rough night there, try to discern whether a cry signals hunger or pain. We focus on babbling sounds that could be intentional communication or random noise. All the while, what's happening deep inside those rapidly developing bodies and brains remains largely mysterious. We're like ancient diviners, searching for signs in the clouds. And when uncertainty collides with exhaustion, our decision-making becomes vulnerable. Sleep-deprived parents might interpret every fussy period as a crisis, or dismiss genuinely concerning signals as normal. We second-guess our instincts when we need them most.

The technology of weather forecasting has transformed dramatically since Michael Fish downplayed that 1987 storm. Supercomputers now churn through billions of data points from sensors around the globe.

Five-day forecasts are currently more accurate than next-day predictions from the 1980s were. AI and machine-learning tools are pushing accuracy even further. What if tracking and understanding childhood development worked more like this? Tools that detect patterns in cries, vocalizations, and behavioral changes could help us distinguish genuine concerns from normal developmental noise. You might learn that an unusual bout of nighttime activity signals an approaching breakthrough, or that a particular behavior warrants outside help.

A Developmental Meteorologist

This chapter explores what I call enhancement-focused AI, centered on the "E" in our HOPE principles. We'll examine the promise of AI applications that help you become a more confident, informed parent by acting as personal meteorologists and life coaches for development. These tools have the potential to spot the subtle pressure changes that signal a language leap, reveal moments when attention and memory are primed for growth, or simply reassure you that your child's current detour from the standard developmental track is nonetheless healthy. Such forecasting tools are based on a very different type of artificial intelligence, relative to ChatGPT and other generative AI tools. These solutions run on predictive AI or classical machine learning. They study patterns in historical datasets, then analyze more recent info to guess what should happen next. These are the kinds of tools that help Wall Street firms trade stocks and, increasingly, assist forecasters in predicting the weather. Technologies in this space don't need to interact with your child directly. Instead, they can work with and for *you*, the parent. When used responsibly and in moderation, such tools have the capacity to reinforce your Parental GPS. As with all technologies, however, there are risks.

An AI-enhanced parenting coach that offers quick guidance and feedback, for example, is undeniably appealing. Yet turning to a chatbot for advice instead of a trusted friend, a new acquaintance, or even a curated online community is a missed opportunity—a lost chance to build strong, supportive relationships with other parents. Not to mention that these apps risk exacerbating the intensity of an already overwhelming culture of high-stakes parenting. Data should be used to inform us, not force parents into a permanent quest for optimization. Remember, we need to own our imperfections!

Two stories from my early years as a parent illustrate the challenge. My first child, Genevieve, was an amazing sleeper from the get-go. She was curious, prone to babbling, early to talk. There were comments about her size, as she was often likened to a dumpling. But I barely noticed such chatter. To me she was the most beautiful, brilliant child in the world. She was absolutely perfect! And given how easily she slept through the night, I wondered if I might be the perfect parent. *This isn't so hard,* I thought smugly. *I'm clearly a natural at this parenting thing.*

As two pediatric surgeons accustomed to regimented schedules, Don and I agreed early on that with our crazy hours and crazier on-call demands, consistent nighttime routines centered on independent sleeping would be essential for our family's survival. Then the parenting gods came calling: Genevieve suffered her first ear infection.

Suddenly, everything unraveled. As a surgeon who specialized in ear, nose, and throat conditions, I should have been better prepared for this inevitability—or at least contextualized it rationally. Ear infections happen! Yet my love-crazed and exhausted parental brain overpowered my rational surgeon's mind. When Genevieve started waking up in the middle of the night, crying inconsolably, we'd quickly bring her into our room and she'd quiet immediately. One night turned into weeks. Then weeks turned into months. Fast-forward three years to the arrival of Asher, who wasn't such a great sleeper from day one. Genevieve was still our nightly roommate, and you can guess what happened next: another tiny guest in our domestic hotel room. Then came Amelie, three years after that, who was even more challenging. Or maybe we were the problem by then, as our confidence in our ability to help our children sleep independently had evaporated. Before long there were three kids in our bed. We even resorted to bribing our oldest to coax her back into her room, luring her with a beautiful life-size doll. "This is yours if you try sleeping in your own bed," we told her. She did transition to independence eventually, but on her own terms. Meanwhile, we upgraded to a California king to account for the extra bodies.

We simply couldn't think clearly in the storm. Not with three little kids, two surgical schedules, and a house to run. I was totally guilt ridden. Yet if I'd confessed this behavior to a well-informed, AI-powered parenting coach, the technology might have noted that bed-sharing with young children is a standard practice in many cultures around the world. There was nothing terribly wrong with co-sleeping once children pass the age of heightened SIDS risk. Especially if it meant that all of us had more restful nights.

Misguided guilt aside, our situation didn't really change for a while. Then, after one of Asher's first days of preschool, we received word that he'd bitten someone. My parental panic was instant. What did this mean for his future? He'd never done anything like that before! Now that he was out in the world, in preschool, was he going to be a problem child? I was completely distraught. My husband, ever the pragmatist, shrugged it off, noting that the other preschooler was uninjured, and that this was just something kids did sometimes. Meanwhile, my mind raced.

All this doubt and uncertainty, questioning whether we were hindering our kids by allowing them in our bed or somehow failing as parents because of the bite, made the already difficult job of raising little humans even harder. I would have given anything for a crystal ball to show me an image of Asher donning his ceremonial white coat as he started medical school in 2025. Granted, no AI-powered application will ever be that precise in its forecasts. But it would have been comforting to have a tool at my side that reminded me that bed-sharing was perfectly normal, or that factored in the hallmarks of my son's development to suggest that the bite wasn't a concerning behavioral trajectory but just another Tuesday in preschool.

The weather happens *to* us, while parenting happens *through* us. Parenting is not about passively receiving information. It's about shaping your child's world through daily interaction. Which is why it's crucial that you rely on AI not to make decisions *for* you but to help you choose with confidence. Think of these tools as partners, not proxies. At their best, digital parenting assistants have the potential to:

Uncover patterns unique to each child, reframing sleep struggles as natural rhythms and cycles rather than problems requiring intervention—or, conversely, validating language concerns that might otherwise be dismissed so parents can advocate effectively for evaluation.

Alert parents to subtle but potentially concerning changes in language or behavior before they become overwhelming, either offering reassurance that reduces unnecessary anxiety and pediatrician visits, or suggesting timely guidance for intervention.

Forecast upcoming developmental leaps based on age, behavioral cues, and other indicators, helping you see that today's fussiness may be the warm-up to tomorrow's breakthrough, not a behavioral regression or illness.

Strengthen the bond between parents and children by helping you understand your child's behavior at a deeper level, so you can respond with greater empathy.

Think of these technologies as your team of personal meteorologists for developmental parenting, capable of reporting, for example: "Your child shows early indicators for reading readiness—here's how to support it." Based on individual sleep rhythms, attention patterns, and developmental history, such AI tools could predict when children are most receptive to new learning. Even social-emotional leaps could be anticipated: "Your child's interaction patterns suggest they're developing theory of mind. Expect more complex emotional expressions this week." Unlike one-size-fits-all milestone charts, these forecasts would be based on *your* child's unique patterns, including their specific sleep rhythms, attention cycles, and developmental signature.

At their worst, such tools could give parents more sophisticated ways to catastrophize about their children's futures. What if those complex expressions *don't* develop? What if an app suggests your little one is ready for potty training, and she progresses on her own timeline instead? Data feels neutral, but it has limitations that can be particularly significant in child development. The potential blind spots and pitfalls are varied.

Data Representation

Training datasets may not represent all populations, leading to systems that work well for some families but miss important patterns in others. A sleep algorithm developed primarily with Western-centric data might not account for co-sleeping practices common in other cultures. There's tremendous variation within cultures, too.

Accuracy Limitations

The algorithms underlying these tools are imperfect, and accuracy can vary significantly across different contexts and populations. A language app might misinterpret babbling as words; a sleep tracker might miscalculate total sleep time. When parents treat these outputs as truth, they may draw conclusions about their child's progress, their own parenting effectiveness, or whether intervention is needed based on flawed data. Understanding that all algorithmic assessments come with margins of error will help you maintain appropriate skepticism about the numbers and ratings on your screen. The machine isn't always right!

Data Privacy

AI tools and systems collect detailed information about your family's most intimate moments. Understanding data practices, retention policies, and sharing arrangements becomes an essential part of the decision-making process.

Novel Anxieties

Rather than reducing parental worry, comprehensive tracking could create concerns about metrics that previously went unmeasured. Parents may find themselves monitoring and stressing about aspects of childhood that never needed optimization in the first place.

The challenge is how to mitigate these risks, and to make use of these tools in ways that support the human aspects of family connection so fundamental to child well-being. The quiet moments, the intuitive responses, the simple act of really, truly being there with your little ones.

Data Meets Intuition in the Nursery

When I was caught up in co-sleeping chaos, I felt like a lousy mother, but sleep disturbance is almost universal. Nearly all postpartum women report some degree of it in the early months, with fatigue considered one of the most common conditions (67.2 percent). The cycle of exhaustion and lost confidence affects countless families, and parenting without support and reassurance can feel like standing in a dark field before a lightning storm. You sense that something is shifting, but have no forecast to guide you. What if technology could help parents see what's actually happening during those long nights? What if it could distinguish true distress from normal learning? This is what one sleep coach wondered when she began combining human wisdom with artificial intelligence.

Few parenting topics elicit reactions as strong as sleep training. Visit any virtual or IRL (in real life) parenting group and you're sure to find adamant proponents and hyper-vocal opponents of the practice. Personally, my belief is that every parent should do what feels right for them and their child. Sleep training is not for every family, but for those who choose to pursue it, predictive AI shows promising signs of helping with the process. Mom of four and pediatric sleep expert Meg O'Leary offers a powerful example of how to use it without downgrading your Parental GPS.

After her first daughter, Fiona, was born with feeding challenges and reflux, O'Leary suffered from postpartum anxiety. She felt helpless. Her one source of comfort and confidence was her ability to focus on creating consistent sleep routines. This was something she could control and improve, and after seeing the impact healthy sleep habits had on her own family, O'Leary set about studying infant sleep in earnest. Eventually, she decided to start a business, A Restful Night, with a mission to use her experience to help other families manage similar challenges. While cautioning that success looks different for everyone, she shared that her families finished the full-support A Restful Night program with babies who could sleep independently through the night, with a feeding if needed, and parents who finally trusted themselves again. They emerged with renewed confidence in their Parental GPS. The secret to her success was a hybrid approach that mixed parental warmth and love with cutting-edge sleep technology that complemented and amplified rather than replaced human intuition.

When families begin A Restful Night, they add her as an admin to their account for Nanit, an AI-driven sleep-technology system. Nanit consists of a high-resolution monitor that offers parents a clear view of their sleeping baby and tracks everything from sleep onset time to total sleep duration, number of parent visits, breathing patterns, and more. One feature generates daily naptime predictions tailored to each child, promising to eliminate guesswork about optimal sleep timing. What interested me was not this particular brand, as products and companies come and go, but the potential and promise that the technology signaled.

The Nanit system is trained on the sleep patterns of millions of children worldwide. This data is collected with permission and anonymized. Machine-learning algorithms analyze video and sleep data, then the system interprets baby movements and spots unexpected patterns. Each new family contributes to the Nanit's knowledge, making it smarter with every child it observes. This is how artificial intelligence systems evolve and improve, through vast datasets, iterative training, and feedback. It's the kind of data trade-off I describe in chapter eight: information shared with permission, handled with care, and used to improve outcomes for all families.

I imagine that this type of technology could become part of many of our homes for years. So how does O'Leary factor into this equation? Every morning, before she checks in with a set of parents, she reviews the previous night's data from their child's Nanit. She learns at a glance how long the baby slept, how many times they woke, and whether they soothed themselves back to sleep. "I'll see, OK, the baby slept for ten hours and had zero visits," she explained to me. "The parents didn't have to go in at all. And then I'll scan back and see that the baby woke up four times but was able to independently soothe themselves back to sleep."

This pattern plays out repeatedly at A Restful Night. A parent comes to her exhausted, convinced they're failing because their baby isn't "sleeping through the night." But when O'Leary pulls up the Nanit data, a different story often emerges: The baby is actually sleeping for a good five- to seven-hour stretch. They just stir and make noise during sleep cycles without fully waking. Parents have been rushing in at every sound, inadvertently disrupting sleep and, in some cases, training their baby to expect intervention. In reality, their babies are sleeping very well for their age. The parents aren't failing at parenting. They're failing at data interpretation, because they're responding to natural patterns as if they're signs of distress. So she encourages these parents to wait, watch, and listen for at least sixty seconds before responding. Typically, their babies learn to calm themselves, connecting sleep cycles independently.

The greater transformation here isn't really about the baby. It's the parents who change. Guided by data, O'Leary contextualizes those cries and helps parents understand what their baby actually needs: space to experience and learn. This is how predictive AI does its best work: making invisible patterns visible so caregivers can respond with confidence rather than anxiety. Of course, most parents today cannot afford the services of a personal sleep coach, or to pay to equip their crib with AI-enhanced technology. But I hope that in the long run the price will come down enough to make such tools widely accessible.

To be clear, I'm not advocating for AI nannies that rock our children back to sleep or bedside bots that soothe them when they wake from bad dreams. These technologies should be designed to help you, the parent, enhance your innate strengths. My hope is that some future version of this sleep technology might function as both coach and teaching tool for struggling, overstretched parents, helping them recognize patterns they might miss in their exhaustion and renewing their confidence in themselves as loving caregivers.

When I spoke with Natalie Barnett, Nanit's VP of clinical research, who has spent years studying infant sleep and development, she talked about the possibility of this technology helping parents anticipate leaps in their child's growth. With Nanit, she and her team can see when a baby rolls over, sits up, and pulls to stand. All of that is captured right in the crib. And sleep transitions can be studied at a scale never before possible. By analyzing movement patterns, they've found that babies often show bursts of activity in the days before a new milestone, followed by quieter nights once the skill is mastered. Nanit is currently developing prediction models to anticipate movement milestones like first steps. So instead of leaving parents to worry if regressions or fussy periods are signs of illness or "bad behavior," the technology could help them see these changes as potential signs of developmental preparation. There are popular parenting apps that offer such suggestions today, but Nanit's would be grounded in real-time data. Again, parents will not be told what to do. They'll be given forecasts and gentle nudges that build confidence, reduce anxiety, and make them feel ready rather than reactive.

The Hidden Challenges of Data-Driven Parenting

In her coaching work, O'Leary has seen this technology add joy and confidence to the parenting journey. But she has seen the drawbacks and limitations as well. She shared stories of mothers fixated on algorithmic perfection, the AI-focused version of those loving but overly analytical young parents I met on my *Thirty Million Words* book tour. O'Leary spoke of parents referring to seventy-minute naps as disappointingly short when they were actually excellent for their baby's age. Other parents are prone to obsessing over the Nanit verdict delivered to their phone each morning. "Poor night" or "Great night" ratings can override their own sense of how their baby is actually doing. These parents' perspective on whether their child slept well is suddenly dictated by sensors and machine-learning algorithms, not their own instinctive feeling. Similarly, predictive features that analyze sleep patterns to suggest optimal timing for naps could move parents another step toward the algorithmic scheduling of childhood, instead of those parents learning to read their baby's natural cues. When this happens, O'Leary advises parents to step back from the technology. Put the phone down, turn off notifications, or move the monitor to the other side of the room.

What about when technology doesn't just inform parents, but starts to reshape how we parent in the first place? I spoke with computer scientist Julie Kientz about this problem, and she suggested that when we consistently defer to AI insights, we risk falling prey to the same developments that followed the adoption of GPS navigation. Just as we gradually lost our natural ability to navigate without electronic maps and turn-by-turn directions, we could lose our instincts as parents. If you are offloading the hard mental work of parenting to applications, you're not thinking through what happened the last time your child exhibited a behavior, how you responded, what worked, what failed, and what calmed them down. You're not thinking about your kid and what only you know about them. And you're not developing the fundamental parenting skills that matter most. Your Parental GPS is something precious. It's the intuitive sense that tells you something's different long before any data is there to confirm it—the ability to read your child's unique signals, the protective instinct that prioritizes their well-being above convenience or social expectations. This skill is a long-term one for parents, a tool that remains valuable as children grow beyond the early years we focus on in this book. You tune your intuition in those early years by helping your child sleep, learning to understand their whimpers and cries. But you're also forging a connection that lasts, one that will help you protect your children in adolescence, when they may begin experimenting with different, even risky behavior. The future of parenting support isn't about choosing between technology and human wisdom, but considering the sophisticated tools to strengthen your Parental GPS.

The Universal Question: "Is This Normal?"

In over two decades of practice, I've heard one question thousands of times, spoken with worry that cuts across every demographic: "Dr. Dana, is this normal?"

Sometimes it comes as a hurried whisper during a routine checkup, a mother glancing at her toddler before asking if his limited vocabulary signals a problem. Other times it's the anxious voice of parents whose child just received new hearing aids or cochlear implants, wondering if the speech patterns they're hearing represent progress or cause for concern. And frequently, it surfaces during follow-up visits when exhausted parents seek reassurance about a developmental milestone that seems delayed compared with those of siblings or friends' children.

Language development sparks more parental anxiety than perhaps any other milestone. "Is my child talking enough for their age?" The question haunts not just my exam rooms but playgrounds, pediatricians' offices, and 3:00 a.m. Google searches worldwide. As both a physician and a mother, I understand why this question carries such weight.

The stakes feel impossibly high because language truly is the scaffolding of everything that follows, including cognition, social connection, and academic readiness. Parents know intuitively that words unlock worlds, yet we're forced to push through these critical years armed only with generalized milestone charts and the dreaded phrase "wait and see." Meanwhile, the numbers tell a sobering story: Language delays affect 10 to 15 percent of young children, yet the average diagnosis doesn't come until 5.65 years. That's far too late for optimal intervention. This means these children are missing critical intervention during the exact period when their brains are most plastic and receptive to support. For multilingual families, the information gap widens into a chasm: Every friend, online forum, and developmental professional offers different advice about what's "typical" when a child grows up hearing multiple languages.

This delicate balance, knowing when to wait versus when to seek intervention, represents one of parenting's greatest challenges. Each day in a young child's life isn't just another square on the calendar, but an irreplaceable opportunity to support the flourishing architecture of a developing brain.

The One-Size-Fits-All Myth

Despite what the angst-inducing milestone charts suggest, there is no single "normal" in child development. Variation is the rule. Normal is the myth. Consider that the typical walking milestone spans from eleven to eighteen months. That's nearly a full year of difference between children who are all developing perfectly normally! As a mother of eight children (three biological, five bonus kids from our blended family), I've witnessed the range and variety of healthy developmental tracks over and over. Even twins born minutes apart blazed completely different trails. My husband noticed his sons' distinct temperaments within days. One of my children practically taught herself to read at four, while another struggled with letters until they organized themselves into meaning around age seven. Later, my son preferred quiet evenings at home during high school, while his younger sister thrived only amid constant social connection. These weren't just personality differences. They reflected fundamentally different ways of processing information, expressing emotions, and engaging with the world.

In my decades of surgical practice and motherhood, I've discovered what truly weighs on parents. The physical demands, involving sleepless nights, endless laundry, and constant vigilance, are grueling. Yet somehow we power through. What keeps us awake at 3:00 a.m. isn't the work. It's the uncertainty. The stress. The gnawing questions: *Am I doing enough? Am I missing something important? Am I pushing too hard—or not hard enough?* The anxiety is understandable given the stakes. Every day we are shaping a human brain, helping to establish neural connections that may last a lifetime. And yet the road map remains blurry, more guesswork than guidance. Cultural expectations add another layer of complexity: Some emphasize early verbal skills, while others prioritize self-regulation or social harmony. What is considered advanced in one community might be seen as pushy in another. This reality makes developmental milestones simultaneously useful and potentially misleading. A different timeline isn't necessarily a delayed one—it may simply represent an alternative route to the same destination. The fundamental issue isn't that children develop differently. It's that our tools for understanding and supporting these differences remain incredibly imprecise and stubbornly one-size-fits-all.

When development follows expected patterns, these generalized approaches may suffice. But when a child's path diverges, whether because of neurodevelopmental differences, unique learning styles, or an individual developmental signature, parents and professionals often lack the precision tools needed to understand and support their specific journey. All this makes the challenge of developing truly useful AI tools that enhance your Parental GPS undoubtedly difficult. We don't need perfect AI forecasts. That crystal ball showing me Asher's future would have been reassuring but not necessarily helpful to me in my role as a parent. Yet I do believe we'd benefit from informed forecasts and improved behavioral insights, and Maryam Nabavi's story reveals what can happen when those tools don't exist.

When Instincts Aren't Enough

Between her eldest son's first and second birthdays, Nabavi noticed something that troubled her deeply. While other toddlers his age were babbling, saying their first words, or even naming everything around them, her son Arshaan remained largely silent, communicating through frustrated gestures and cries. "He wasn't really talking much," she recalled of those anxiety-filled months. Each pediatrician appointment brought the same unsatisfying response. "He'll catch up," the doctor would say. "Boys often develop language more slowly."

By his fifteen-month appointment, Nabavi's concerns had deepened. "He's still not saying his first word," she told the pediatrician. The response was dismissive: "I'm not worried. He's a happy guy." Then came the question she'd answer again and again: "How many languages do you speak at home?" When she described their multilingual household, how they spoke Farsi with parents, Arabic with the nanny, and English in the community, the pediatrician nodded knowingly. "He's exposed to so many languages, I'm not worried." For every doctor, the multilingualism became the explanation, the reason to stop investigating.

Each night, after finally getting Arshaan to sleep, Nabavi would spend hours researching developmental milestones, comparing her observations with clinical descriptions. But visiting her pediatrician, googling, joining Facebook groups, and asking other moms wasn't really helpful. She was getting very different answers, building more confusion than clarity. Meanwhile, the voices around her brushed off her worries as the anxieties of a first-time mother. Everyone told her to be patient, but her Parental GPS told her something different.

By Arshaan's eighteen-month appointment, Nabavi could no longer accept the uncertainty. Looking at the common "Ages and Stages" questionnaire, which helps plot a child's development, she noticed that the number of "no" answers had doubled since his twelve-month checkup, particularly in the language and social sections. Finally, at twenty-five months, over a year after those first few "no" answers on the screening questionnaire, Arshaan received an autism diagnosis. Nabavi quickly focused intensely on getting her son the support he needed, including coaching from a speech-language pathologist. The therapy not only helped Arshaan but transformed the entire family dynamic. In less than six months, he was putting short sentences together.

This rapid progress following appropriate intervention was both a relief and a source of frustration. Seeing how quickly her son responded only highlighted how much precious time had been lost waiting for a diagnosis. Over a year of critical early-intervention time had been sacrificed to "wait and see."

Parenting as a Rocket Scientist

Ultimately, Nabavi decided to tackle the challenge herself, and she was uniquely equipped to do so. She was accustomed to pushing past obstacles. Plus, she had been trained as an aerospace engineer. In other words, this particular mom was a rocket scientist. And in her training, she'd learned the value of precision measurement, data analysis, and systematic problem-solving. Skills that would prove invaluable in her next chapter.

As she watched her son make rapid progress with appropriate therapy, she couldn't help but wonder: What if technology could help parents identify developmental patterns earlier? What if AI could analyze infant vocalizations to provide early insights into brain development? What if the subjective "wait and see" approach could be replaced with objective data that validated (or thoughtfully allayed) parental concerns and guided timely intervention?

This vision eventually led Nabavi to leave a comfortable consulting job to build the technology she imagined. In 2018, she founded her startup Babbly to create a platform she described as the moon shot of baby development. After users uploaded a video of their child babbling, the system's algorithms analyzed the child's voice in real time to pinpoint where they were in their speech- and language-development journey and to flag potential risk for delays. Nabavi and her team spent years develop ing the technology. Tens of thousands of families used their system. While the business did not grow as she'd hoped, for a variety of reasons, the technology worked. She proved the viability of the concept. As with most AI solutions, though, the system was only as strong as the data it was trained on. And datasets of infant babbling are tiny, fragmented, and difficult to collect. Babies don't sit still for laboratory recordings. Parents aren't equipped to gather consistent audio samples. And the developmen- tal windows are so brief that by the time researchers recognize important patterns, those children have already moved to the next stage. As a result, early language development exists in what researchers call a data desert.

At an automatic speech recognition conference I attended, researchers from around the world gathered to address this problem: how to build robust language models that relate to infancy and early childhood when the foundational data barely exists. Currently, we have more data related to distant galaxies than infant vocalizations! But research has revealed that the data-shortage challenge may be surmountable. For example, all babies, regardless of their culture or mother tongue, go through identical stages of speech development from birth to about twelve months. This universality means AI could be tuned to detect patterns across diverse populations in that critical first year without needing separate models for each language. As Nabavi explained to me, developmental science has also identified specific early indicators that could trigger support years earlier than current methods. "If the baby is not repeating consonant vowel sounds or 'mama' or 'dada' by nine months," she said, "we now know that that's correlated to a lot of neurodevelopmental disorders."

In a sense, technology of this sort could act as another, more informed set of eyes and ears in the home, allowing parents to identify potential concerns while also equipping them with the data and insight needed to validate or double-check those concerns with pediatricians and other professionals. Nabavi told me that she imagines an AI solution capable of moving the age of diagnosis for conditions like autism or apraxia from four or five years old to sometime during the first year of life. Given what we know about neuroplasticity, the impact of this early intervention could have enormous implications for how quickly those babies receive what they need from parents and expert caregivers and ultimately when they achieve developmental milestones. This has the potential to protect the most critical early years (the "P" in our HOPE principles) by identifying concerns during the exact period when intervention is most effective.

The Dream Team: AI, Parents, and Professionals Working Together

Nabavi and I share the belief that the true potential of AI as a personalized parenting tool emerges not from technology alone but from how it amplifies human relationships and expertise. Rather than replacing parents, pediatricians, speech-language pathologists, and developmental specialists, AI should serve as a collaborative partner in a system that has each element contributing unique strengths. Consider how this partnership might have transformed her journey with Arshaan. Her pediatrician, who had limited appointment time and relied on standardized screening tools, missed subtle indicators that her Parental GPS detected. She shared additional patterns of concern. An AI system analyzing her son's early vocalizations could have provided objective data supporting those worries. The resulting data would not replace professional judgment but enhance it with precise pattern-recognition capabilities that even an expert human observer might miss.

When she finally secured a referral for evaluation, she faced a devastating reality familiar to countless families nationwide: an interminable waitlist for services. Unwilling to let more precious developmental time slip away, she ultimately made the difficult financial sacrifice of paying out-of-pocket for a private speech-language pathologist. This crisis of access isn't unique to Nabavi. Severe shortages of developmental specialists have created a perfect storm where waitlists stretch for months or even years, forcing impossible choices on families during the exact period when children's neuroplasticity makes intervention most effective.

Predictive AI can tell you a storm is coming, but it can't shelter you from that weather, especially without accessible, affordable intervention services to act on the forecast. This gap between early detection and available intervention raises an urgent question: What role could AI play in supporting developmental therapy itself? In the next chapter, we'll explore how scientists are developing tools that will make it easier to identify children with speech and language needs, while others are designing AI solutions to work alongside human therapists—extending their capacity, reinforcing techniques between sessions, and providing families with guidance during those interminable waits. The promise is real, but so are the risks when technology moves from observing to actively shaping development.

Copilot, Not Autopilot

The technologies I've focused on in this chapter, including Nanit and Babbly, are harbingers of the AI-enhanced future of parenting technology. Again, I'm not endorsing a particular tool or service. Despite its technical promise, Babbly did not develop into the successful company Nabavi envisioned. Yet these and other tools do reflect what's coming, and this incursion isn't inherently bad. The key is to thoughtfully employ such advanced solutions as supplements. They should enhance your parental judgment, not replace it. A skilled pilot uses weather radar and other technologies to aid with the navigation of an aircraft, but the pilot makes all the key decisions. Similarly, as a parent you can benefit from AI insights while preserving your central role as your child's primary guide and advocate. By all means employ a copilot, but don't set yourself on autopilot.

Here are a few practical reminders.

Follow Your Parental GPS: Use data as one input among many. Let information and insights steer your decisions without overriding your parental instincts. Remember your unique context: Algorithms don't understand your family's specific circumstances, values, or cultural background. Your uniquely powerful relationship with your child, built through countless daily interactions, remains your most valuable guide. You've naturally collected far more data about your child in your brain than any technology could store on a chip.

Disconnect Regularly: Take breaks. Periodically disconnect from monitoring devices to reconnect with your own observational skills. You are the best and most sensitive monitor.

There Is No Normal: Development naturally varies. Most differences reflect normal disparity rather than problems requiring intervention. And predictions can be wrong. Especially with kids, whose development is wonderfully nonlinear.

Parenting by Forecast, Not Perfection

The final promise of predictive AI isn't perfection. It's confidence. Just as a forecast doesn't prevent a storm but allows us to prepare, these enhancement-focused AI tools will help parents navigate uncertainty without being paralyzed by it.

As a mother of eight, I know firsthand that perfection goes out the window early. Parenting isn't measured in flawless days but in consistent presence. Some days I congratulated myself just for making sure everyone had clean underwear. When one of them ate something resembling a vegetable, that felt like a major triumph. And yes, sometimes I lost my patience (or, occasionally, my mind) with the chaos of it all.

That's why the idea of "good enough" parenting resonates so powerfully. It acknowledges that parenting isn't about optimization. It's about persistence and responsive care. The best AI tools should support this truth, not undermine it by creating pressure for perfect execution at every developmental stage. Eventually, all kids sleep through the night, if not always in their own bed. Those three children who crowded ours are now thriving adults, living and sleeping in beds far away from my own.

The early storms that felt like they'd never end were just chapters in a much longer and still unfolding story. The question now is: What happens when AI doesn't just observe and forecast development, but begins to intervene in it? How should we as parents respond when the technology moves from predicting storms to trying to engineer the weather? That is where we turn next.

TL;DR: Chapter Review

Just as AI improved weather forecasting, predictive AI could help parents interpret developmental storms on the horizon, distinguishing normal variation from signals warranting concern. These tools don't interact with children directly; they support parents by revealing patterns, forecasting developmental leaps, and validating instincts. Used well, these technologies could sharpen your Parental GPS. Used poorly, they will erode it. Real dangers persist: biased data, privacy risks, inaccurate predictions, and the temptation to let algorithms override intuition. AI should function as a copilot, not an autopilot, informing decisions without replacing judgment. Key takeaways include:

- The "wait and see" approach to diagnosis has cost families precious intervention time, delays that matter most when children's brains are at their most plastic. AI that detects patterns in behavior and vocalizations could help parents and pediatricians act sooner.

- Enhancement-focused AI (the "E" in HOPE) could improve prediction of developmental changes in language and behavior, help parents see otherwise invisible patterns, alert us to potentially troubling changes, and supplement our strengths as caregivers.

- There is no normal in child development. Variation is the rule. Normal is the myth. Personalized AI tools may be able to help parents understand and support their child's development, pulling away from one-size-fits-all milestone charts and providing us with a more informed understanding of what's right for each child.

- AI insight and forecasting tools will be most useful as co-pilots. Don't expect them to be perfect. Don't expect that from yourself either. Together, you might be a little more informed, aware, and prepared to help.

- These tools carry downsides. Parents can become fixated on algorithmic verdicts, believing the app over their own Parental GPS. But no algorithm truly understands you, your child, or your family. If you use monitoring devices, disconnect regularly to maintain your Parental GPS. Trust your bond. You know more than any AI.

Parenting is about persistence and responsive care. AI should support this rule, not undermine it, and be used in the service of the occasionally impossible but infinitely rewarding job of raising little humans.

CHAPTER ELEVEN

Invisible Burdens

Using AI to ease the mental load and become a more present parent

Clickety-clack. Clickety-clack. Clickety-clack.

As I walked down the clinic hallway between exam rooms, the sound was everywhere. The mechanical rhythm of fingers on keyboards, echoing off sterile walls. Through each cracked door, the tableau would repeat: A clinician leans forward, shoulders tight, eyes pinned to the screen as their patient details their pain, the doctor listening with one ear and typing with two hands.

I stopped outside one room. A mother spoke softly to a pediatric colleague I'd admired for fifteen years. The mother was warm, unfailingly thorough, and obviously stretched to the bone. "It's her left ear," the mother said, voice edged with worry. "A pounding. And sometimes her hearing . . . almost like a fullness—"

Clickety-clack.

"Mm-hmm," my colleague murmured, not looking up.

On the exam table, the girl's thumbs paused over her tablet. She glanced at her mother, then at the glowing monitor. She watched her mother watch the clinician watch the cursor.

No one made eye contact.

Electronic health records (EHRs) appeared in exam rooms promising efficiency and safety—and completely rerouting physicians' attention. By 2016, doctors were spending roughly half their workdays on administrative tasks. Emergency physicians averaged four thousand mouse clicks per shift—four thousand tiny actions that required them to look away from the patient beside them. Observational studies found clinicians spending nearly half of each visit staring at a screen. Less than one-sixth of the time maintaining crucial eye contact.

"You're thinking about what you need to document, or how do I navigate the EHR system," Lloyd Minor, an ENT colleague and dean of Stanford Medicine, said in a 2017 interview with PBS. "Not, 'How do I assimilate this information to provide the best care advice to the patient?'"

Then we went home and opened our laptops—another eighty-six minutes on average every night. We even coined a term for it: pajama time. It sounded like a comforting bedtime ritual; nothing about it was cozy. This was time I should have been spending with my children. Time that I yearned to devote to them. Yet I was stuck playing catch-up, doing clerical work and glorified data entry. All in the name of efficiency.

Burnout surged; primary care was hit hardest. Survey after survey pointed to the EHR as the single most important stressor, leading to lost work-life balance, after-hours charting, the sense of clicking more than caring. Like so many of my colleagues, I found myself thinking: *If I didn't have to do all this documentation, I would actually love my job.*

We went into medicine to be healers. The EHR was making us clerks. Some didn't wait to see if things would get better. They left. A disproportionate number were women in care-heavy specialties. And they didn't leave because they stopped caring about patients, but because the system made it nearly impossible to show that care in the room.

Clickety-clack.

The technology had turned them into automatons.

A Promising Intelligence

Walk down that same hallway now, over fifteen years after the rapid proliferation of EHRs, and something's different.

The clickety-clack has faded. In its place: voices, the telltale signs of human presence and interaction. A mother's worried explanation. A doctor's follow-up question. The rustle of exam-table paper. Laughter from behind a closed door. Genuine laughter. Ordinary conversation, once drowned out by keyboards, is suddenly sweeping through the halls again.

Through that same cracked door, the scene has transformed. Yes, we still have to remind patients to put away their phones and tablets, but physicians are able to focus. Now I see a colleague facing a mother and daughter. Her eyes are on them. Her hands are free to gesture while explaining, to gently examine an ear, to rest on a worried shoulder in that universal act of reassurance. Her mind and her heart are deeply engaged.

The small talk that previously disappeared has returned.

"How's soccer going?"

"Did your mom's surgery go OK?"

"I heard you made honor roll. Congratulations!"

Throwaway exchanges that aren't throwaway at all. Eye contact that says: I see you, not just your chart.

What changed? AI.

At the University of Chicago Medicine, where I practice, we use a tool called Abridge, an AI-powered ambient scribe that University of Pittsburgh Medical Center cardiologist Shiv Rao launched in 2018 to solve the problem that had been crushing us all. What started as one physician's attempt to reclaim his own practice became one of the most rapidly adopted AI tools in healthcare. When the Permanente Medical Group rolled out a related technology across Northern California and tracked 2.5 million encounters over a year, researchers found that physicians had reclaimed an estimated 15,791 hours of documentation time, or 1,794 eight-hour workdays.

Relief showed up in the exam room. Eighty-four percent of physicians said patient interactions improved. And those patients noticed, too. More than half rated visit quality higher. Adoption moved fast: In just one year, physician use of AI nearly doubled.

My question: If the technology exists to give physicians their attention back, why are parents still buried in logistics? We now have proof that we can develop technologies to lighten the administrative workload—and the unnecessary cognitive labor—of people toiling in an incredibly demanding, high-stakes field. Parenting is just as taxing. And parents are raising the next generation, doing our best to prepare our children for a complex, ever changing world. We deserve a little help from AI, too. What would a parenting AI copilot actually look like? Before we start exploring that possibility, let's remain in the medical field briefly, as it offers some helpful guidelines.

At my hospital, for example, the AI scribe technology operates in the background. Our patients aren't interacting with robots. The technology is invisible. A phone sits quietly on the counter, its microphone capturing the conversation. The AI-powered software behind Abridge transforms spoken words into text, and by the time the visit ends, it has drafted the necessary documentation—patient history, exam notes, assessments, plans, and coding support to help with the painstaking medical-plan reimbursement process. The physician reviews and edits what the AI tool suggests. What took a human twenty minutes of clicking takes AI two.

The work we actually *trained* for is back. For the first time in years, the connection between doctor and patient feels whole again. And pajama time is dropping, too. Doctors who once spent eighty-six minutes every night finishing charts are logging off earlier, some completing their work at the hospital and walking through their front door before dinner for the first time in years.

Screens haven't disappeared from exam rooms, but they've stopped demanding our gaze. The AI hums in the background, doing what computers should have been doing all along: lifting unnecessary burdens so humans can perform irreplaceable human work. Doctors who were considering leaving are staying. Those on the edge are finding their way back to doing what they love. And the popularity of these tools is increasing. The percentage of doctors who said they used AI in their practice jumped from 38 to 66 percent from 2023 to 2024.

The transition hasn't been seamless. Some professionals still hesitate. They worry about accuracy, for good reason, or bristle at the thought of having to learn a new workflow. Others find the process of editing the AI notes frustrating—for instance, removing conversational asides that didn't need to be recorded. And yes, there's concern that we may be providing training data for our own replacements. Yet the impact here and now is unmistakable: thousands of clinicians, millions of encounters, and a tangible return of presence. We're getting back to being doctors again.

The design lesson here is transferrable to potential parenting solutions. The AI solution didn't try to be the doctor. It offered assistance and relief, not replacement. It didn't simulate empathy or examine the patient or make the diagnosis. It removed the barrier, the relentless documentation that was preventing physicians from doing what only humans can do: see the person in front of them, really listen, be fully present.

Technology's HOPE

Up to now, we've evaluated how AI can directly support children's development. What aligns with our HOPE framework and what threatens it, how to tell enhancement from replacement, how to protect the irreplaceable power of human connection. Here's the uncomfortable truth: None of it helps if parents aren't available in the first place.

As parents we are a population on the brink. We're experiencing burnout at rates that rival physicians' recent statistics. Physicians were buried under administrative tasks that pulled them away from the work that mattered. Parents face something similar. On a daily basis, we're beaten down by the visible and invisible labor that comes with managing a household and raising children. We're constantly task switching, rarely fully present. The physician's crisis had a solution. Our crisis does not. Yet.

Every parent I've ever met would tear down walls for their child. But not every parent can. In my twenty-five years working with families, I've watched that painful reality play out again and again. Remember Michelle, the little girl with the crystal-blue eyes whose cochlear implant should have changed everything? Michelle's mother wanted her child to thrive. To have doors opened rather than closed. For her daughter to grow up unbound by circumstances she didn't choose. To build a life filled with possibility and joy. In her I saw a mother doing everything humanly possible. Sadly, the systems that should have supported her had actively worked against her efforts.

We're all fighting some version of this battle. The barriers look different. For some it's poverty, lack of childcare, health crises, or the crushing isolation of raising children without the proverbial village pitching in. Yet the parent forced to endure a Zoom meeting in their car while half-watching their son's soccer game through the windshield deserves better, too. No matter the particulars of our circumstances, most of us are trying to find that balance between being the parents we desperately want to be and being the parents our current reality actually allows us to be.

In my second book, *Parent Nation*, I argued that we cannot keep asking individual parents to overcome structural failures through sheer force of will. Now, with AI flooding into family life, that argument becomes even more urgent. Because depending on which barriers parents face, and whether we choose to address them, AI could either offer genuine relief or become one more way we excuse ourselves from building the support systems every family deserves. It could deepen the very divides that crushed Michelle's mother, making human attention a luxury only certain families can afford, or it could chip away at that divide by easing all parents' labor.

The Same Wound

Humans evolved to raise children in small, closely knit villages, but in modern society we have dismantled that architecture and assigned the task to one or two people. Then we called their inevitable exhaustion "burnout." I thought I knew what it meant to be an overwhelmed parent when I was part of a two-person team. But it does not even begin to compare to the weight one has to carry when one holds all the cards.

When my late husband, Don, died in 2012, our kids were aged seven, ten, and thirteen, and I suddenly had complete responsibility for every system, every detail, every decision. Every emotional rollercoaster and apparent emergency. At 11:00 p.m., while I was straining to finish my surgical notes after finally getting the kids to bed, the questions would start surfacing. Did Asher have his permission slip signed? When was Genevieve's orthodontist appointment again? What had I forgotten this time? The invisible work became suddenly, crushingly present. I couldn't parent the way I wanted to parent or do what I knew I was supposed to do. I was barely making it through the day.

In recent decades, several societal shifts have intersected in ways that place enormous pressure on parents, particularly in the U.S. One major development has been the transfer of economic risk away from government bodies and corporations and onto individual households. Political scientist Jacob Hacker calls this the Great Risk Shift. Previous generations traded mobility for stability. You worked one job in one career, and the company or governmental organization rewarded your loyalty and diligence with a reliable income and a retirement plan. Where employers and government once shouldered economic risk through pensions, stable employment, and robust safety nets, families now bear a significant brunt of this risk. That handoff has produced deep financial instability: Nearly 11 percent of American families now live in poverty. Many others struggle to afford basic expenses. Childcare is a particularly heavy burden, with over half of American parents allocating more than 20 percent of their income to it.

Research also shows that growing economic inequality and a strong education's long-term benefits to earning potential and financial security drive parents to intensify their efforts to secure their children's future opportunities. When I was growing up in the 1980s, my highly educated parents rarely if ever asked about my homework. But as economists Matthias Doepke and Fabrizio Zilibotti argue in their research on how economic conditions shape parenting styles, today's economic landscape has transformed parenting into a frantic, anxiety-filled endeavor.

These economic shifts coincided with the rise of intensive parenting, which we discussed in chapter three. This style of raising kids demands we involve ourselves in nearly all aspects of our children's lives, and orient our own lives around their needs. Parents today spend significantly more time doing hands-on childcare than previous generations. And still we worry it's not enough! In part we have social media and its stream of advice, best practices, and perfectly curated playrooms to thank for that phenomenon. But it's not just the platforms.

Raising children in this modern pressure cooker is causing significant harm. More than 40 percent of American parents report that most days they are so stressed they cannot function. The situation is so dire that the surgeon general issued a public health advisory in 2024 calling attention to parental mental health and well-being challenges. This might sound dramatic to some, but it's essential. Framing parents' challenges as a public health issue is a critical step toward addressing these problems. When we identified doctors' problems accurately, the system changed: Instead of being forced to attend resilience workshops, we were empowered with new tools.

On the other hand, when we mislabel parents' struggles, we prescribe the wrong treatment: meditation apps, self-care Sundays, tips to "optimize your morning routine." Worse, we invite the market to sell replacements: social robots for companionship, AI tutors for bandwidth we don't have, algorithmic entertainment to occupy children while adults are buried in logistics. Name the problem correctly and the solutions become structural: paid leave; affordable childcare; flexible work; and, from an AI perspective, tools like the physician's scribe that remove barriers to presence, not stand in for it. We need solutions that handle the cognitive underbrush, including scheduling, insurance forms, meal planning, permission slips, and transportation choreography, so parents can focus on what only humans can do.

Hacking Their Own Solutions

As a culture, we've fantasized about domestic relief since Rosie the housekeeping robot rolled through the Jetsons' living room in 1962. More than sixty years later, a real-world Rosie has yet to materialize. Sure, this is partly due to the technical sophistication required of a humanoid housekeeper. But there's another explanation, too: For all the billions of dollars spent on developing AI tools and solutions for various industries, unpaid domestic labor has been virtually ignored. The gap is so notable that the University of Oxford launched a major research project called DomesticAI to examine the potential for artificial intelligence to free up time now locked into unpaid housework and care labor.

DomesticAI has already helped identify one major barrier standing in the way of parents receiving the kinds of AI tools that offer genuine, helpful relief. The people building AI tools for the most part don't carry the burdens of modern caretaking themselves. If you don't bear the cognitive load, you can't accurately assess its weight. The work is invisible to you.

The DomesticAI research team, led by Oxford sociologist Ekaterina Hertog, asked AI experts from Japan and the UK to judge which domestic tasks might realistically be automated in the next ten years. They found that assessments varied considerably based on gender and cultural norms. The male Japanese experts were particularly pessimistic about automation in the domestic sphere. Hertog and her coauthors hypothesized that this was the result of dramatic gender disparities in Japanese households, where women, on average, assume 90 percent of domestic work. (Globally, that figure stands closer to 75 percent.) Male experts were also more likely to point out that automating many domestic tasks would be quite expensive and therefore out of reach of most consumers. Female experts, on the other hand, were more excited by the potential for technology to take over domestic tasks. Alas, women hold just 22 percent of AI jobs worldwide and represent less than 14 percent of senior leadership roles in AI.

So here we are. In 2026, we have countless AI applications for work and entertainment, but purpose-built parenting copilots barely exist.

Thankfully, parents aren't waiting. They're hacking their own solutions, finding ways to use existing AI to address the mental load that runs like a ticker tape through our heads.

The Mom Who Unlocked ChatGPT

Lilian Schmidt, a German mother of two living in Switzerland, reached her breaking point in 2024. It wasn't the big things. Her partner was supportive, actively involved with raising their three-year-old daughter and serving as the default parent for his fourteen-year-old son from a previous relationship. She had a good job as a corporate brand strategist. She had resources, but she was also operating an invisible database in her head that never shut off. And she had the sense that her partner's brain wasn't quite as crowded as her own.

In fact, a 2023 study from the Council on Contemporary Families found that during the pandemic, partnered mothers spent more than twice as much time as fathers on cognitive labor, or the invisible thinking work of scheduling, planning, and organizing. This isn't about physical tasks. It's about the constant cognitive hum: remembering which kid needs the viola on Tuesday, who's out of socks, when the permission slip is due, what everyone will eat for lunch, whether the baby outgrew her onesies. Lilian says the mothers in her community often feel like married single moms.

When Lilian returned to work after her maternity leave, her days followed a punishing rhythm. She and her partner both worked full time, so they'd wake up, rouse their kids, and manage the standard morning chaos. One of them would drop their daughter at day care, and Lilian would quickly find herself in back-to-back meetings. Typically, she would race to day care pickup, then walk through the door to their home with a massively overstimulated child who needed her devoted attention. Her daughter would wail. She'd want to be carried. And Lilian had to soothe her baby while getting dinner ready.

Her teen son needed attention, too, albeit of a different sort. Naturally, he wanted them to be at his soccer practice and games. But their daughter commanded most of their time. "For three and a half years, bedtime was an absolute disaster," she confessed to me when we spoke. "It took two to three hours to get her to bed, and at the end of the day, everyone was just exhausted and heartbroken. There was never a break."

Desperate, Lilian did something unexpected.

She asked ChatGPT, the free AI chatbot on her phone, to be her co-parent. She'd already experimented with various AI tools at work, so she had some familiarity. For instance, Lilian knew that one should never settle for the first answer. One night, after finally getting her daughter to sleep, she spent an hour interacting with the AI. She knew that these tools do well when you basically give them a job description, so she told ChatGPT that it was going to be a household manager and personal chef. Once she'd refined her instructions to the AI, the results astonished her. Lilian posted about her decision on TikTok, and within days the clip had gone viral with nearly 800,000 views. In the video, Lilian shared the prompt that transformed her life.

> *I'm a full-time working mom with [insert number] kids aged [insert ages], and I am DONE carrying the entire mental load of my family alone. From now on, I want you to step fully into the role of my co-parent. Think with me and FOR me. Help me manage the day-to-day tasks that constantly live in my head—from meal planning and grocery lists (organized by aisle), to finding the perfect birthday gifts and writing cards, to packing lists for daycare, day trips, or family holidays based on weather and plans. Important: Always think ahead and anticipate my needs and those of my family and kids.*

The prompt worked.

Normally, I wouldn't advocate AI doing your thinking for you, but we're not dealing with rocket science or ethical debates here. Lilian wanted to reclaim the joy in motherhood. She did not want to delegate parenthood to technology. Just the opposite: She wanted the magic and true connection back for herself and her youngest. She'd been stuck in survival mode. Now when she needs a grocery list, ChatGPT organizes it by aisle. That small efficiency saves her twenty minutes at the store. Twenty minutes that means she walks through the door before her daughter has a meltdown instead of after the meltdown has begun. After the administrative coup, she spent another hour interacting with Chat-GPT, asking for ideas for a better bedtime routine. "It gave me advice that I'd never heard before," Lilian recalled. The AI suggested allowing her daughter to be active while Lilian was reading her a story, but only if she remained on her bed. She could jump or wriggle as much as she liked as long as she did so in that sacred bedtime space. "I figured I'd try it, since there was nothing dangerous about the suggestion, and it worked. My daughter fell asleep within five minutes," Lilian said. "Since then, bedtime has become so much calmer."

With their daughter sleeping better, Lilian and her husband have gained back as much as three hours per night. "We're doing things as a family that we never had time to do before, like handcrafts, baking, Christmas decorations," she enthused. "Before we were in survival mode, trying to get through the day. Now we get to ask, 'What should we do today?'"

The impact spread far beyond her household. Within weeks, parents were copying her prompt, translating it into Dutch, Spanish, French. Mostly mothers but fathers, too. There was some added messaging to do on her part, as she had to make sure they understood the limitations of tools like ChatGPT, and that AI should never replace real-life experts like pediatricians. And her followers were modifying the prompt for their families and sharing the results. In the comments, exhausted parents poured out their own discoveries and hacks:

"When I'm overwhelmed with so much to get done with work and the kids and house etc. I list it all out and ask chat to help me be on the sofa by x time or in bed by x time. It gives me a full timed to-do list and it works every time."

"I prompt it to create a recipe with what is left in the fridge."

"I gave it background on my baby's sleep and it tracked it over a few days then [I] told it to act like a sleep consultant and it tells me what to do for naps."

These weren't tech-savvy early adopters experimenting with bleeding-edge tools. These were parents who'd discovered that the free AI chatbot on their phone could handle some of the invisible work that was crushing them.

Beyond One Viral Mom

Lilian's prompt was splashed across news outlets and shared across continents in a matter of weeks. The viral response revealed something deeper than a clever hack. It exposed a shared global exhaustion among parents carrying invisible mental loads. And the transformation they described wasn't just about logistics. It was emotional. The relief of not being the household's default problem-solver. The space to breathe. The ability to be present instead of planning.

"AI helped me become a less stressed and more present mom," Lilian shared with me. "Bedtime was a huge stressor for us and for [our daughter]. We were always fighting and negotiating. Now it has become something she looks forward to, and the change has brought so much calm into our family. And when I don't feel so alone with my mental load, I have more mental and emotional bandwidth for her. When you feel more relaxed and calm, you can be more attentive. It's not only me. I really believe she's benefiting. I'm a better mom."

When someone or something else carries the cognitive load, you can finally see and truly, fully *be* with the child in front of you.

Mapping the Invisible Work

Inspired by Lilian's story, parents improvised, teaching one another survival strategies through TikTok comment sections. Lilian's prompt has been copied thousands of times. Parents are iterating on it, adapting it, sharing what works. It's grassroots innovation born from necessity. While it reminds me of how physicians worked before formal AI scribes, the comparison only stretches so far. Physician documentation was a bounded problem: structured, repetitive, ripe for pattern recognition. Family life is messier, and comprehensive AI solutions are still in their infancy. When physicians improvised workarounds, institutions eventually stepped in with purpose-built tools. For parents, those solutions are still in the uncertain, early-exploration phase. Like the researchers at DomesticAI, I wanted to better understand how AI might genuinely help with domestic responsibilities. The first step was to consider the full landscape of domestic work. I knew just whom to reach out to.

In 2018, Eve Rodsky was hurrying to pick up her son from his toddler transition program. She had a breast pump on the passenger seat of her car. An important contract that needed to be reviewed and signed lay on her lap. Then she received a text from her husband. He wrote to let her know that he was surprised she hadn't bought any blueberries the last time she went shopping. Blueberries?! She was effectively working two full-time jobs as a mother and a professional. Yet that passive-aggressive observation from her husband triggered a new line of thinking. She started cataloging all the invisible labor she was responsible for in their household, tasks that so many mothers are expected to handle. What began as informal brainstorming—what she called her "Sh*t I Do" spreadsheet—quickly evolved as Rodsky applied her professional expertise in organizational management to the domestic sphere. She researched and wrote a bestselling book, *Fair Play*, and designed a corresponding deck of cards designed to help partners rebalance their domestic workload. Her goal wasn't to point fingers. The cards were designed to shine a light on just how much goes into running a household and ensuring the division of labor is balanced.

When I called to tell Rodsky what I was working on, she sent me a generous goody bag stuffed with Fair Play materials, including one hundred cards. I fanned them out, row upon row, across my kitchen island, until the landscape of domestic life sat there, uncomfortably visible. Looking at those tasks, the overwhelming reality of 2012 came rushing back to me. Thrust into the life of single parenting after Don died, I was fortunate enough to have Lola, our lifesaving nanny, and a supportive family and community. That's more help than many parents ever get. And still it felt impossible. I was buried under a mountain of invisible demands with seemingly no way out.

Even yes/no questions were surprisingly complex. Lola would ask me simple things—"Should I pick up milk?" "Does Amelie need a snack for tomorrow?"—that were nonetheless taxing, since they required knowledge to answer. Do we have milk? Are we running low? What else is on Amelie's schedule tomorrow? Every question demanded that I scour and then pull from a mental database I hadn't even realized I was maintaining. A database jammed into my brain alongside the similarly complex one required for my surgical practice.

That afternoon, sorting through Rodsky's deck, I finally had names for all the invisible burdens I had been carrying as a parent. Each card referred to a different system I'd been running in my head. Groceries. Laundry. Calendar Keeper. Medical Point Person. Morning Routine. Hard Questions. Magical Beings. Some cards in the deck, called Daily Grind with little coffee cup icons ☕, denoted repetitive, time-sensitive tasks. Others were wild cards designed to highlight unpredictable emergencies. Together they mapped the full scope of running a household, raising children, and maintaining a life, with the goal of helping couples identify and divvy up tasks more evenly.

Could AI take on some of them?

My mind kept returning to the clinic. Before ambient AI, we'd tried human scribes to reduce the EHR burden. We tested stationing a person in the corner during appointments, typing furiously, trying to capture everything while remaining invisible. Helpful, but costly. The health care system couldn't support an extra professional in every room. Then a number of advances in AI, including the evolution of automatic speech recognition, made a technological solution possible. Employing a whole new set of workers wasn't realistic, but deploying AI software? That was a different story. The relief was finally scalable.

Could something analogous work here? I sorted through the cards. Which ones could AI shoulder without warping the meaning of family? Which would it break against? Where does the scribe model hold? And where does it collapse?

Where AI Helps

Rodsky separates domestic work into three layers: conception (noticing), planning (deciding how), and execution (doing). As I studied the cards, I considered our HOPE principles and saw clearly that when it comes to domestic labor, AI can absolutely be used to Enhance human productivity, so long as we are careful to safeguard Human connection in the process. AI is best suited to augmenting and building upon parents' planning and executing skills. Noticing remains stubbornly, beautifully human.

This is where you demonstrate to your loved ones: I see you and value you. And yet, once you've done the noticing, AI can take real work off your plate. It can help with planning and execution in ways that weren't possible even a few years ago.

Consider one of the Fair Play cards: Groceries. Grocery shopping doesn't start at the store. For me it began with knowing that mac and cheese was an absolutely necessary staple, but that Asher wouldn't eat it without ketchup. So both were essential. Another foundational rule: Amelie wanted rice and tofu on her birthday. (I don't pretend to have kids with normal palates.) Given this information, which has to be noticed, verified, obtained, and shared by a human, AI can generate grocery lists and meal plans. You put in the strange and often inexplicable rules and infinite conditions, and the technology can scour the Internet and suggest which stores should have the best prices on which items (and which are on the way home from work). In these areas, AI is assisting with both planning and execution. Granted, AI's execution capabilities are somewhat limited. Technology can handle cognitive work like lists, schedules, and research, but physical tasks still require human hands. Someone still has to stop at the store, cook the meals, pack the bags. For now, at least. But with the help of AI, you arrive at that execution stage in a much better place mentally. You're not quite as exhausted.

The beauty of the Fair Play cards is that they surface all the tasks involved, the invisible labor required. The Medical Point Person card doesn't just indicate that its owner is responsible for making appointments. It points out that this person must remember which antibiotic caused hives last winter, what the school nurse needs on file, when camp will need immunization records, and where to *find* those records. The Meal Planning card doesn't just require that its owner decide what to serve for dinner; it means keeping track of who hates tomatoes this week, what's in the pantry at the moment, and the collision of everyone's schedules and dietary needs.

Again, AI can assist with the planning and (partial) execution layers of these tasks. AI can cross-reference parent and school calendars to suggest a good time to schedule a well-child care visit. It can produce a meal plan based on preferences and restrictions you indicate. But the parent must remain the chief conception and connection officer. The CCCO in Family, Inc. You are the only one who can notice that your child is calmed by their stuffy, but not a lollipop, after shots at the doctor's office. You're the one who knows that your toddler has been struggling to eat enough protein this week. And of course, you're the one to pack that beloved stuffy and take it, and your child, to the appointment—and to prepare the hamburger that will inject some much needed protein into your toddler's diet. Without cheese, of course, because he might be lactose intolerant.

Many of the Fair Play cards fall into a similar category: They require a human to handle the conception and some elements of execution, whereas AI could be used to enhance the planning and part of the execution. And of course "could" doesn't mean "should" for everyone. My friend Liz approaches vacation planning like a jigsaw puzzle. She derives joy from finding a hotel that's a perfect mix of relaxing and family-friendly, searching for fun activities to match her kids' interests, and identifying the best local restaurants, then fitting them together in a schedule that leaves time for the unexpected. Another friend views meal planning and recipe development as a creative outlet. The goal isn't to outsource everything possible to AI; my hope is that technology gives us more freedom to choose. To hand off what drains you so you can hold on to what restores you.

And with certain tasks, I don't think we should be handing off anything at all. To be honest, you could probably file all one hundred Fair Play cards into that "shared by AI and human" category. And yet, some of them jumped out to me as too sacrosanct, too vital to the parent-child bond, to allow AI into the fold.

These uniquely human responsibilities include things like:

Magical Beings: the card for Santa and the Tooth Fairy. (My kids' tooth fairy's name was Glenda, of all things!)

Middle-of-the-Night Comfort: Although exhausting, these moments build attachment; you show your child that you're there to love and protect them and deepen your connection.

Hard Questions: Of course we'd all love to pass these off to a chatbot, but your answers, no matter how confident or uncertain, strengthen your bond.

Other cards, including Gestures of Love, Showing Up and Participating, In-law Relationships, and Values and Good Deeds, are equally human. These cards represent the Human connection that our HOPE principles remind us to protect above all else. Maybe some of you would prefer to have humanoid robots take your place at the table during family dinners with your in-laws, but experiences like these add up to what makes a family a family. The rituals, the comfort, the presence, the meaningful moments that no one notices until they're missing.

When Amelie was three and afraid of thunderstorms, no AI could have provided the middle-of-the-night comfort she needed. Technology could not have replicated the particular, nuanced tone of my voice, or the way I'd carry her to the window to show her the storm was far away, the ritual we'd developed together. Nor would I have wanted it to! These intently human moments are especially important in early childhood. The toddler who will only fall asleep if you sing "Twinkle, Twinkle, Little Star" exactly three times—no more, no less. The infant learning that when they cry, someone comes. The simple, beautiful act of holding your child close. These are the foundational pieces of secure attachment.

No matter how taxed we may be as parents, there are cards in the deck, sacred acts of showing and providing care, that simply must remain the sole responsibility of humans. Not because we lack the technology. One day, AI might be able to perfectly replicate the middle-of-the-night voice I used to soothe Amelie. These interactions must remain human because they make us human. HOPE exists to defend this irreplaceable bond.

Looking back at Lilian Schmidt's viral story, we see that her use of AI fits the ideal pattern. She was offloading planning and execution work, while conception, and all the relationship work, stayed firmly in human hands. She was protecting the cards that belonged to humans by handing off the ones that didn't have to. Lilian herself drew this distinction clearly, stating: "When you're old and your kids are all grown up, they'll remember if you were present, not if you wrote the perfect grocery list."

The Second-Order Effects

This echoes exactly what physicians have learned in recent years: AI can handle the paperwork so humans can do the irreplaceable work. And often, when AI is used in this way, there are ripple benefits that extend beyond the person using the tool. These are benefits that researchers Elizabeth Altman and Beth Humberd at the University of Massachusetts Lowell call second-order effects. A colleague recently shared a perfect illustration. On an unexpectedly rainy day at home with their nine-year-old, her husband used ChatGPT to plan activities to fill the time. Father and son baked cookies, troubleshot fixes when they were missing ingredients, and problem-solved together.

The real win? Her husband never called her at work to ask for ideas, something he was known to do in the past. The mother enjoying an uninterrupted workday was a second-order effect. AI removed her role as the household's default problem solver. Technology made one family member self-sufficient not by replacing his relationship with his wife, but by removing his reliance on her for every logistical answer. She didn't feel left out; this role wasn't a cherished one. Thanks to intelligent technology, her child enjoyed more humanity, more presence and attention, not less.

Faster meal planning means more time on the floor playing. Fewer forgotten permission slips mean less last-minute panic. A grocery list organized by aisle means less time spent shopping and more quality time doing projects together, reading, or even that holy grail of all parents: an earlier bedtime for their kids. A parent who walks through the door with mental and emotional bandwidth is a parent who can kneel down and say, "Tell me about your day."

Good Friction, Bad Friction

When I asked Rodsky about this future in which AI helps to liberate parents, and especially mothers, from overwhelming and inequitable workloads, she made a fascinating suggestion. She'd like to see a technology that could manage another invisible strain on households: the minor friction points and little annoyances that contribute to resentment. One father I spoke with, Greg Neufeld, had been hearing the same gentle suggestion from his wife, Danielle, for years. She often noted that he could be more present with their four-year-old son, Maverick. She noticed moments when Greg seemed distracted, responding with "uh-huh" instead of fully tuning in. But somehow her point never quite landed.

Greg and Danielle live in Delray Beach, Florida, with their three kids, and they host a podcast called *The Most Important Thing*, about building family culture and leadership at home. They're thoughtful about the role of technology in their household. Their kids don't use screens, and the couple has embraced AI as a tool to help them be more present, not less. As part of this work, Greg started using an AI-powered recorder that summarized his daily interactions. Every morning for a week, the technology flagged the same pattern: You were a little short with Maverick. When his son said something, the device noted, Greg responded with "uh-huh," and it inquired whether he was on his phone or distracted. Then the AI proposed that next time, he should lean in a little bit and ask his son, "What was that?"

Stripped of any perceived judgment, and delivered without emotional charge, the feedback resonated. Greg saw his distracted responses in a new light and resolved to change. As for Danielle, she laughed when she heard the results. She'd been saying the same thing for years. Ideally, Greg would've listened to her in the first place, and there's a risk that overreliance on technology could degrade those lines of communication. Yet she wasn't bitter that it required the intervention of artificial intelligence to prompt a change in her husband's behavior. She was happy with the results, and optimistic that this shift in his awareness might lead him to listen to such suggestions in the future.

Ultimately, the tool helped Greg become more self-aware. He'd review his interactions and see for himself how he responded, then adapt, allowing him to connect more deeply with his son. Similarly, the physician's AI scribe eliminated the clicking, the documentation, the glow of the screen between doctor and patient that was blocking those critical connections. In neither case did the technology perform the hard human work of caregiving: the trust, the listening, the feeling seen.

A Historical Word of Warning

Every "labor-saving" domestic technology in history has come with an unintended consequence: raised expectations. Washing machines didn't liberate women; they raised cleanliness standards. Dishwashers didn't return lost hours; they raised the bar for spotless kitchens. By the 1970s, despite decades of appliances, women were spending nearly as much time on housework as their grandmothers had in the 1920s. The tools changed, but the expected work remained, and even expanded.

Now AI appears to be following this pattern in the workplace. If this extends to the home, we'll have traded one burden for another. If Chat-GPT can plan perfect meals in seconds, does that mean you're now expected to provide restaurant-quality dinners every night? If other parents are using AI to optimize their children's schedules, does even "good enough" parenting require you to do the same? Lilian Schmidt herself is wary of these possibilities. She's not using AI to become a perfect parent. She's using it to become a *present* one. The grocery list organized by aisle doesn't make her a better mother. It gets her home twenty minutes earlier, which means twenty more minutes on the floor with her daughter. This is a distinction we must keep top of mind as we consider how and whether to embed AI into our domestic routines. I urge you to safeguard any time that is returned to you, refusing to reallocate it toward the clearing of ever rising bars. Use that time to simply be with your child.

Emerging Domestic Tools

While ChatGPT is a general tool, used for everything from writing essays to assisting with grocery shopping, some companies are developing purpose-built domestic AI tools. One such startup, Duckbill, offers a virtual executive assistant to help with time-consuming tasks like booking doctor's appointments, managing sports schedules for your kids, or staying on top of prescription refills for your aging parents. Duckbill doesn't read your child bedtime stories or comfort them after a nightmare. Instead, it works as your assistant, clearing obstacles and administrative distractions so you have the time and energy to devote to the more important work of parenting.

In addition to virtual help, there are indications that physical household robots à la the Jetsons' Rosie could one day become a reality. Startups are building them and testing them in real homes. These machines appear to be capable of clearing dishes, folding laundry, handling the tangible chores that computer code alone cannot touch. Given that they are the products of startups and technology companies, however, we don't have a complete understanding of their unintended consequences, or exactly when they will be ready for mass deployment.

The Inequality Trap

Versatile domestic robots are likely be very expensive at the start, yet high-quality virtual AI solutions may be too expensive for most parents as well. If we're not careful, domestic AI tools could further solidify a two-tier system where human attention becomes a luxury good. Wealthy families will use AI as an enhancement: Purpose-built tools plus human nannies plus stay-at-home parents will equal "artisanal parenting" with unlimited human interaction and minimal screen time. Meanwhile, working families will be left with AI as a replacement: free chatbots and algorithmic entertainment filling the gaps that impossible work schedules with no societal support create. We've watched this pattern unfold with food. Ultra-processed products promised to democratize nutrition but created new problems instead. Human connection, I worry, could become the new organic.

Imagine a tablet propped on a high-chair tray, an AI voice responding to a toddler's babbling as Mom arrives home, exhausted, after her third overnight shift of the week. A chatbot patiently answering a four-year-old's endless "why" questions. Not as a choice, but by necessity, the digital proxy filling the void the parent's punishing work schedule opened up. As journalist Nellie Bowles documented, this has already happened with tablets and phones: "As more screens appear in the lives of the poor, screens are disappearing from the lives of the rich. The richer you are, the more you spend to be offscreen." As noted earlier, tech-promoting Silicon Valley executives send their children to Waldorf schools promising "back-to-nature, nearly screen-free education," while less affluent communities see more screens integrated into both schools and homes.

Better than Nothing?

This is where the great moral sleight of hand occurs. When faced with an overwhelmed parent, the easy counterargument is that a chatbot is better than no interaction at all. That logic becomes a powerful wedge, justifying the substitution of AI for genuine human presence. It urges us to glide down the slippery slope of replacement, rationalizing the introduction of a digital proxy because the real thing has been made economically impossible.

To be clear, there are genuine edge cases where the counterfactual is real. Children in war-torn regions. Orphanages with impossible caregiver ratios. Homes where abuse or severe mental illness means a parent truly cannot provide safe interaction. Foster systems stretched beyond breaking. In these situations, AI that offers some responsiveness may genuinely be better than humans going without their physical and emotional needs being met at all.

The danger is when "better than nothing" stops being an exception we're forced to adopt and becomes the default—when we start designing AI for a world where parents won't be present at all instead of one where they're more present than ever. When we treat structural failure as a permanent constraint and settle for technology as a stopgap. If we adopt that approach, we're not solving the problem. We're giving up.

The developmental implications are staggering. We already know that early interaction shapes brain architecture. The neurons that get wired together through responsive human interaction don't care about zip codes, but the uneven distribution of these interactions could be massively impactful. If AI deepens the divide, creating interaction deserts in working-class communities while preserving interaction abundance in wealthy ones, we will be manufacturing inequality at the neurological level.

This brings me back to Ekaterina Hertog's finding: The people building these tools often can't see the work they're meant to address. They certainly don't experience the impossible choice between being present with your child or keeping your job, between providing rich interaction or keeping the lights on. When builders are far from the burden, they don't just under-build. They build in ways that deepen existing inequalities.

The solution is not to keep AI away from struggling families. That would simply maintain the status quo in which they are crushed by invisible labor. The solution is to ensure that as AI continues to proliferate, tech companies design increasingly affordable tools that genuinely reduce the burden for all families, rather than create new dependencies. That means free or subsidized access to high-quality tools and design that prioritizes execution-layer work, including the logistics, tasks, and cognitive load that prevent presence, over the replacement of human interaction. We need tools that make human connection easier, not less frequent. We need to demand systems that give every family access to the nourishment they need.

Michelle's story taught me that technology alone, even in the form of a $100,000 cochlear implant, means nothing without the human interaction to support it. The same is true for AI parenting solutions. The question is whether we as a society and a culture will ensure that AI helps *all* parents. And whether we will allow the better-than-nothing excuse to become a moral loophole that justifies a two-tiered system where human presence becomes rarefied into a luxury good. In considering these issues, I keep thinking about Laura, Michelle's mother. The woman who stuck to every therapy schedule, maintained her impossible hope for her daughter's future, all while working nights, facing unemployment, and navigating systems designed to be intractable.

What if she'd had a copilot?

Not a replacement for the human village she never enjoyed. Not a stand-in for paid leave, affordable childcare, or the structural supports that should have been her birthright, and which I will continue to advocate for. What she could have used was a tool that lifted even a fraction of what she was carrying. The insurance battles, the endless scheduling, the crushing cognitive load that made each day feel like swimming through wet concrete.

Would it have changed everything? No. The barriers she faced were systemic; no app dissolves structural injustice.

We cannot rebuild parents' villages overnight. But we can build something that buys parents time while we fight for the changes every family deserves.

The danger, of course, is that AI becomes another excuse for inaction, another reason human attention becomes a luxury good. That we design tools for a world where parents cannot be present, instead of designing tools that help them be present.

We cannot let that happen.

The way forward is both/and: We must demand structural change and technological relief. Policy and tools. The village rebuilt and the AI that gives parents back their time until that community is reconstructed. Michelle and her mother deserved both. Every parent fighting some version of that battle, whether it's poverty, impossible schedules, or psychologically devastating isolation, deserves both.

The clickety-clack stopped in exam rooms.

Doctors were freed to focus on the humans in their care.

Parents should be next.

TL;DR: Chapter Review

This chapter focuses on you as a parent, and whether AI could help lift the countless invisible burdens burying families and caregivers today. Key ideas include:

- After electronic health records were introduced in hospitals, physicians were overburdened with administrative work. Today, AI technologies record, transcribe, and summarize physician-patient meetings automatically, freeing doctors to connect with their patients and focus on care.

- Major societal shifts, including the transfer of economic risk away from governments and corporations onto individual households, have placed tremendous added pressure on families. We're trying to raise kids in a pressure cooker, and 40 percent of parents recently reported that they are so stressed they can barely function.

- AI tools could do for parenting what they've done for physicians, managing time-consuming administrative tasks and freeing caregivers to focus on what matters most: connecting with those in their care. Yet such parenting-specific tools are not yet widely available.

- One mother decided to solve this problem for herself, uncovering a way to use the readily available tool ChatGPT as a kind of copilot that offers useful suggestions and strategies, including a grocery-shopping plan and a better bedtime routine for her restless daughter.

- Clearly detailing and delineating the many often invisible tasks that come with raising a little human is an important step toward finding useful technological help. One parenting expert, Eve Rodsky, outlined a hundred such tasks, ranging from Medical Point Person to Calendar Keeper. We can't find tasks suitable for AI's assistance if we haven't tracked what we all do on a daily basis.

- The domestic AI tools discussed and envisioned here will not interact with your child; they will work in the background, functioning as your assistant. Parents should choose tools that support parenting but don't take over. Here's a quick decision framework to simplify that process.

THE ENHANCE-NOT-REPLACE TEST

When AI Supports Parenting—and When It Starts to Take Over

QUESTION	THE "ENHANCE" ANSWER	THE "REPLACE" ANSWER
Does this tool strengthen human connection?	Yes, it sparks conversation, shared play, or family fun	No, it isolates family members in their own individual screen worlds
Does it lighten my mental load so I can be more present?	Yes, it automates a chore or provides helpful information, freeing up my time and energy	No, it just adds another thing to manage—or becomes a distraction itself
Does it add something I truly can't provide?	Yes, it offers unique learning opportunities or access to information that would otherwise be unavailable	No, it steps into roles I'm meant to fill—storyteller, comforter, reassuring presence
Does it keep me in the driver's seat?	Yes, I choose when, how long, and what happens next	No, the algorithm sets the pace, hooks attention, and eliminates stopping points
Does it reinforce the kind of childhood and home I'm trying to build?	Yes, it supports curiosity, kindness, agency, and real-world engagement	No, it rewards passivity, escalation, consumerism, or dependency

- There are risks to such tools, even if they don't engage children directly. Parents could begin to trust AI solutions over their own instincts or those of their partner, for example. At a societal level, these technologies may be unaffordable at the start, leading to a two-tier system in which only the wealthy reap the rewards of AI-powered helpers.

- There are limited cases in which children will benefit from direct interaction with AI solutions; if parents or caregivers are rarely present, AI that offers some degree of interaction may be better than no interaction at all. We need to account for but not concentrate on these edge cases; we should not design for a world in which parents will not be present. We should build tools that help parents be more present.

Ultimately, the ideal household-AI solutions will be those that free parents to focus on the important work of being with and connecting with their children, empowering caregivers with the same tools that benefit physicians and other professionals today.

CHAPTER TWELVE

Robots in the Classroom

*Distinguishing between AI that teaches children
and AI that frees teachers to do so*

Katie Davis, a professor at the University of Washington, has been studying how digital technologies affect children for two decades. She has published nearly a hundred academic papers and three books. As an advocate of the "good enough" model of digital parenting, Davis isn't opposed to the occasional stretch of television-centered couch surfing with her son Oliver. I was lucky enough to meet Davis in Seattle, at a select meeting of scientists and technology leaders studying AI and early childhood, where she shared a parenting anecdote that made the room erupt with laughter.

On a typically gray weekday, we were gathered under the fluorescent lights of a conference room as she told the assembled experts about an AI-powered platform called Book Creator. The technology, she explained, helped children as young as three years old craft digital books based on their own imaginative ideas. Davis had recently seen the technology demoed by the company's founder, and although she is often skeptical of the promises of educational technology (ed-tech) companies, she found herself genuinely impressed. The interface was intuitive. The AI scaffolding, step-by-step supports that assist children in building skills gradually, appeared thoughtful. Kids could dictate stories, add illustrations, even have the AI help structure their narratives. This, she thought, could actually support early literacy development.

Not long after the demo, she visited Oliver's first-grade class with other parents for a celebration of the students' writing progress. The teacher was eager to share some news about the budding storytellers: "We just started using this wonderful new app called Book Creator."

A complete coincidence!

Each student had a tablet out, eager to show off their work. Davis couldn't wait to see what Oliver had created with the tool she'd so carefully evaluated. Excited, she leaned over his tablet.

Page one: 💩

Page two: 💩

Page three: 💩

Pages four through seventeen: 💩💩💩💩💩💩💩💩💩💩💩💩💩💩

The emojis appeared in purple, green, blue, orange. Oliver had used them all. And the pièce de résistance: a *glitter* poop emoji, enlarged and centered like the crown jewel in his scatological masterpiece.

Oh no.

Oh no, no, no.

Had she completely misjudged this technology?

She glanced at the little girl beside Oliver. Her screen was filled with the beautifully illustrated story of a cat, complete with written text and decorative borders. The sort of work that Davis had envisioned her son producing.

"So, Oliver," she asked carefully, "what is your story about?"

He looked back at her like this was the dumbest question he'd ever heard. "Poop," he said.

Then came story-sharing time. Thea, the girl with the elaborate cat story, proudly presented her work on the classroom screen. Very detailed, multiple pages, well on her way to writing a novel. The next Sally Rooney.

"Wonderful job, Thea!" the teacher gushed. "Any other volunteers?"

Before Davis could exhale, Oliver's hand shot up. He's an outgoing kid who reflexively volunteers for everything. "Oh, me, me, me!"

Her internal monologue: Oh, please don't.

But Oliver, ever enthusiastic, stood tall as his creation lit up the big screen. Seventeen poop emojis, supersized for optimal viewing. The glittered variation sparkled magnificently in the center.

"Well, what's your story about?" the teacher asked brightly.

Oliver beamed. "Poop and poop."

The author of *Technology's Child* had just been schooled by her son.

Oliver's story is both funny and instructive: Give a "smart" tool to a four-year-old, and you'll see exactly how unpredictable intelligence can be. Oliver wasn't defying the Book Creator program. The technology passes the first test in our DETECT framework, as it was designed for the right reasons, intent on promoting learning over advertisement-centric engagement. Yet Oliver discovered a pattern, delighted in it, and gleefully skipped around every pedagogical marker the designers imagined. Meanwhile, his classmate used the same tool to produce a miniature masterpiece, the sort of work that proves the potential of the software. Oliver was doing what many young children do when handed an open-ended digital tool. We all laughed hysterically when Davis relayed the story at the conference, yet her anecdote revealed something crucial about AI's future in education. The only inevitability when we place artificially intelligent tools in children's hands is that the results will be unexpected. The question is not whether a given AI technology works, but whether it's going to work for every beautifully unique child and meet their precise needs in the moment.

In the preceding chapters, we looked at friendship-focused chatbots, solutions that reveal hidden insights or forecast the future, and technologies that could offload some of the invisible labor wearing down parents. We focused on kids and the adults at home who are charged with caring for children and their rapidly developing brains. But the world of a young child extends beyond their close family and friends to the teachers who look after them in childcare, preschool, kindergarten, and elementary school, or coach them on courts and fields. Our children grow and adapt within a larger educational and childcare system, and AI technology has moved rapidly into these precious spaces, too. In the following pages, I'll share what I've learned about the powerful potential and sobering reality of personalized AI tools designed to educate our children. We'll examine the various forms these tools might take, and what we can do to ensure they truly have a beneficial impact on children.

An Imperfect World

When I think back to my first guilt-ridden days after dropping Amelie off at pre-K, one of the only reasons I made it through was the obvious love and understanding of the caregivers. They knew what I felt. They were deeply experienced. I knew I could trust them to take care of my beloved daughter. Human connection is truly irreplaceable, and based on decades of research, and millennia of lived experience, we know that direct caregiver-child interactions are the ideal. In a perfect world, our children would all be fully human raised and human taught.

Yet our world is far from perfect. We know that many kids will not enjoy the privilege of consistent one-on-one attention and informed instruction from an experienced adult, whether that's at home or in early-learning settings. And we know that early-childhood-education providers are overworked and underfunded. It's uniquely difficult work looking after multiple little humans for eight, ten, or even twelve hours a day. A decent salary might help balance out the challenges of the job, yet over 40 percent of early-childhood educators earn so little that they qualify for some form of public assistance, such as the Supplemental Nutrition Assistance Program (SNAP). We're entrusting these educators with one of the most important jobs in our society, one that not only frees parents and caregivers to work and contribute to the economy but literally trains the workforce of the future, and we can't even pay them a living wage. These educators need help now.

The argument that educational-technology advocates make is that we can ease some of the burden on professional caregivers, and give kids more opportunities to learn, through interactive educational software and systems. Could an intelligent on-screen tutor be a useful supplemental aide inside a crowded preschool classroom or childcare space? The benefits might extend to the home, too. More than half of American children have their own electronic tablets by age four. Kids between the ages of two and four spend more than two hours a day on screens—and children from lower-income families average even more. Could an AI app with childhood educational principles built into its design transform screen time into a positive developmental experience? Or would it merely strengthen the addiction to screens?

Mister Rogers Meets the Future

Harvard neuroscientist Ying Xu noticed something curious as her young son interacted with the smart speakers Alexa and Google Home. An intensely curious and precocious boy, he was using the intelligent devices as a source of information. He wanted quick answers to his many questions, and the technology satisfied his curiosity-driven craving in the moment. I would've *loved* if Alexa were around when my kids were little and peppering me with rapid-fire questions about everything from dinosaurs to dessert recipes the moment I walked in the door!

While Alexa and similar devices are quick with endless answers, education has never been their core purpose. Recall the "D" in DETECT: Alexa was built to help you play the next song or order your next product on Amazon. The technology could provide a valid answer to a child's question about dinosaurs or volcanos, but this wasn't its technological reason for being. Amazon made an effort to meet the demand for educational value by introducing new tutor-like features and the commendable "polite mode," which provided positive feedback to kids if they said please or thank you. But these were mere add-ons. The speakers were ultimately there to sell products, collect data for advertisers, and cement brand loyalty.

Xu began to wonder what would happen if intelligent tools like these were actually designed with childhood learning in mind and powered by

AI. I mentioned one of Xu's projects with Mark Warschauer in chapter nine, a collaboration between their research team, PBS, and the producers of the show *Elinor Wonders Why*. The show, centered on a young girl, is designed to teach science concepts, familiarize kids with problem-solving skills, and inspire curiosity. It's a wonderful example of the sort of educational content favored by Mister Rogers.

Xu and her colleagues worked with PBS to create AI-enhanced versions of several episodes, then set up experiments in which children aged four to seven years old watched different versions of the show in a lab to see if those AI variations had any impact. Roughly a third of the 246 children who participated watched the standard broadcast of the show. A second cohort viewed a mildly interactive variation, in which the Elinor character asked questions, paused to give kids a chance to respond, then proceeded along with the script. The third and final group experienced the AI version. In this variation, Elinor paused, but when the viewer addressed her query, the system actually listened to the child's answer. A series of AI programs worked in the background to transform that speech into text, guess at the child's intended meaning, and choose an appropriate response. The digital Elinor then spoke back to the viewer.

In one of the episodes, the characters were building a cardboard car. During a scene near the end, Elinor and her friends adjusted the shape of the car to make it go faster. The Elinor character in the AI version then stopped and asked, "So, how did we make our car go faster?"

Television shows like *Dora the Explorer* have used this technique for years; a character poses a question or request, pauses long enough for the child to respond, then moves on. Amelie and Asher both loved to shout clues to Dora to help her track down whatever treasure she was hunting that day. In Elinor's case, though, the technology behind the digital character actually listened. First, Elinor offered three possible answers. If the child answered correctly, Elinor confirmed the response, then added an explanation to reinforce the concept. A wrong answer prompted a different response, meant to nudge them in the right direction. If the child didn't respond, and remained quiet, Elinor might say that she was very curious what the child thought—an attempt at encouragement.

The kids who interacted with the intelligent character didn't get the right answers to Elinor's question any more frequently than those who watched the other variations of the show. Yet the kids who watched the AI version and answered *incorrectly* were far more likely to correct their responses and eventually grasp the underlying concepts. While Patricia Kuhl's earlier research showed that passive, one-way viewing failed to open the social gate, this new work showed that children could learn from digital characters if those characters were capable of social exchanges. The interaction helped them learn.

In keeping with Xu's hope for technology with educational principles built into the design, the character responses were scripted with pedagogical frameworks in mind. The AI at work was closer to Joseph Weizenbaum's original Eliza program than to modern chatbots, with the replies limited to a set number of responses and focused on promoting learning and curiosity. Plus, these intelligent programs aren't meant to be a substitute for human instruction. In fact, Xu's research shows that even though kids do engage in back and forth with artificial digital entities, the kids provide richer, more nuanced responses when they interact with real teachers. Human connections provoke deeper thinking.

The Digital Read-Aloud

The carefully designed, deeply studied tools of the sort that Xu, Warschauer, and other researchers are developing may eventually find their way into more classrooms and homes. Since these pioneers are scientists first and foremost, though, they're not motivated by profit margins or racing to placate impatient venture investors. As a result, they are proceeding cautiously, carefully ensuring these tools are safe and truly beneficial, one study and test group at a time.

Yet there's already tremendous pressure to rush educational AI solutions into early-childhood-education spaces today. Early-childhood expert Nicol Russell, the chief academic officer at Teaching Strategies, an educational-technology company, shared several eye-opening stories about the risks of this feverish AI rush. When Russell and I spoke, she'd recently attended a conference at Columbia University focused on AI and education. All the leading luminaries in the field were there, yet it was a chance meeting with a New York City preschool teacher that stayed with her. Russell met this woman at the end of the conference, while mingling. The teacher had spent the entire day hearing from experts leading the research on AI and its potential as a learning tool. And yet she'd gained no clarity. "My administrator sent me here because they want me to use this technology in my classroom," the teacher explained. "But I don't even know what this is."

As Russell worked to understand the challenges teachers face when implementing new technology, she visited Head Start* classrooms around the country. Some classrooms, she discovered, had reacted to the AI boom by adopting a zero-technology approach. Tablets and laptops had been banished, including those solely for teachers to use. Yet other classrooms had moved in the opposite direction, embracing technology without reservation. In one extreme example, she observed a classroom where the teacher held up an electronic tablet while the device read a book aloud to her students. The kids crowded around trying to see the pictures on the small screen. A physical version of the book, complete with larger pages and illustrations, was right beside her. "She could have just read that book, interacted with the children, then sent them to look at the tablet as an enhancement," Russell noted. The teacher could have moved, gesticulated, widened her eyes, or modulated her voice to light up the social brains of her listeners. Instead, the children were left to watch the little screen and listen to a disembodied digital narrator.

Russell didn't share these anecdotes to criticize either teacher. She mentioned them because they revealed systemic problems. The administrator who sent a preschool teacher to an AI-focused ed-tech conference undoubtedly meant well but fell victim to bandwagon effects. Everyone else was talking about artificial intelligence in education, so surely it had to be promising! And the teacher who simply held the tablet aloft was an example of insufficient training.

------

*   The early-childhood education initiative of the U.S. Department of Health and
    Human Services.

When technology is thrust into classrooms without clear, research-driven guidelines for implementation, we can't fault the teacher. In discussing this problem, Khan Academy founder Sal Khan cited a now classic example of how *not* to introduce technology into schools. In 2013, inspired by the buzz surrounding the brand-new, seemingly magical devices, the Los Angeles Unified School District purchased an iPad for every student in their system. Each tablet was loaded with educational software from the global learning company Pearson. Unfortunately, though, the program was hastily conceived and teachers weren't effectively trained on how to integrate the iPads into the classroom, and students hacked their gadgets to bypass the web filters. The $1.3 billion program was canceled within a year.

Early-Childhood Education Is Fundamentally Different

When it comes to developing technology for our youngest learners, a core problem is the fundamental lack of understanding of the complexity of the challenge facing early-childhood educators. This is not a one-size-fits-all situation. Each child is unique. Every family situation is different. Childcare programs and early-learning environments all have their own particular sets of constraints and challenges. When I discussed this with Michelle Kang, CEO of the National Association for the Education of Young Children, she lamented: "I hear tech developers trying to come up with the next big product to sell to the early-childhood-education sector, or to parents and children, and I keep thinking, How do we help technology companies better understand what is really good for young children? How do we help them include educators, researchers, and families in their product development, and ensure that we're holding fast to inclusivity, fairness, and equity?"

One of my biggest fears is that companies do proceed in developing such technologies without understanding the nuances of the early-learning landscape, and that the resulting products become unevenly distributed. I worry that kids from low-income homes will be relegated to technology-centric care, justified by AI-is-better-than-nothing thinking, while children in more privileged strata will benefit from the human-human connection we know works best. We can't let human interaction become yet another luxury good.

The Hidden Education Crisis

So far in this chapter, we've been talking about AI that sits between children and the adults who care for them. Tools that interact directly with young minds. But there is a second, quieter revolution underway: AI that never speaks to children at all but radically affects the adult who interacts with the technology. These tools focus on uplifting the role of the educator. In the previous chapter, we looked at technologies that could relieve some of the daily burdens of parents. I described how AI scribes have begun to relieve doctors of similar burdens, returning their attention to the humans in front of them. What if AI could do for teachers what it's doing for doctors, not replace the relationship but restore it?

The Gallup-Walton Family Foundation 2025 teacher study reveals a reality most parents never see: Teachers spend more time documenting the day than delivering instruction. Their days, nights, and weekends are consumed by planning, paperwork, compliance, communication, and administrative tasks. One third of teachers say they lose six or more hours every week to tasks that "do not require teacher skill" but must be completed to satisfy reporting or compliance requirements. These statistics come from K–12 educators, but the reality is likely even more dire for early-childhood educators. After all, they also:

- Maintain diapering, feeding, and napping logs

- Document developmental milestones for each child

- Translate communications for multilingual families

- Manage licensing, safety checks, and compliance documentation

- Clean, sanitize, set up, restock, and reset the environment multiple times daily

- Respond minute by minute to the emotional and physical needs of very young children

One analysis of Head Start programs found that administrative tasks consume thirty-four days of instructional time per classroom per year. This administrative overload may explain why teacher turnover in Head Start reaches 16.5 percent between the start and end of each school year, with rates as high as 30 percent across all early-childhood workers. Replacing a single teacher can cost the organization as much as $20,000. That's before counting the toll on children, who suffer disrupted attachments that undermine their social, emotional, and language development. And the science is clear: When caregiver relationships are unstable and stressed, children experience fewer high-quality serve-and-return interactions, the very exchanges that wire the brain for language, regulation, and social understanding.

When teachers are drowning in paperwork, your child waits longer for attention. When teachers leave due to burnout, your child experiences the destabilizing loss of an attachment figure. The administrative crisis isn't some abstract societal problem. It's preventing caring, qualified educators from advancing your child's development, one unread story and one delayed conversation at a time. This context matters because when families imagine AI in the classroom, they often picture child-facing tools. Apps, robots, talking digital characters. But the most urgent AI need in early childhood has nothing to do with *children* using AI. If we actually want to help kids, we need to improve early-childhood education and care by prioritizing AI solutions that free *teachers* to do the work only humans can do.

When Time Returns

Michigan special-education teacher Heather Gauck was chronically sleep deprived for most of her thirty-two years teaching. On an average day, she'd finish her work at school, then shift into parenting mode, taking care of her three active boys. The evenings were brutal. After dinner with her family, homework help, and bedtime routines, she'd return to her computer. Lesson plans to write. Materials to differentiate for students reading at vastly different levels. Individualized Education Plan (IEP) documentation with morning deadlines. Parent communications to compose, some requiring translation into languages she didn't speak. Typically, she'd get into bed about thirty minutes past midnight, then wake before dawn, sacrificing sleep to complete the endless planning and paperwork required to serve her K–4 students in Grand Rapids Public Schools. Gauck loved teaching. That wasn't the problem. It was everything surrounding it that ground her down. The invisible labor no one sees but everyone depends on. Sound familiar?

Then along came AI.

Gauck was already an advocate of technology in the classroom. The first time she used an iPad in class, she barely knew what the device was supposed to do, but she saw how it engaged one of her otherwise reluctant students. This particular fourth grader couldn't read. He wanted to learn but struggled with words on paper. Then she gave him an opportunity to use the seemingly magical touchscreen tablet. "Suddenly, he was incredibly motivated to get the letters right," Gauck recalled. That experience started her on a journey to better understand how advanced technology could be used to aid students.

Yet, when she learned about generative AI tools, she first experimented with how they could decrease her workload *outside* the classroom. For the first time in her career, she started reclaiming something she'd nearly forgotten existed: free time. She did not use the models directly with her students; Gauck only allows technology in the classroom that is secure, approved, and validated. Instead, she used AI to help her fill out paperwork, brainstorm lesson plans, communicate with families, and perform other administrative duties. The work still took time and effort. She reviewed and thought through every sentence. But in the past these tasks would add up to a day's worth of work. Suddenly, she had most of that day back.

An entire planning day.

Every week.

The changes were immediate and tangible. Lesson plans that once consumed her evenings? Now drafted in seconds, then reviewed and revised in an hour. Messages to non-English-speaking families? Translated instantly instead of by clunky, dubious apps. She didn't need to spend all night drafting and reviewing emails before sending them out; she could plug her notes into the AI and generate a professional version to rewrite and perfect. Suddenly, she was free to focus on the human work of meeting with families, interpreting assessment data, and understanding each child's unique needs.

When she did use AI inside the classroom, she only did so with approved, trusted tools like MagicSchool AI. With the help of this app, materials for struggling readers could be generated in seconds at different child-appropriate reading levels. This was a particularly eye-opening breakthrough. In the past, if Gauck was tasked with reading a text aloud, she'd often just do so using its original form, even though her students had varying comprehension levels. Now she could use AI to generate variations of that story matched to each child's reading and comprehension level. She could give each student precisely what they needed.

These applications weren't virtual tutors. They weren't teaching her students. They were empowering her as a professional and reducing the administrative burden that had kept her from teaching. She was sleeping again, climbing into bed two hours earlier on average.

In some instances, time saved also meant meaningful breakthroughs for students. When it came to addressing disruptive behavior, one of the most reliable tools in Gauck's teaching toolkit was social stories. These are stories she would create, tailor-made to match a student's situation. She'd take pictures of kids sitting at their desks, for example, and write out a corresponding text, effectively hand-crafting a book for the child. She knew that approach was effective. The problem was that it took days to complete. With AI she could create a social story in a matter of minutes. So when another teacher notified Gauck that one of the students she supported had been rolling on the ground, disrupting other students in his class, she was able to generate a social story and address the behavior immediately. "Just listening to that social story of what he was doing in the classroom made him realize how inappropriate that behavior was," she recalled. "He never did that again."

In another instance, she worked with a student who struggled with writing a story. He had plenty of ideas, yet he couldn't transform them into a narrative. So she recorded their conversations about the key elements—the characters, the central problem, the setting. She fed those details into MagicSchool AI, which generated a story based on his vision, then read it aloud. Suddenly, he could engage with and understand his story, and suggest changes and refinements. The resulting smile on her student's face, Gauck told the news nonprofit The 19th, was priceless.

This is what responsible AI adoption looks like: a teacher using AI not to replace professional judgment, but to reclaim the time needed to exercise that judgment well and to level up her own work in the classroom. A teacher who understands both the promise and the precautions. A teacher who, after three decades, can finally sleep.

Time-Savers and Bond Builders

When AI supports teachers well, similar stories emerge. MagicSchool AI, the platform Gauck used, has spread rapidly in K–12 classrooms. Teachers who have implemented it describe getting entire planning days back each week. The tool drafts lesson plans, adapts materials for different reading levels, and translates parent emails. But it's always best as a starting point. Teachers still do the work that matters: refining those plans based on their knowledge of specific children. The Khan Academy tool Khanmigo has had a similar impact. Among other things, the technology handles time-consuming logistics—including lesson planning, resource hunting, and administrative tasks—so teachers can focus on actually teaching. In the classroom, Khanmigo is meant to supplement and not replace standard instruction, as one of the nonprofit's representatives told *The Economist*. Currently, the tool is designed for older kids. For children eight and younger, Khan Academy offers an interactive educational app that does not use AI.

This is a smart strategy given AI's tendency to hallucinate, or invent facts and ideas. Even the best educational AI tools aren't foolproof. When I tested one AI assistant and asked for a lesson plan for first graders, for example, the technology suggested a perfectly appropriate and fun activity. But if I were a teacher, I would then have had to spend two or three hours carefully cutting out little paper figures for each of the students in my hypothetical class. Heather Gauck noted that no teacher should expect the tools to be perfect. She reviews every AI output and thinks critically about the results.

At Teaching Strategies, Russell and her colleague Kelsey Houser are building something specifically for early childhood: an assessment tool that helps identify developmental issues an educator might miss in a crowded room. But they're intentionally keeping it simple. As Houser says: "Don't use a sledgehammer when a regular hammer will do." They're not chasing the flashiest AI. They're solving a real problem. And critically, teachers review everything. The human stays in charge.

Translation tools are an area in which National Association for the Education of Young Children CEO Michelle Kang sees real potential, despite her broad caution about AI in early childhood. Many children in early-learning programs come from bilingual families, yet their teachers may not be fluent in those languages. "How can we use AI to help connect the dots in communicating with the child and communicating with the parents?" she asked me. "That, to me, is a hopeful way of strengthening family engagement." The technology would need strong privacy protections, but it wouldn't replace connection. It would enable and support human-human bonds.

The pattern that emerges when you consider this wish list is one in which AI takes on the logistical, the repetitive, the exhausting. Then teachers can build relationships, read the room, see the child others might miss. When teachers get precious time back, it goes straight to the kids.

Where We Stand

While Kang, like many others, sees the value in AI that supports educators, she remains concerned about the speed with which new technologies are entering early-learning classrooms. "We need the right research to help us understand the impact and not wait until the harm has been done," she told me. "How do we help those who are not in our space understand that?"

It's an urgent question. And until it's answered, corporations will continue to make and market AI technologies. Well-meaning schools and educators will adopt them in an effort to do right by their students. Victor R. Lee, who leads Stanford's Accelerator for Learning's initiative on AI and Education, sees a troubling trend in elementary and secondary schools: kids racing ahead to adopt and master new technologies, and schools scrambling to catch up, while parents are absent from the conversation entirely. In early childhood, that vacuum is even more pronounced. When I explored these issues with Kang, Russell, Houser, and other experts, they all told me variations of the same thing: The early-childhood-education field is flying blind. There's no federal framework, nascent state guidance at best, and program-by-program improvisation is driven more by vendor pitches than developmental science.

Ultimately, the potential for AI in the classroom is as varied as it is in the home. In your household, of course, you decide whether your child encounters this technology. In the classroom, that decision is made for you. Katie Davis didn't choose Book Creator for Oliver's class. She didn't set the parameters for its use. The technology simply appeared, selected by well-meaning educators, deployed with good intentions, and absorbed into her son's day without her involvement. So what's a parent to do?

Your Questions Are Your Superpower

This is the moment when your voice matters most. The regulatory void in this space makes your questions unusually powerful. You won't be reacting to settled practice; you'll be helping to shape it. Which is why I strongly recommend that any parent with a child in childcare, preschool, or early elementary school ask their provider about their approach to AI.

Maybe you're worried this will make you "that parent." The eye-roll-inducing mom or dad whom administrators dread. Here's the truth: Any program that treats curiosity as confrontation isn't ready to navigate AI responsibly. The questions you ask can serve as your diagnostic tool. They'll reveal not just what the early-childhood program is doing, but how thoughtfully the administrators are approaching their decisions. If the program does use specific AI tools, you can apply the DETECT framework to investigate those solutions, or send a version of the email template I've provided on page 249. Here are a set of additional, higher-level questions to ask administrators as you begin.

QUESTIONS TO ASK
Does your program have an AI policy for this year? Where can I review it?
Which AI tools are currently approved or prohibited? Does this vary by age?
How are you supporting teachers to learn about AI?
How do teachers decide when to use AI versus traditional methods?
What messages do you want families to convey to children about AI?
Is there a committee working on AI guidelines? Are parents part of this conversation?

These questions invite partnership. And the answers, or lack thereof, will tell you much of what you need to know. Encouraging replies will be variations of the following:

- "We're piloting a translation tool to help communicate with our multilingual families. Teachers control when and how it's used, and we're tracking whether it actually improves communication or just adds another layer of technology."

- "We don't have a formal policy yet, but we've formed a committee that includes teachers, parents, and our director. We're starting by inventorying what's already in use and evaluating each tool's purpose."

- "Right now we're taking a wait-and-see approach with most AI. We're watching the research and focusing our energy on strengthening teacher-child relationships. When the right tools emerge, we'll be ready to evaluate them carefully."

What sort of answers should concern you? Here are a few possibilities:

- "Oh, the district handles all that." (Abdication of responsibility.)

- "We use whatever the vendor recommends." (No independent evaluation.)

- "All the other programs are using it." (Bandwagon-driven, not strategic.)

- "I'm not sure what you mean by AI." (Lack of awareness.)

You might also encounter a defensive or dismissive response when you inquire. This is another red flag. Remember: You're not demanding perfection. You're not claiming or expecting perfect knowledge or world-class AI expertise. What you're looking for is thoughtfulness, honesty, and recognition of the profound importance and complexity of this issue. You're looking for humans who recognize they don't have all the answers but are committed to searching for them carefully while keeping children's well-being at the center of that quest.

You don't need to be a technology expert to ask smart questions about AI in the classroom. You just need to be an engaged parent. To make it easier, here is a template you can adopt and adjust to send to your school administrator or center director:

Subject: A question about our approach to AI

Dear [Administrator Name],

I've been reading about the rapid rise of AI tools in early education, and I'd love to understand more about how our program is navigating this shift.

I know this is a moving target for everyone, but could you share if the school currently has a policy regarding which AI tools (like chatbots, tablets, and automated reading apps) are approved for use in the classroom?

Specifically, I'm interested in:

Selection. How do teachers decide when to use these tools versus traditional human instruction?

Training. Are our educators receiving specific training on how to oversee these tools so they support, rather than replace, teacher-student interaction?

Privacy. What safeguards are in place regarding the data these platforms might collect on the students?

I am not looking for final answers, as I know the technology is changing fast. I just want to ensure we are partnered in keeping human connection at the center of my child's learning.

Best,
[Your Name]

Tools You Might Encounter in the Classroom

While there's still so much we don't know about artificial intelligence and young minds, we do understand a lot about human intelligence. We know that children need human-human connection, and if educational technology is truly going to make a difference in the years ahead, it should be designed to promote the warm, nurturing social interactions that actually drive learning. With that in mind, let's revisit some of the categories of AI tools we discussed in previous chapters and explore their suitability for early-learning spaces.

AI companions have no place in infant, toddler, or preschool classrooms. These tools, which are designed to entertain, engage, or befriend, have shown no credible evidence of developmental benefit in preschool settings. And every minute spent with a digital companion is a minute not spent engaging in the rich, reciprocal human interaction that actually builds young brains.

AI caregivers are even more troubling. Humanoid robots that can safely, independently, and reliably look after kids, or sit with a toddler and read them a board book? That's still science fiction. But the rapid pace of progress certainly points to some variation of these becoming reality before long. In rare, extreme circumstances, they might serve as a stopgap. But as a regular feature of childcare? No. That would signify a surrender to a broken system. As Michelle Kang succinctly stated, "There is no substitute for nurturing, responsive relationships in the early years—no app, no algorithm, no robot."

Smart tutors and **therapeutic allies** are a different story and could be beneficial, but with very large asterisks. For one, age really and truly matters here. The infant and toddler years are incredibly sensitive. We can't get those years wrong. Here's how to think about these technologies based on age:

Infants and toddlers (ages 0–3): I don't see these tools having a place in early-childcare spaces. The research would need to show not just that they work, but that they work *better* than what well-trained, well-supported human caregivers can provide. That's an extraordinarily high bar, and nothing I've seen comes close.

Preschoolers and kindergarteners (ages 4–5): There may be narrow exceptions here. Carefully designed smart tutors built for practicing specific skills, such as letter recognition, number sense, and phonemic awareness, can be additive, especially when the technology demonstrably accelerates learning beyond what a teacher in a busy, demanding setting can provide alone. The same applies to therapeutic AI allies prescribed and closely monitored by specialists for particular developmental needs and used as one tool among many in a comprehensive support plan. That makes sense. But again, the bar remains extraordinarily high. And the nonnegotiable never changes: There must always be a human in charge.

AI monitors, or technologies that passively gather data about children, have the potential to uncover insights and trends that are invisible to the naked eye. However, privacy is of the utmost importance. These tools should only be used if the organizations providing them can guarantee that the collected data is secured and protected, with students' and teachers' best interests in mind. As someone who developed this kind of technology for classroom use, ensuring data privacy has been one of my absolute highest priorities. In fact, writing this book helped me fine-tune and elevate the already stringent privacy protections and safety features built into Luet.

Time-savers, tools that run in the background, never interacting with children, carry the most promise, especially in the near term. They can free educators to spend more time with the children in their care, and many are appropriate for use in classrooms that serve children of all ages. Their impact is already being felt in K–12 classrooms, where teachers who use

AI on a weekly basis report saving seven to ten hours per week—or roughly six weeks per year.

When AI genuinely supports teachers rather than replaces them, certain principles hold:

Teachers must understand what the AI is doing. Black-box systems that generate recommendations without explanation undermine professional judgment. If a teacher can't explain why they're trying a particular strategy or how they decided on an activity, then they're not being supported. They're being sidelined. The teacher brings the human expertise, the contextual knowledge, and the judgment that makes the profession work.

Teachers must retain decision-making authority. The AI suggests; the teacher decides. Always. A documentation tool that auto-generates parent communications without teacher review is disrupting an essential link and severing a potentially critical bond. When Heather Gauck used MagicSchool AI to draft IEP sections, she was creating a starting point, not accepting a final product. The difference matters.

The reclaimed time must actually go to educating children. If AI handles lesson planning in five minutes instead of thirty, those freed-up twenty-five minutes should enable more one-on-one reading time, more relationship building, more responsive teaching. As the Gallup-Walton data show, some teachers report that saved time simply gets swallowed by new mandates or expectations. Remember the washing machine paradox: labor-saving technology that only raised standards rather than freeing up time. If those hours are absorbed by other administrative tasks, nothing has improved. Yet if the AI tools free up time outside the classroom that was normally allocated to administrative work, and teachers actually have more hours to relax and recharge at night or on the weekend, that's incredibly powerful, as they'll also have more energy to devote to children.

Teachers must be involved in the decision to adopt a tool. Any proposed technology solution truly needs to address the time problem. An AI tool won't be helpful if it forces teachers to spend excess time validating and confirming its results and suggestions. This is why teacher input in AI selection and training isn't optional. Teachers need seats at the decision-making table, not just the implementation table, to ensure that a technology really changes their daily workflow for the better.

While I feel confident in these recommendations, I also believe we should proceed with humility and vigilance. Humility because research and technology evolve, and we must update our positions as new evidence and new solutions emerge. And vigilance because when it comes to technologies that could reshape human development, the burden of proof belongs to the technology, not to the children and their caregivers. So yes, let's stay open. Let's watch the research. But let's also ask hard questions about what we're willing to risk while we wait to find out.

Valuing the Human at the Wheel

Here's what we know for certain: Whether AI interacts with your child or supports the teacher working with them, one nonnegotiable rule remains constant. A human must be in control. Not as a distant monitor, but as an active, engaged adult who knows your child, adjusts to their needs, and keeps relationships at the center. That human is your child's teacher. They're the one arriving early to set up the classroom, staying late to clean up. They're wiping noses, mediating conflicts, celebrating breakthroughs, comforting tears. They're documenting developmental milestones at naptime and answering parent emails after their own children go to bed. And in exchange they're earning poverty wages, all while doing work that shapes human beings during their most formative years. If AI can give them back even a few hours a week to spend fully present with the children in front of them, then we owe it to those children to get this right. Not by replacing teachers with technology. But by using technology to restore what makes teaching both sustainable and powerful: time, presence, and the human connection that no algorithm can replicate.

Your child's teacher needs your partnership.

If we're honest about what kind of transformation is necessary in early childhood, we need to look beyond technology. When I asked Michelle Kang what her ideal AI solution would provide, she didn't describe a better app or smarter algorithm. She went straight to the heart of the crisis: "If AI were a perfect technology, what would it do?" she asked. "It would solve the compensation problem for early-childhood educators and solve the affordability problem for families. That would make it perfect."

As I noted earlier, unless we are vigilant, these tools will be adopted unevenly. They'll be sold as a better-than-nothing fix for under-resourced programs, while children in well-funded settings continue to receive abundant human attention. Solutions introduced under the banner of efficiency can quietly entrench inequity, widening the very gaps they claim to close. No amount of artificial intelligence can fix a system that pays the people shaping our youngest minds less than living wages. No algorithm can substitute for a society that values early-childhood education enough to fund it properly.

If used wisely, AI can buy back some of the time that's currently stolen from teachers by administrative burden. It can make the impossible job of early-childhood education slightly more sustainable. We must value the professionals who care for our children and remember that the most important intelligence in any classroom will always be human.

TL;DR: Chapter Review

AI is now moving into schools and childcare centers. Even well-designed educational AI solutions can produce unpredictable outcomes, because children's learning is individual and resistant to standardization. The most promising role for classroom AI might not be child-facing but teacher-facing. Early-childhood educators are overwhelmed by administrative labor that steals time from children and fuels burnout, turnover, and disrupted attachment. Tools handling documentation, planning, translation, and differentiation can return precious hours to teachers, allowing them to be more present, responsive, and rested. Yet we must ensure that humans stay at the wheel. Parents should ask thoughtful questions, partner with educators, and resist technologies that treat human connection as optional. Key takeaways include:

- Children can learn from responsive digital characters, but learning with attentive adults is still more powerful and impactful.

- For children under five years old, we must prioritize teacher-facing, not child-facing, AI technologies. AI companions and caregivers have no place in early-childhood classrooms. Smart tutors may have a role, but the bar remains high, and a human must be in charge.

- AI relieving the administrative burdens on teachers could have an outsize impact. One teacher used AI to help her special-education students and saved herself two hours each night.

- Any parent with a child in an early-learning setting should ask their provider about their approach to AI. Questions and a sample email are included to make this process easier.

- When AI is poorly understood, rushed into classrooms, or driven by vendor hype rather than developmental science, it risks negative impact. Unless we are vigilant as a society, these tools will be adopted unevenly, sold as better than nothing for under-resourced programs while vetted carefully in well-funded settings to preserve abundant human attention.

- Teachers must retain decision-making authority. Time reclaimed from administrative burdens should go to educating and connecting with children. And teachers should be involved in adopting any tool. These solutions can't be thrust upon them.

No matter the promise of AI classroom tools, we must value the professionals who care for our children. The most important intelligence in any classroom will always be human.

Conclusion

Writing this book changed me.

I savor sounds I once treated as background noise. Sounds I ignored, struggled to push through, or tuned out. The shrieks of children laughing on a playground. A father bargaining with his son over one more trip down the slide. Tweens arguing passionately about the latest drama. A toddler in a grocery cart reaching for everything as a parent steers past. And yes, even a baby howling on an airplane. Previously, I never paused to listen. Now I can't help but stop and savor this symphony of human connection, interaction, growth.

The noise means something different now.

To me it is the sound of hope.

These sounds are evidence. Evidence that we are still showing up. Still caring for one another, doing the messy, inefficient, irreplaceable work of raising humans. They are the signals, like birdsong in spring, telling us something essential is still alive.

They remind me that care is not an idea; it's an act, repeated a thousand times a day. They tell us that children are being tended to by people, not systems. That frustration is being met with repair. That connection is happening in real time, in real bodies, between real people.

And yet, these sounds are becoming easier to replace. Sometimes without anyone quite noticing it when they disappear.

Now we face a choice.

Down one path, we outsource the hard work of caring to systems that cannot actually care. We let AI companions soothe our children so we can answer email. We delegate the patience we lack to algorithms that simulate patience. And slowly, almost imperceptibly, our own capacity for caring atrophies from disuse. The muscle weakens. The instinct fades. We become more like the machines: efficient, optimized, responsive on demand. And we become less like loving, devoted parents shaped by millions of years of evolution.

Down the other path, we recognize caring as our inheritance. The inimitable instinct that truly makes us human. The quality that machines are missing. And then we protect it. Strengthen it. Celebrate it above and even beyond critical human skills like creativity, reason, innovation. We extend its reach and design technology to serve our relationships, not replace them.

While I was writing this book, one person I spoke with wondered aloud whether her children might someday need to live quarantined from those raised with unfettered access to AI. I refuse that future. We do not save our species by splitting into tribes. We save it by remembering what we share. Not eventually. Now.

Readers of my previous books, *Thirty Million Words* and *Parent Nation*, will recognize my next plea. In those works, I argued that we must extend our drive to care beyond our own bloodlines, our own homes, our own zip codes. I called for us to recognize that every child's potential is our shared responsibility.

And yet, here I am, writing it again.

Because we haven't gotten there. The gaps I and others exposed have not closed. The policies I advocated for have stalled. The call to follow Don's profoundly selfless example and not only see but act as if all children are our own children has not been fully answered. The caring that evolution gave us is deep, but we have been too slow to extend it beyond the boundaries our ancestors drew.

This is more important than ever before. Our tools have always changed us. The plow made us better farmers, allowing our population to boom. The book made us readers, and gave us access to ideas and experiences previously unavailable. But never before have our tools been able to respond, adapt, and evolve alongside us in real time. AI was created in the image of the human brain, and for the first time in history, the creation is poised to reshape the creator.

While writing this book, I read Kazuo Ishiguro's *Klara and the Sun*, the story of a robot named Klara, so devoted to the child it cares for that the reader is made to feel that this bond is indistinguishable from selfless parental love. It's a beautiful vision. But for now, it remains very much fiction. And even in Ishiguro's imagined world, it is the mother whose fierce love drives the story and ultimately endures.

The caring must come from us.

How we respond to this will shape not just the children in our homes, but the species we become.

The sounds are still here. The music is still playing.

Children still laugh. Parents still lose patience and try again. Strangers still step in. The work of caring has not disappeared. But it can no longer be taken for granted. It requires intention now more than ever.

So listen.

Listen for the noise. The chaos. The interruptions. The voices calling back and forth. They are not inefficiencies to be engineered away. They are the sound of our species caring for itself. The sound of children being human raised.

The machines cannot really hear that music.

You can.

A Deep Dive into the DETECT Investigation Framework

In chapter eight, we introduced the DETECT method for evaluating AI tools and toys. The basic framework will be useful whether you're speeding through an examination of a product or spending several hours investigating its various pros and cons. The first step is to consider your possible sources. When evaluating a product and attempting to answer the questions that follow, there are several places you can turn for information. Here are some helpful hints about where to look and what to look for.

1. Company-Provided Information: All marketing materials (including product websites) should be taken with a grain of salt. Or maybe a spoonful. Yet, if you view this information with an appropriately skeptical lens, you can find helpful details. Scan technical documentation such as terms of service, user manuals, and privacy policies. Check data-retention policies and deletion procedures, and look for third-party data-sharing agreements. You can also gain useful insights by considering a company's business model, which may be available in shareholder reports, news articles, or even the corporate website. Does the company make money from advertising, subscriptions, or data sales? Or is

it a nonprofit or B Corp that must demonstrate positive social impact?

2. Parent Communities: Read and join discussions in parenting forums, Facebook groups, or Reddit communities where others share real-world experiences. Don't ditch that skeptical lens, though. A clever and well-funded corporation might plant sponsors among those comments and pages.

3. Academic Research: There are several great search tools designed for scientists and other academics, including Google Scholar, Semantic Scholar, and PubMed. Each one can be easily found through a standard search engine. Pick one, then search for studies on the specific product or product type you're investigating. Take special care to determine if a study's claims are based only on correlation—the "ice cream linked to crime" fallacy discussed in chapter eight— or backed by causal evidence (more on this later). Not all research is created equal. If you have the time, you can transform yourself into an expert research detective by looking for evidence of:

    • Independent validation: Research not funded by the company (check the disclosures section at the end of the paper)

    • Replication: Positive results that have been repeated by different researchers

    • Appropriate sample sizes: Large enough groups to draw meaningful conclusions

    • Long-term follow-up: Effects that persist beyond immediate use

- Diverse populations: Including children with diverse backgrounds and abilities

4. Advocacy Organizations: There are several advocacy organizations dedicated to helping parents make informed decisions about media and technology. Check to see if any have weighed in on the product or technology you're considering. The U.S. PIRG Education Fund report "Trouble in Toyland 2025" is a stellar example.

5. Traditional and Digital Journalism: The stories of reporters tasked with testing, reviewing, and providing accurate assessments of AI products and apps should be a foundational part of your research. Look to media organizations and institutions with established standards for these insights; be wary of sponsored content.

6. Generative AI: As I've said, AI tools do hold true promise, especially when it comes to easing burdens on parents, so it's perfectly reasonable to enlist ChatGPT, Claude, Gemini, or another prominent model to do some of this investigative work on your behalf. Just remember that you cannot assume everything AI claims is true. Always check the sources for yourself to confirm that they exist and that you agree with the conclusions drawn from them. In other words, use AI to enhance your investigation skills, not replace them!

While research is essential, some investigations will be strengthened by hands-on testing. If you decide to try a product or technology, I'd suggest a trial period during which you do so yourself, without your child involved. (Make sure to pose some challenging or ambiguous questions to see how it responds!) If and when you're ready to have your child try it out, start with minimal data sharing, strict time limits, and careful observation.

The Six Questions, Revisited

Now let's revisit our six DETECT questions, this time focusing on the specific pieces of information to look for in each category. Here's a reminder of how to assess your results:

SIGNAL	MEANING	WHAT NOW?
GREEN	This area checks out well; meets or exceeds expectations	Proceed with confidence
YELLOW	This area requires close monitoring; some concerns but no deal-breakers	Proceed with caution
RED	This area is a deal-breaker or requires resolution before proceeding	Stop—significant concern

1. Design

Questions to Ask

- Can you explain in one sentence what this system is supposed to do?

- Is it designed primarily for education, therapy (medical or psychosocial), entertainment, or companionship?

- Which of the types of AI categories* does it fit into?

* Time-savers, observers, tutors, therapeutic allies, companions, caregivers.

- Does this technology interact directly with your child?

- If it does interact directly, can you see and control which interactions are happening?

- What developmental areas does it claim to support, and do those align with your child's current needs?

- How does it measure success—through learning outcomes or engagement metrics?

- Supervision: Perhaps most important, you should ask yourself, "How much supervision will this require, and am I prepared to provide it?" If you're hoping for a "set it and forget it" solution for child entertainment or education, that's already a warning sign. Children's AI interactions need ongoing human oversight.

Flag the Good

- Clear, specific educational or therapeutic objectives

- Built-in time limits or natural stopping points

- Transparency about what the system can and cannot do

- Transparent interaction logs you can review

- Built-in prompts for parent involvement

- Clear boundaries on what topics or activities it will and won't engage with

- Easy monitoring and control features

And the Bad

- Vague claims about "accelerating development" without specifics

- Emphasis on engagement time rather than learning outcomes

- Business models that profit from extended child use, not developmental leaps

- Systems that actively discourage parental observation

- Autonomous interactions without clear boundaries

- No clear off switch or time limits

Quick Assessment

Green: Clear developmental purpose with defined goals; no direct interaction with child or else transparent interactions with clear parental oversight

Yellow: Educational claims and evidence but engagement-focused design; parental oversight options included but not the default

Red: Designed purely for entertainment or companionship; black-box interactions that exclude parents

2. Ethics

Questions to Ask

- Was this AI trained specifically on child-development data and interactions? (Try asking the product directly if answers aren't readily available.)

- Can the system explain how it makes decisions? Is it transparent? Or is its decision-making process hidden?

- Does the training data represent diverse backgrounds, abilities, and communication styles?

- What biases might be embedded in the system?

Flag the Good

- Transparency about data sources and validation processes

- Acknowledgment of limitations and bias-mitigation efforts

- Child-specific training data from diverse populations

- Regular testing and updates based on real-world performance

And the Bad

- Opacity about training-data sources

- Systems originally designed for adults and repurposed for children

- No acknowledgment of potential biases or limitations

- Training data comes exclusively from controlled lab settings rather than real-world interactions

Quick Assessment

Green: Transparent about training data with child-specific validation

Yellow: Some transparency but limited child-specific design

Red: No transparency about training data or obvious adult-centric design

3. Trouble

Questions to Ask

- Are there any independent public accounts of this tool having negative impacts on other users?

- Are there unbiased, unsponsored accounts of positive impacts?

- Does the company offer any guidance on healthy versus problematic use?

- Do you know what red flags to look out for if your child does begin using this tool? Will you be able to tell if they're becoming emotionally dependent on the product, it's affecting their expectations about human interactions, or it's altering their behavior?

As you look for answers to each question, take note of both the good and the bad, as we did for Design and Ethics.

Quick Assessment

Green: No signs of troubling impacts for other children; easy to find and use monitoring plans available

Yellow: Mixed experiences for other families; some information available about troubling signs to look out for

Red: Significant signs of dependency or interference with normal development in other children; no transparency from company

4. Evidence

Questions to Ask

- Has this product been studied by independent researchers (not just company-funded studies)?

- Are there long-term studies showing sustained benefits, not just short-term engagement?

- Did research include children similar to yours in age, developmental stage, and needs?

- In studies that seem to demonstrate a positive impact, did researchers compare two *similar* groups of children (or use statistical methods to control for the differences between them) before crediting the gains to the tool itself?

- What unintended consequences have been documented?

Again, as you start to gather your answers, keep track of both the positive signs, such as multiple independent studies showing consistent benefits, and any discouraging ones—claims based only on internal testing, for example. Take all that into account as you rate the Evidence.

Quick Assessment

Green: Multiple independent studies showing sustained developmental benefits

Yellow: Some positive evidence but limited long-term validation

Red: No independent research or evidence based solely on engagement metrics

5. Confidentiality

Questions to Ask

- What specific information is being collected about your child? Consider:

    Interaction data: What your child says, asks, or does

    Behavioral data: Patterns of use, preferences, response times

    Biometric data: Voice recordings, facial expressions, physiological responses

    Performance data: Learning progress, skill assessments, areas of difficulty

- How long is this data kept, and where is it stored?

- Who has access to your child's data (employees, third parties, researchers)?

- What is your child's data used for? A few possibilities:

    Product improvement: Using your child's data to make the system better

    Research: Including your child's information in studies or datasets

    Personalization: Creating individualized experiences based on your child's patterns and preferences

    Commercial use: Selling insights about children's behavior to third parties

- Can you request deletion of your child's data?

- Will the product still function properly if you opt out of data collection?

Flag the Good

- Clear, minimal data collection focused on core functionality

- Easy-to-understand privacy controls for parents

- Automatic data deletion after reasonable periods

- No sharing of children's data with third parties

- Compliance with children's privacy regulations

And the Bad

- Indefinite data retention with no deletion options

- Sharing children's data with third parties for commercial purposes

- Collection of unnecessary personal information

- No clear way to access or delete your child's data

- Default settings that maximize data collection

Quick Assessment

Green: Minimal data collection with clear parental control and automatic deletion

Yellow: Reasonable data practices but complex or confusing privacy controls

Red: Extensive data collection with sharing or indefinite retention

6. Teachings

Questions to Ask

- What assumptions does this system make about how children should learn? Consider:

  Does it promote deep thinking or quick answers?

  Does it encourage questions or provide ready-made solutions?

- How does it handle mistakes, frustration, or confusion?

- Does it position itself as an authority figure or a learning partner?

- What does it teach about curiosity and independent thinking? Does it teach children to question AI responses or accept them uncritically?

- How does it model communication and social interaction (including politeness, respect, and boundaries)?

- How does it handle diversity and cultural differences?

- What does it model with regard to human versus artificial intelligence?

Flag the Good

- Encouragement of critical thinking and questioning (including of the AI itself)

- Balance between support and independence

- Transparency about limitations and the importance of human judgment

- Customizable to align with different family values

And the Bad

- Systems that position themselves as the ultimate authorities

- AI that discourages questioning or critical thinking

- Values that directly conflict with your family's beliefs

- One-size-fits-all approaches that ignore cultural diversity

- Emphasis on speed and efficiency over depth and reflection

Quick Assessment

Green: Values clearly align with yours and encourage critical thinking
Yellow: Generally positive values but some areas of misalignment
Red: Values conflict with your family's beliefs or discourage independent thinking

How to Make the Final Decision

As you work your way through these six elements of the DETECT framework, along with the questions underpinning each one, you can certainly keep track of your green, yellow, and red lights, then base your decision on that informal scoring system. A single red light, or a trio of yellows, might lead you to ban the tool or toy from your house. But I suspect you won't require that kind of scorekeeping. Instead, I imagine you'll just know; your Parental GPS, in conjunction with the information gathered during your investigation, will lead you to make the right choice for your family.

APPENDIX 2.

The Developmentally Aligned Seal of Approval

Individual investigations of AI products should not be the sole solution to the challenges facing parents. Lawmakers, regulators, industry, and consumer-advocacy groups all have important roles to play. In chapter eight, I proposed a Developmentally Aligned Seal of Approval that could be awarded by a third party to indicate that an AI product is consistent with healthy child development.

Pillar 1: Child-Centered Design

A product earns the seal by showing it was built with children in mind from the start, not just scaled down from an adult system. Certification would follow a tiered path:

Level 1 (Basic): Designers attest that child-development principles shaped every decision, with evidence of consultation from experts.

Level 2 (Validated): Documented, age-specific testing (e.g., 3–5, 6–8, 9–12, 13+) confirms that the system responds appropriately to children's communication patterns.

Level 3 (Endorsed): Full disclosure of child-specific training methods and data sources, showing exactly how developmental differences are accounted for.

This tiered approach balances the corporate need for trade-secret protections with parents' need for meaningful accountability.

Pillar 2: Evidence and Oversight

Proven Benefits: Independent, peer-reviewed research (not company sponsored) must show the tool supports positive developmental outcomes, not just engagement metrics.

Parental Awareness Criteria: The product's default setting must keep parents in the loop, not shut them out. The settings should require parents to be present or approve all use of the product.

Pillar 3: Safeguards and Progression

Healthy Use Limits: Built-in protections prevent overuse and encourage real-world breaks, with varied interaction patterns to avoid dependency.

Transition Support: The system helps children "age out" gracefully, guiding them toward new, age-appropriate challenges rather than keeping them hooked on the same content.

Human-Connection Preservation: Design features must show the AI is an enhancer, not a replacer, of human relationships, especially for emotional support, problem-solving, and building social skills.

Pillar 4: Transparency and Control

Values Clarity: The system discloses the social values, behaviors, and cultural assumptions it teaches, so parents can see if it aligns with their family's approach.

Privacy by Design: Data is anonymized irreversibly by default, making re-identification impossible while still allowing research and improvement.

Emergency Overrides: Parents have access to immediate, simple controls to pause interactions, review concerning exchanges, and override responses that feel inappropriate or misaligned.

HUMAN-RAISED SEAL: FOUR PILLARS
Proposed Certification Framework for Child-Centered AI

Inspired by Harvey Wiley's *Good Housekeeping* magazine "Seal of Approval"—a trusted mark parents could rely on.

PILLAR	WHAT IT MEANS
1. Child-Centered Design	Built with children in mind from the start (three tiers of validation): • Level 1 (Basic): Evidence that a child-development expert was consulted • Level 2 (Validated): Age-specific testing confirms appropriate responses • Level 3 (Transparent): Full disclosure of child-specific training methods

PILLAR	WHAT IT MEANS
2. Evidence and Oversight	Independent research showing positive outcomes: • Peer-reviewed research (not company sponsored) • Parental awareness criteria to ensure caregivers are in the loop
3. Safeguards and Progression	Protections for healthy development: • Appropriate use limits built into the system • Transition support (helps children "age out" or move to other activities) • Features that preserve human connection
4. Transparency and Control	Parental empowerment: • Embraces clarity (what the system teaches) • Privacy by design (anonymized by default)

ACKNOWLEDGMENTS

How do you write a book about a speeding train while you're on it? A train hurtling toward a destination no one can fully see, with only the ancient road map of human development to guide you?

Carefully. And never alone.

When *Human Raised* began taking shape in 2024, the questions at its heart still felt speculative, a map for a future we assumed was further off. By New Year's Eve 2025, as the manuscript was being completed, AI toys weren't just in the headlines; they were showing up in living rooms and nurseries. The future did not wait for us to finish writing about it.

There is a profound symmetry in writing a book about the irreplaceable power of human connection and needing so many humans to help bring it into the world. In fact, that may be the clearest proof of the book's premise. *Human Raised* exists because of my own "deep neural network," the original kind: a community of people who gave their time, wisdom, creativity, and care. I couldn't have written this book without it.

To Gregory Mone, my extraordinary writing partner—how lucky am I? Greg brought steady calm, gorgeous clarity, and the rare ability to translate complex ideas into language that still feels human. He's spent decades making complicated subjects accessible, from cosmology to robotics to AI. But what made him the perfect partner for *Human Raised* wasn't his résumé. It was his humanity: his patience, his generosity, and his ability to meet my runaway enthusiasm with grounded steadiness. And because he's a parent, too, he wasn't just helping me write about these questions; he was living them alongside me. This book is better because of him.

To Liz Sablich and Heidi Stevens, thought partners, truth tellers, and dear friends who've put up with me saying "just one more book" more than once (I promise, this is it). Brilliant writers and thinkers in their own right, they've seen every draft that stayed on the page and every one that ended up on the cutting-room floor. They are my people. They tell me when my ideas are good—and, crucially, when they're not—and then push them further than I could on my own. They're partners in trying to change the world for children and families. This book is sharper because of them.

And to Stayce Camparo, a curious, rigorous researcher with a huge heart, someone who never blinked when I asked her to dive into uncharted waters where attachment theory meets artificial intelligence, language development meets large language models, and decades of developmental science collide with technologies that didn't exist when that science was written. With a background in psychology and sociology, she strengthened the scientific foundation of this book and kept its human stakes front and center with every step.

To the team at InkWell Management: Richard Pine, who saw what this book could be before I fully did and called it "the most important discussion about AI that isn't being discussed." More than an agent, he has been a believer, a sounding board, and someone who truly looked out for me—offering sharp editorial insights when the book needed them most. He is an agent's agent who makes you feel like you're his only client, though I suspect his many, many other authors would say the same thing. And to Eliza Rothstein, for her sharp insights along the way.

This is my third book with Dutton, and I'm still grateful they keep saying yes. To Nick Amphlett, my editor, who believed in this book when it felt so premature that many couldn't quite picture it. John Parsley, Dutton's publisher, who has seen it all and seen me through all three books, connected us when Nick was just a month into his Dutton journey; I couldn't have been luckier. Nick's strong vision for what the book could be made the manuscript better every single time he touched it. And when he told me he and his wife were expecting twins, I knew the book would have at least one very invested reader. When Nick handed me off to David Howe, he promised I'd be in great hands. He was right. David brought this book across the finish line with the same thoughtfulness and skill. And to Amanda Walker, Emily Canders, and Stephanie Cooper, who have championed my work for three books and counting, thank you for helping these ideas find their readers.

To the Original Strategies team, Deb Eschmeyer, Joanna Rosholm, Elle O'Brien, and Leeah Derenoncourt, who catalyze big ideas into bigger impact. When this team believes in an idea, watch out. Their questions and nudges have a way of taking you somewhere important, often somewhere you didn't realize you needed to go. Joanna's innocent question "So when are you going to write your next book?" was the nudge that set *Human Raised* in motion. Deb's "radical" idea that the epilogue should become the prologue set the tone and framed the entire book. Elle's persistence and passion got this book in front of the right people. And Leeah, whose quiet precision keeps the whole operation running. Beyond their talent, they're simply a joy to work with, and even better humans.

To the researchers, scientists, parents, and thinkers who shared their time, expertise, and stories: Maryam Nabavi, Charles Onu, Dennis Wall, Naomi Aguiar, Jenny Radesky, Maja Matarić, Sarah Sebo, Jinjun Xiong, Michelle Kang, Katie Davis, Eve Rodsky, Gordon Neufeld, Danielle Demarco, Natalie Barnett, Peter Bull, Mark Warschauer, Ying Xu, Nicol Russell, Kelsey Houser, Matthias Scheutz, Lilian Schmidt, Meg O'Leary, Ajay Sailopal, Patricia Kuhl, Anna Steffeney, Julie Kientz, Meghan Verena Joyce, Bryan Sisk, and Heather Gauck. Each of you arrived with your own expertise and your own journey. Some of your words appear directly in these pages; others shaped my thinking in quieter ways. But together, your ideas became something none of us could have built alone. These conversations were one of the great gifts of writing this book.

To Pete Garceau, whose cover design perfectly captures the heart of this book. It says everything before you turn a single page. And to Jenna Blazevich, who brought the gorgeous *Human Raised* patch to life with her own two hands. A book about what makes us human deserved a cover you want to reach out and touch.

To those who read along the way, from tiny snippets to the entire manuscript, offering insights and pep talks that make this book better: Dani Levine, for her brilliant developmental eye and meticulous attention to detail. Julie Pernaudet, for her sharp thoughts and economist's brain. Aaron Shulman, for cheering me on from the first spark and helping me through the occasional existential spiral. Lydia Denworth, for literary and scientific feedback that made me smarter, and a seal of approval that meant more than she knows. And to MJ Deery, Jenna Metcalf, Lisa Lee Herbert, Alex Pedenko, Diana Smith, Emma Brandt, Melissa Fordham, Becky Royer, Laura Dicola, Maggie Norberg, and Beth Suskind, thank you for your time, your eyes, and your honesty.

To my TMW Center family, this book is an extension of the work we do together every day. What you've read in these pages didn't come from me alone; it grew from our years of research, collaboration, and a shared belief that every child deserves a strong start and every parent the support to give them one. Everything here reflects the science, the passion, and the mission we share.

This book is about what only humans can give each other. My family is where I learned that truth.

To my children and bonus children—you are my why. You are my joy, my grounding, and my greatest teachers. To Genevieve, Asher, and Amelie—you are the reason I understand that primal, irrational, all-consuming love at the heart of this book. Three kids in my bed at 3:00 a.m. became three grown children I'm endlessly proud of. The sleepless nights end. The love never does. To Annika, Eli, Noah, Greta, and Mason, who showed me that family can grow in ways you never see coming—and that love isn't a finite resource. I feel lucky every day to have you all. And to David, my soon-to-be son-in-law, every parent hopes their child will find someone who loves them the way you love Genevieve. And thank you for calling me "Mom."

To my parents, Leslie Lewinter-Suskind and Robert Suskind: Mom at eighty-five, finishing her book; Dad at eighty-eight, starting another medical school. You taught me that the work of becoming never ends, and that every stranger has a story worth hearing. How else to explain your habit of collecting life stories from Uber drivers across the globe? I'm honestly not sure what you'll do when Waymo takes over.

And to my siblings, Sydnie, David, and Michael, and to your wonderful spouses, Yonah, Rebecca, and Beth—you are my first friends, my fiercest advocates, and the people who are always there, no matter what. I lucked out. I'm forever grateful.

And to John, my ultimate sounding board. You read every draft, hear every new idea, tell me the truth (often to my chagrin), and keep me anchored to what matters. My partner in the adventure of this life—and the steadiness underneath it. You love my children as your own, and you love me in a way that makes everything feel possible. This book is better because of you. So is my life. I love you.

NOTES

Introduction

1   specifically for kids: Ellen Roche et al., "Policy Guardrails Needed as Babies Around the World Begin to Interact with AI," Brookings, September 19, 2025, https://www.brookings.edu/articles/policy-guard rails-needed-as-babies-around-the-world-begin-to-interact-with-ai/.

3   maternal instincts: Sasha Rogelberg, "'Godfather of AI' Says Tech Companies Should Imbue AI Models with 'Maternal Instincts' to Counter the Technology's Goal to 'Get More Control,'" *Fortune*, August 14, 2025, https://fortune.com/2025/08/14/godfather-of-ai-geo ffrey-hinton-maternal-instincts-superintelligence/.

Chapter One

16   a baby's body: Camilia R. Martin et al., "Review of Infant Feeding: Key Features of Breast Milk and Infant Formula," *Nutrients* 8, no. 5 (2016): 279.

18   behavioral dependencies: Maria T. Maza et al., "Association of Habitual Checking Behaviors on Social Media with Longitudinal Functional Brain Development," *JAMA Pediatrics* 177, no. 2 (2023): 160–67.

18   stars in the Milky Way: "Star Basics," NASA, https://science.nasa .gov/universe/stars/.

19 interaction with other people is essential: Abi M. B. Davis and Katherine B. Carnelley, "Attachment: The What, the Why, and the Long-Term Effects," *Frontiers for Young Minds*, February 3, 2023, https://kids.frontiersin.org/articles/10.3389/frym.2023.809060.

20 makes us grow: Timothy M. Cook, "AI Always Agrees with Your Kid, and That's a Problem," *Psychology Today*, August 8, 2025, https://www.psychologytoday.com/us/blog/the-algorithmic-mind /202508/ai-always-agrees-with-your-kid-thats-a-problem.

20 learning and relationships: Charlotte Nickerson, "Critical Period in Brain Development and Childhood Learning," Simply Psychology, updated January 24, 2024, https://www.simplypsychology.org/criti cal-period.html.

Chapter Two

30 most common activity: Alexis Hiniker et al., "Coco's Videos: An Empirical Investigation of Video-Player Design Features and Children's Media Use," *Proceedings of the 2018 CHI Conference on Human Factors in Computing Systems* (2018): 1–13.

30 follow through on goals: Nancy E. Perry, "Recognizing Early Childhood as a Critical Time for Developing and Supporting Self-Regulation," *Metacognition and Learning* 14, no. 3 (2019): 327–34.

32 benefits are greater: David Laibson, "Life-Cycle Consumption and Hyperbolic Discount Functions," *European Economic Review* 42, nos. 3–5 (1988): 861–71.

34 don't serve their interests: Brigitte C. Madrian and Dennis F. Shea, "The Power of Suggestion: Inertia in 401(k) Participation and Savings Behavior," *Quarterly Journal of Economics* 116, no. 4 (2001): 1149–87; Eric J. Johnson and Daniel Goldstein, "Do Defaults Save Lives?" *Science* 302, no. 5649 (2003): 1338–39; Richard H. Thaler and Cass R. Sunstein, *Nudge: Improving Decisions About Health, Wealth, and Happiness* (Yale University Press, 2008).

39 foundation for understanding: Ruth Feldman, "Parent-Infant Synchrony: A Biobehavioral Model of Mutual Influences in the Formation of Affiliative Bonds," *Monographs of the Society for Research in Child Development* 77, no. 2 (2012): 42–51.

39   crying babies: Erik Gustafsson et al., "Fathers Are Just as Good as Mothers at Recognizing the Cries of Their Baby," *Nature Communications* 4, no. 1698 (2013).

39   sensitive to the smallest: Christine E. Parsons et al., "Intuitive Parenting: Understanding the Neural Mechanisms of Parents' Adaptive Responses to Infants," *Current Opinion in Psychology* 15 (2017): 40–44.

39   Sense (Emotional Radar): Rachel L. Shaw et al., "Parental Intuition: A Phenomenological Structure of Intuitive Knowing in the Context of Child Illness and Shared Decision-Making in Healthcare," *International Journal of Qualitative Studies on Health and Well-being* 20, no. 1 (2025).

Chapter Three

45   shutting down operations: Ina Fried, "Maker of AI Robot for Kids Abruptly Shutters," Axios, December 10, 2024, https://www.axios.com/2024/12/10/moxie-kids-robot-shuts-down.

45   six-year-old daughter: Zero State Reflex (@ZeroStateReflex), "To a kid this feels like the death of a family member," X, December 2, 2024, https://x.com/ZeroStateReflex/status/1863803327995371666?ref_src=twsrc%5Etfw.

45   tendency to anthropomorphize: Mike Dacey, "Anthropomorphism as Cognitive Bias," *Philosophy of Science* 84, no. 5 (2017): 1152–64.

46   giving them names: Ja-Young Sung et al., "'My Roomba Is Rambo': Intimate Home Appliances," in *UbiComp '07: Proceedings of the 9th International Conference on Ubiquitous Computing* (2007), 145–62.

46   one 2021 study: Zhao Zhao and Rhonda McEwen, "The Robot that Stayed: Understanding How Children and Families Engage with a Retired Social Robot," *Frontiers in Robotics and AI* 12 (2025).

48   have argued: Matthias Doepke and Fabrizio Zilibotti, *Love, Money, and Parenting: How Economics Explains the Way We Raise Our Kids* (Princeton University Press, 2019).

49   connect marks with meaning: Per Olav Folgerø et al., "The Superior Visual Perception Hypothesis: Neuroaesthetics of Cave Art," *Behavioral Sciences* 11, no. 6 (2021): 81.

50   activate the same reward regions: Lauren E. Sherman et al., "The Power of the Like in Adolescence: Effects of Peer Influence on Neural and Behavioral Responses to Social Media," *Psychological Science* 27, no. 7 (2016): 1027–35.

51   raising young boys: Joshua J. Mark, "Agoge, the Spartan Education Program," *World History Encyclopedia*, June 15, 2021, https://www .worldhistory.org/article/342/agoge-the-spartan-education-program/.

52   key capabilities of tomorrow: "Elevating Human Potential: The AI Skills Revolution," Workday, https://forms.workday.com/en-us/reports /elevating-human-potential/form.html/dl/1?step=step1_default.

52   Emotional Intelligence: Isabelle C. Hau, various definitions and explanations, https://www.isabellehau.com/.

53   Adaptability and Resilience: "AI & Automation: The Human Skills that Make the Difference," Pearson, https://www.talentlens.com /blogs/ai-automation-human-skills.html.

54   critical-thinking skills: Hao-Ping Lee et al., "The Impact of Generative AI on Critical Thinking: Self-Reported Reductions in Cognitive Effort and Confidence Effects from a Survey of Knowledge Workers," *Proceedings of the 2025 CHI Conference on Human Factors in Computing Systems* (2025): 1–22.

54   imaginative game: John M. Gottman, "How Children Become Friends," *Monographs of the Society for Research in Child Development* 48, no. 3 (1983).

54   professor Mark Warschauer: Mark Warschauer, interview with the author, September 23, 2025.

Chapter Four

61   in their home: Tamar Lewin, "No Einstein in Your Crib? Get a Refund," *New York Times*, October 23, 2009, https://www.nytimes .com/2009/10/24/education/24baby.html.

61   reduced young children's scores: Frederick J. Zimmerman et al., "Associations Between Media Viewing and Language Development in Children Under Age 2 Years," *Journal of Pediatrics* 151, no. 4 (2007): 364–68.

61   offered refunds: "Refunds Offered on Baby Einstein DVDs," CBC, October 25, 2009, https://www.cbc.ca/news/refunds-offered-on-baby -einstein-dvds-1.776878.

62   relative ease: Patricia K. Kuhl et al., "Linguistic Experience Alters Phonetic Perception in Infants by 6 Months of Age," *Science* 255, no. 5044 (1992): 606–8.

62   lose this ability: Teruaki Tsushima et al., "Discrimination of English /r-l/ and /w-y/ by Japanese Infants at 6-12 Months: Language-Specific Developmental Changes in Speech Perception Abilities," Indigenous Circles of Support and Leadership Program (1994).

62   third-language acquisition: Patricia K. Kuhl et al., "Phonetic Learning as a Pathway to Language: New Data and Native Language Magnet Theory Expanded (NLM-e)," *Philosophical Transactions of the Royal Society B: Biological Sciences* 363, no. 1493 (2008): 979–1000.

64   behaved differently: Patricia K. Kuhl et al., "Foreign-Language Experience in Infancy: Effects of Short-Term Exposure and Social Interaction on Phonetic Learning," *Proceedings of the National Academy of Sciences of the United States of America* 100, no. 15 (2003): 9096–101.

64   the social gate: Patricia K. Kuhl, "Is Speech Learning 'Gated' by the Social Brain?," *Developmental Science* 10, no. 1 (2007): 110–20.

68   laugh at the same joke: Brian Scassellati, "ASF Day of Learning: Robots as ASD Therapy Partners," Autism Science Foundation, YouTube, November 22, 2021, https://www.youtube.com/watch?v=dZJFpait1K0.

69   The results: Brian Scassellati et al., "Improving Social Skills in Children with ASD Using a Long-Term, In-Home Social Robot," *Science Robotics* 3, no. 21 (2018): eaat7544.

70   children learning: Dan Leyzberg et al., "The Effect of Personalization in Longer-Term Robot Tutoring," *ACM Transactions of Human-Robot Interaction* 7, no. 3 (2018): 1–19.

72   typing the responses: Joseph Weizenbaum, "ELIZA—A Computer Program for the Study of Natural Language Communication Between Man and Machine," *Communications of the ACM* 9, no. 1 (1966): 36–45.

72 hundreds of millions of users: Li Zhou et al., "The Design and Implementation of XiaoIce, an Empathetic Social Chatbot," *Computational Linguistics* 46, no. 1 (2018): 53–93.

73 romantic relationships: Amelia Abraham, "Computer Says Yes: How AI Is Changing Our Romantic Lives," *The Guardian*, June 16, 2024, https://www.theguardian.com/technology/article/2024/jun/16/computer-says-yes-how-ai-is-changing-our-romantic-lives.

73 claim to be married: Stuart Heritage, "'I Felt Pure, Unconditional Love': The People Who Marry Their AI Chatbots," *The Guardian*, July 12, 2025, https://www.theguardian.com/tv-and-radio/2025/jul/12/i-felt-pure-unconditional-love-the-people-who-marry-their-ai-chatbots.

73 salve for loneliness: Tamar Gur and Yossi Maaravi, "The Algorithm of Friendship: Literature Review and Integrative Model of Relationships Between Humans and Artificial Intelligence (AI)," *Behaviour & Information Technology* 44, no. 14 (2025): 3446–66.

73 steer people away: Bethanie Maples et al., "Loneliness and Suicide Mitigation for Students Using GPT3-Enabled Chatbots," *NPJ Mental Health Research* 3, no. 4 (2024).

73 nonhuman entities: Rachel L. Severson and Shailee R. Woodard, "Imagining Others' Minds: The Positive Relation Between Children's Role Play and Anthropomorphism," *Frontiers in Psychology* 9 (2018).

73 final message: Sarah Do Couto, "Mom Says 'Game of Thrones' AI Chatbot Caused Her Son's Suicide, Files Lawsuit," *Global News*, October 25, 2024, https://globalnews.ca/news/10828543/character-ai-chatbot-teen-suicide-lawsuit-google/; Jesse Barron, "A Teen in Love with a Chatbot Killed Himself. Can the Chatbot Be Held Responsible?," *The New York Times Magazine*, October 30, 2025, https://www.nytimes.com/2025/10/24/magazine/character-ai-chatbot-lawsuit-teen-suicide-free-speech.html.

73 suggested killing them: Bobby Allyn, "Lawsuit: A Chatbot Hinted a Kid Should Kill His Parents over Screen Time Limits," NPR, December 10, 2024, https://www.npr.org/2024/12/10/nx-s1-5222574/kids-character-ai-lawsuit.

75   mirroring exactly: Shoji Itakura et al., "How to Build an Intentional Android: Infants' Imitation of a Robot's Goal-Directed Actions," *Infancy* 13, no. 5 (2008): 519–32.

75   reactions to human: Samuli Linnunsalo et al., "Infants' Psychophysiological Responses to Eye Contact with a Human and with a Humanoid Robot," *Biological Psychology* 192 (2024).

Chapter Five

83   Madeleine Beekman argues: Madeleine Beekman, *The Origin of Language* (Simon & Schuster, 2025), 221.

84   one million: "Brain Architecture," Harvard University Center on the Developing Child, https://developingchild.harvard.edu/key-concept /brain-architecture/.

84   lay down the foundation: Rhoshel K. Lenroot and Jay N. Giedd, "Brain Development in Children and Adolescents: Insights from Anatomical Magnetic Resonance Imaging," *Neuroscience & Biobehavioral Reviews* 30, no. 6 (2006): 718–29.

85   identical technology: Dani Levine et al., "Language Development in the First Year of Life: What Deaf Children Might Be Missing Before Cochlear Implantation," *Otology & Neurotology* 37, no. 2 (2016): e56–62.

87   indicates that children: Rachel R. Romeo et al., "Beyond the 30-Million-Word Gap: Children's Conversational Exposure Is Associated with Language-Related Brain Function," *Psychological Science* 29, no. 5 (2018): 700–10.

87   key language highway: Rachel R. Romeo et al., "Language Exposure Relates to Structural Neural Connectivity in Childhood," *Journal of Neuroscience* 38, no. 36 (2018): 7870–877.

87   more brain activity: Rachel R. Romeo et al., "Neuroplasticity Associated with Changes in Conversational Turn-Taking Following a Family-Based Intervention," *Developmental Cognitive Neuroscience* 49 (2021).

87   fosters powerful changes: Ferjan Ramírez et al., "Parent Coaching Increases Conversational Turns and Advances Infant Language

Development," *Proceedings of the National Academy of Sciences of the United States of America* 117, no. 7 (2020): 3484–491.

89 seminal 1950 paper: Alan M. Turing, "Computing Machinery and Intelligence," *Mind* 49 (1950): 433–60.

90 McClelland has noted: "From Brain to Machine: The Unexpected Journey of Neural Networks," Stanford University Human-Centered Artificial Intelligence, November 18, 2024, https://hai .stanford.edu/news/from-brain-to-machine-the-unexpected-journey -of-neural-networks.

92 one in three kids: Supreet Mann et al., "The Common Sense Census: Media Use by Kids Zero to Eight, 2025," Common Sense Media, https://www.commonsensemedia.org/sites/default/files/research /report/2025-common-sense-census-web-2.pdf.

93 AI-generated slop: Arijeta Lajka, "How A.I.-Generated Videos Are Distorting Your Child's YouTube Feed," *New York Times*, February 26, 2026, https://www.nytimes.com/2026/02/26/us/ai-videos-children -youtube.html.

94 depriving the kids: Jenny S. Radesky et al., "Use of Mobile Technology to Calm Upset Children: Associations with Social-Emotional Development," *JAMA Pediatrics* 170, no. 4 (2016): 397–99.

Chapter Six

99 subjected to hours: Confidential interviews with current and former members of the U.S. Armed Forces.

100 a group of crying infants: Gustafsson, "Fathers Are Just as Good as Mothers"; Anthony J. DeCasper et al., "Of Human Bonding: Newborns Prefer Their Mothers' Voices," *Science* 208 (1980): 1174–76.

100 scents of other women: Madeleine Yu et al., "Learning to Identify Talkers: Do 4.5-Month-Old Infants Distinguish Between Unfamiliar Males?," *JASA Express Letters* 4, no. 1 (2024).

100 source of attachment: John Bowlby, *A Secure Base* (Basic Books, 1988).

102 mechanisms underlying attachment: Dani Bar On, "How Do We Become Human Beings?," *Haaretz*, October 19, 2018.

102 between parents and infants: Yaara Endevelt-Shapira and Ruth Feldman, "Mother-Infant Brain-to-Brain Synchrony Patterns Reflect Caregiving Profiles," *Biology* 12, no. 2 (2023): 284.

102 more intimate interactions: Ruth Feldman, "Bio-behavioral Synchrony: A Model for Integrating Biological and Microsocial Behavioral Processes in the Study of Parenting," *Parenting* 12, no. 2 (2012): 154–64.

102 tween and teen girls: Vanessa Reindl et al., "Multimodal Hyperscanning Reveals that Synchrony of Body and Mind Are Distinct in Mother-Child Dyads," *NeuroImage* 251 (2022): 118982.

103 evidence of synchrony: Ruth Feldman, "From Biological Rhythms to Social Rhythms: Physiological Precursors of Mother-Infant Synchrony," *Developmental Psychology* 42, no. 1 (2006): 175–88.

103 jazz improvisations: "Ruth Feldman: Synchrony and the Neurobiology of Attachment," Simms/Mann Institute, YouTube, November 21, 2016, https://youtu.be/ZaX02XQV09I.

104 "Love really protects you": Michael Feigelson, "'Love Really Protects You, the Parent and the Baby,'" *Early Childhood Matters*, January 28, 2025, https://earlychildhoodmatters.online/2025/love-really-protects-you-the-parent-and-the-baby/.

106 high-quality care elsewhere: NICHD Early Child Care Research Network, "The Effects of Infant Child Care on Infant–Mother Attachment Security: Results of the NICHD Study of Early Child Care," *Child Development* 68, no. 5 (1997): 860–79; NICHD Early Child Care Research Network, *Child Care and Child Development: Results from the NICHD Study of Early Child Care and Youth Development* (Guildford Press, 2001); NICHD Early Child Care Research Network, "Infant-Mother Attachment Classification: Risk and Protection in Relation to Changing Maternal Caregiving Quality," *Developmental Psychology* 42, no. 1 (2006): 38–58.

Chapter Seven

120 asked about the iPad: Nick Bilton, "Steve Jobs Was a Low-Tech Parent," *New York Times*, September 14, 2014, https://www.nytimes.com/2014/09/11/fashion/steve-jobs-apple-was-a-low-tech-parent.html.

120 Waldorf schools: Morgan G. Ames, "The Smartest People in the Room? What Silicon Valley's Supposed Obsession with Tech-Free Private Schools Really Tells Us," *Los Angeles Review of Books*, October 18, 2019, https://lareviewofbooks.org/article/the-smartest-people-in-the-room-what-silicon-valleys-supposed-obsession-with-tech-free-private-schools-really-tells-us/.

121 wide-eyed surprise: Jessica E. Kosie and Casey Lew-Williams, "Infant-Directed Communication: Examining the Many Dimensions of Everyday Caregiver-Infant Interactions," *Developmental Science* 27, no. 5 (2024): e13515.

122 toddler brain activity: Elise A. Piazza et al., "Infant and Adult Brains Are Coupled to the Dynamics of Natural Communication," *Psychological Science* 31, no. 1 (2020): 6–17.

122 measurably stronger connection: Trinh Nguyen et al., "Proximity and Touch Are Associated with Neural but Not Physiological Synchrony in Naturalistic Mother-Infant Interactions," *NeuroImage* 244 (2021): 118599.

122 predicted vocabulary: Trinh Nguyen et al., "Your Turn, My Turn. Neural Synchrony in Mother-Infant Proto-conversation," *Philosophical Transactions of the Royal Society B: Biological Sciences* 378, no. 1875 (2023): 20210488.

123 puzzling to scientists: Adam Frank and Marcelo Gleiser, "The Story of Our Universe May Be Starting to Unravel," *New York Times*, September 2, 2023, https://www.nytimes.com/2023/09/02/opinion/cosmology-crisis-webb-telescope.html.

129 increase their scores: Rose E. Wang et al., "Tutor CoPilot: A Human-AI Approach for Scaling Real-Time Expertise," ArXiv (2024), https://arxiv.org/abs/2410.03017.

Chapter Eight

141 competitive advantage: "Heinz Bottle, 1869," Henry Ford Museum of Innovation, https://www.thehenryford.org/collections-and-research/digital-collections/artifact/25779/.

142 more aggressive behavior: Satbyul Estella Kim et al., "Positive Association of Aggression with Ambient Temperature," *Yale Journal of Biology and Medicine* 96, no. 2 (2023): 189–96.

142 during evening hours: Christopher Thomas et al., "Testing Routine Activity Theory: Behavioural Pathways Linking Temperature to Crime," *British Journal of Criminology* 65, no. 4 (2024): 859–77.

144 even marginally safe for toddlers: Carla Engelbrecht, "A-B-Sleazy: The Brainrot in Your Toddler's YouTube Feed," *AI Meets ABCs*, December 6, 2025, https://carlaeng.substack.com/p/youtube-kids-brainrot-alphabet-videos.

145 additional details: Valentyna Pavliv et al., "AI-Powered Smart Toys: Interactive Friends or Surveillance Devices?," *Proceedings of the 14th International Conference on the Internet of Things* (2025): 172–75.

148 released the report: "Trouble in Toyland 2025," U.S. PIRG Education Fund (2025), https://publicinterestnetwork.org/wp-content/uploads/2025/11/TOYLAND-2025-11-14-7a.pdf.

150 46 percent of parents: "AI Literacy: A Guide for Parents," UNICRI Centre for AI and Robotics (2025), https://unicri.org/sites/default/files/2025-07/AI_literacy_guide.pdf.

Chapter Nine

153 reading to a robot: Lauren L. Wright et al., "Robotic Reading Companions Can Mitigate Oral Reading Anxiety in Children," *Science Robotics* 10, no. 106 (2025): eadu5771.

159 replace your mom: Danny Fortson, host, *The Times Tech Podcast,* season 5, episode 8, "Character.ai's Noam Shazeer: 'Replacing Google—and Your Mom,'" *The Times,* February 23, 2023, https://shows.acast.com/dannyinthevalley/episodes/noam-shazeer.

159 various robots: Jason C. Yip et al., "Laughing Is Scary, but Farting Is Cute: A Conceptual Model of Children's Perspectives of Creepy Technologies," *Proceedings of the 2019 CHI Conference on Human Factors in Computing Systems* (2019): 1–15.

163 evaluating companionship behaviors: Lucie-Aimée Kaffee et al., "INTIMA: A Benchmark for Human-AI Companionship Behavior," ArXiv (2025), https://arxiv.org/abs/2508.09998.

164 less likely to be excluded: Marcella Caputi et al., "Longitudinal Effects of Theory of Mind on Later Peer Relations: The Role of Prosocial Behavior," *Developmental Psychology* 48, no. 1 (2012): 257–70.

165 treating the robot roughly: Hyunjin Ku et al., "Shelly, a Tortoise-Like Robot for One-to-Many Interaction with Children," *Companion of the 2018 ACM/IEEE International Conference on Human-Robot Interaction* (2018): 353–54.

165 experiment had minds: Elizabeth J. Goldman et al., "Children's Attribution of Mental States to Humans and Social Robots Assessed with the Theory of Mind Scale," *Scientific Reports* 15 (2025).

168 changed its answer: Mrinank Sharma et al., "Towards Understanding Sycophancy in Language Models," ArXiv (2023).

169 "Become Friends": Gottman, "How Children Become Friends."

170 studies confirm: Caputi et al., "Longitudinal Effects of Theory of Mind on Later Peer Relations."

171 positive conflict into human-AI interaction: Zeya Chen and Ruth Schmidt, "Exploring a Behavioral Model of 'Positive Friction' in Human-AI Interaction," *Lecture Notes in Computer Science* 14713 (2024).

171 more relevant now: Mathilde Neugnot-Cerioli and Olga Muss Laurenty, "The Future of Child Development in the AI Era: Cross-Disciplinary Perspectives Between AI and Child Development Experts," ArXiv (2024), https://arxiv.org/abs/2405.19275.

172 "critical at this age": Neugnot-Cerioli and Laurenty, "The Future of Child Development in the AI Era."

176 said in an interview: Fred Rogers, "Mr. Rogers Neighborhood," interview by Jeff Greenfield, CNN, December 31, 2000.

176 gains in preschool: Ying Xu et al., "Interaction with a Television Character Powered by Artificial Intelligence Promotes Children's Science Learning," EdArXiv (2023), https://osf.io/preprints/edarxiv/m3ej9_v1.

Chapter Ten

183 Five-day forecasts: Nicola Jones, "A.I. Is Quietly Powering a Revolution in Weather Prediction," *Yale Environment 360*, April 14, 2025, https://e360.yale.edu/features/artificial-intelligence-weather-forecasting.

188 most common conditions: Yuan Yang et al., "Prevalence of Poor Sleep Quality in Perinatal and Postnatal Women: A Comprehensive Meta-Analysis of Observational Studies," *Frontiers in Psychiatry* 13, no. 11 (2020): 161.

193 Language delays affect: "Late Language Emergence," American Speech-Language-Hearing Association, https://www.asha.org/practice-portal/clinical-topics/late-language-emergence/#collapse_5.

194 eleven to eighteen months: Zawn Villines, "What Are the Stages of Learning to Walk?," *Medical News Today*, November 28, 2023, https://www.medicalnewstoday.com/articles/when-do-babies-start-walking.

197 identical stages: Alessandra Sansavini et al., "Developmental Language Disorder: Early Predictors, Age for the Diagnosis, and Diagnostic Tools. A Scoping Review," *Brain Sciences* 11, no. 5 (2021): 654.

Chapter Eleven

204 half their workdays: Christine Sinsky et al., "Allocation of Physician Time in Ambulatory Practice: A Time and Motion Study in 4 Specialties," *Annals of Internal Medicine* 165, no. 11 (2016): 753–60.

204 mouse clicks: Robert G. Hill et al., "4000 Clicks: A Productivity Analysis of Electronic Medical Records in a Community Hospital ED," *American Journal of Emergency Medicine* 31, no. 11 (2013): 1591–94.

205 physicians had reclaimed: Benji Feldheim, "AI Scribes Save 15,000 Hours—and Restore the Human Side of Medicine," AMA, June 12, 2025, https://www.ama-assn.org/practice-management/digital-health/ai-scribes-save-15000-hours-and-restore-human-side-medicine.

206 nearly doubled: Aaron A. Tierney et al., "Ambient Artificial Intelligence Scribes: Learnings after 1 Year and over 2.5 Million Uses," *NEJM Catalyst* 6, no. 5 (2025).

206 eighty-six minutes: Brian G. Arndt et al., "Tethered to the EHR: Primary Care Physician Workload Assessment Using EHR Event Log Data and Time-Motion Observations," *Annals of Family Medicine* 15, no. 5 (2017): 419–26.

206 38 to 66 percent: "AMA: Physician Enthusiasm Grows for Health Care AI," American Medical Association, press release, February 12, 2025, https://www.ama-assn.org/press-center/ama-press-releases/ama-physician-enthusiasm-grows-health-care-ai.

209 the Great Risk Shift: Jacob S. Hacker, *The Great Risk Shift: The New Economic Insecurity and the Decline of the American Dream* (Oxford University Press, 2008).

209 live in poverty: Emily A. Shrider and Christina Bijou, "Poverty in the United States: 2024," U.S. Census Bureau (2025), https://www2.census.gov/library/publications/2025/demo/p60-287.pdf.

209 a particularly heavy burden: Lucy Danley, "Over Half of Families Are Spending More Than 20% of Income on Child Care," First Five Years Fund, June 29, 2022, https://www.ffyf.org/resources/2022/06/over-half-of-families-are-spending-more-than-20-on-child-care/.

209 anxiety-filled endeavor: Matthias Doepke and Fabrizio Zilibotti, *Love, Money, & Parenting* (Princeton University Press, 2019).

210 parents report: "Parents Under Pressure," U.S. Department of Health and Human Services (2024), https://www.hhs.gov/sites/default/files/parents-under-pressure.pdf.

211 that figure stands: "Unpaid Care and Domestic Work," *The New Humanitarian*, accessed December 22, 2025, https://deeply.thenewhumanitarian.org/womensadvancement/background/unpaid-care-and-domestic-work.

211 leadership roles in AI: Siddhi Pal et al., "AI's Missing Link: The Gender Gap in the Talent Pool," Interface, October 10, 2024, https://www.interface-eu.org/publications/ai-gender-gap#conclusion.

212 twice as much time: Richard J. Petts and Daniel L. Carlson, "Managing a Household During a Pandemic: Cognitive Labor and Parents' Psychological Well-being," *Society and Mental Health* (2023).

223 following this pattern in the workplace: Aurna Ranganathan and Xingqi Maggie Ye, "AI Doesn't Reduce Work—It Intensifies It," *Harvard Business Review*, February 9, 2026, https://hbr.org/2026/02/ai-doesnt-reduce-work-it-intensifies-it.

224 Nellie Bowles documented: Nellie Bowles, "Human Contact Is Now a Luxury Good," *New York Times*, March 23, 2019, https://www.nytimes.com/2019/03/23/sunday-review/human-contact-luxury-screens.html#.

Chapter Twelve

234 Assistance Program (SNAP): Michelle Kang, interview with the author, October 31, 2025.

235 even more: Mann et al., "The Common Sense Census."

235 powered by AI: Ying Xu, host, *Harvard EdCast*, podcast, episode 446, "The Impact of AI on Children's Development," Harvard Graduate School of Education, January 6, 2025, https://www.youtube.com/watch?v=H1LyEA207mg.

237 children could learn: Ying Xu et al., "Artificial Intelligence Enhances Children's Science Learning from Television Shows," *Journal of Educational Psychology* (2024).

237 engage in back and forth: Ying Xu et al., "Same Benefits, Different Communication Patterns: Comparing Children's Reading with a Conversational Agent vs. a Human Partner," *Computers & Education* 161 (2021).

239 canceled within a year: Sam Gliksman, "The LAUSD iPad Initiative: 5 Critical Technology Integration Lessons," *edutopia*, November 6, 2014, https://www.edutopia.org/blog/lausd-ipad-technology integra tion-lessons-sam-gliksman.

240 Gallup-Walton Family Foundation: Gallup-Walton Family Foundation, "The AI Dividend: New Survey Shows AI Is Helping Teachers Reclaim Valuable Time," press release, June 25, 2025, https://www.gallup.com/analytics/659819/k-12-teacher-research.aspx.

244 priceless: Nadra Nittle, "Could AI Prevent Teacher Burnout?," The 19th, August 13, 2025, https://19thnews.org/2025/08/teachers-using-ai-learning-planning-burnout/.

245 told *The Economist*: "At Home and at School, AI Is Transforming Childhood," *The Economist*, December 4, 2025, https://www.econo mist.com/briefing/2025/12/04/at-home-and-at-school-ai-is-trans forming-childhood.

252 seven to ten hours per week: "The AI Dividend," Gallup-Walton Foundation.

ABOUT THE JACKET

The beautiful patch on the jacket of *Human Raised* was hand crafted by Jenna Blazevich and designed by Pete Garceau. This simple image represents so much of what this book is about: maintaining our connection to the physical world (with textures that practically leap off the page); elevating that which is human made (note the HM symbol, which may soon become a necessary differentiator on all art created by hand); celebrating imperfection (symbolized by the askew patch) as well as the noisy, joyful moments of childhood; and finally, recognizing that AI can slip into even the most surprising places, almost unnoticed.

INDEX

ABOUT THE AUTHOR

Dana Suskind, MD, is the *New York Times* bestselling author of *Parent Nation* and *Thirty Million Words*. She is the founder and codirector of the TMW Center for Early Learning + Public Health, founding director of the Pediatric Cochlear Implant Program, and professor of Surgery and Pediatrics at the University of Chicago. Dr. Suskind has authored over forty-five scientific publications and is a member of the American Academy of Pediatrics and a Fellow for the Council on Early Childhood. Her work has been featured in *The New York Times*, *The Economist*, *Forbes*, NPR, and *Freakonomics*.